Healing From Hidden Scars

Edward Young

Contents

Foundations of Hidden Scars

Daily Healing Practices

Survivor Voices: First-Person Vignettes

12-Month Healing Plan: Months 1–8

Creative and Relational Healing

Meaning, Identity, and Legacy

Your Charter for Life

Foundations of Hidden Scars

The brain is a complex survival machine that rewires itself in response to chronic threat. For the purpose of this book, CPTSD (Complex PostTraumatic Stress Disorder) is defined as a chronic, pervasive psychological condition that includes emotional dysregulation, negative selfconception, relational difficulties, and altered threat perception, arising from prolonged, repeated exposure to traumatic events. Persistent childhood trauma—whether abuse, neglect, or domestic violence—sets off a cascade of neurobiological changes that create a state of hyperarousal and neurobiological sensitization. The amygdala becomes hyperreactive, the prefrontal cortex (PFC) loses part of its regulatory brake, and the hippocampus struggles to stitch events into coherent narratives. These shifts produce emotional flashbacks that feel immediate, disrupt sleep and focus, and lower the threshold for what counts as danger. The four primary stress responses—fight, flight, freeze, and fawn—are then engaged automatically, sometimes to the point of impairing executive function. When the threat is ongoing across development, as in combat or sustained civilian abuse, these circuits are reinforced, leading to longlasting changes that are shared by veterans with traumatic brain injury and civilians with CPTSD. Shame and silence also play a role, but we will address them in detail later. This foundational understanding of how trauma rewires brain circuits informs the grounding and safety strategies that must precede deeper processing.

What CPTSD Really Means

Imagine a recruit fresh to the platoon who never stopped practicing alert drills because the home front was a minefield. That training—constant scanning, shifting weight from foot to foot, listening for the wrong tone—can start before a rifle is ever issued. Think of early trauma as the first tour of duty your nervous system never signed up for. Whether the mission was neglect, abuse, or abandonment, the persistent danger sculpts the nervous system the way repeated marches shape a soldier's calves, and CPTSD grows out of that chronic childhood trauma.

Chronic trauma rewires the brain, producing hypervigilance and altered neural circuits that mirror the symptoms of battle fatigue, TBI, and CPTSD in veterans.

Emotional flashbacks are not cinematic replays; they are sudden, wholebody reactions that bring back the raw feelings—fear, shame, helplessness—of a past traumatic moment, as if the danger is happening again. Not all flashbacks replay film footage; some are purely emotional. They feel like a mortar barrage of emotion, dropping you into a childhood moment without the visuals. A smell in a crowded market, a raised voice in a board meeting, the angle of a hallway light—any trivial cue can trigger this fullbody response. For soldiers, these can mix with combat triggers, making it hard to tell which event is being answered: a childhood alarm or a convoy ambush.

The 4F stress responses on patrol: fight, flight, freeze, fawn

Bodies have four main battlefield tactics when threatened: the 4F responses — Fight, Flight, Freeze, Fawn. These automatic survival patterns are formed early in life and were designed for lifeordeath situations. In safe settings they often manifest as:

The anger defense is the Fight response: imagine a sergeant who, at the slightest perceived insult, goes on the offensive. That sudden hit of rage is not always about what happened in the room; it often traces back to a time when fighting was literally the only option.

- Flight – The avoidance move. Think of the soldier who refuses to talk about a patrol or avoids reunions. Avoidance buys immediate calm but keeps the hotspot active, so the nervous system stays primed.

- Freeze – Dissociation and alert scanning. One minute you're present; the next you're watching yourself go through motions. The body's way of shutting down, scanning for a route to safety.
- Fawn – Compliance to reduce threat. This is the "please don't shoot me" tactic: excessive peoplepleasing, loss of boundaries, and silencing your own needs to keep the peace.

All were adaptive in the moment. The problem is when they start running on automatic in safe zones—at home, at work, in the mess hall.

Daily effects: mood, connections, and identity. CPTSD can cause affective dysregulation (extreme mood swings and difficulty calming down), relational difficulties (trust fractures and trouble keeping steady bonds), and a fragile sense of self-worth—an identity that shifts with the wind. Combat trauma and TBI often pile on memory gaps, irritability, and cognitive fog, making social and occupational functioning harder. Families pick up the debris; spouses, partners, and children may develop Complex secondary PTSD from living with chronic threat behaviors and erratic coping.

Practical tactics for soldiers and families are summarized below. There is work to do. With targeted tactics, clinical support, and a few good allies, it's possible to quiet the hyperalert networks and create steadier days. These tactics, scripts, and drills will be detailed later in the book, where they can be applied in barracks and living rooms alike.

Childhood Trauma as Root Cause

Early adversity disrupts attachment and regulation: When a child's caregivers are inconsistent, absent, or hostile, the basic training for emotional regulation never happens. Attachment — the blueprint for trusting others and feeling safe — gets scrambled. That's not just a fancy term; it's the difference between having a reliable battle buddy and trying to fight alone in the dark. Soldiers with this kind of early adversity often carry heightened reactivity into adult bonds, making closeness feel risky and safety hard to accept.

Chronic Neglect: Shaping Stress Responses and Regulatory Challenges

Long-term neglect is like running constant drills with no time to rest: the alarm system gets louder and quicker to trigger. The hypothalamic-pituitary-adrenal axis and fear circuits become primed for threat, so small slights or unpredictable events can produce outsized arousal — insomnia, anger, or shutdown. For a troop returning from deployment who also grew up neglected, the combined load can leave them on a hair-trigger, struggling to self-soothe when reminders surface.

Repeated early stress rewires the brain into a state of heightened vigilance. As described in the foundational explanation, the amygdala, PFC, and hippocampus adjust, leading to emotional flashbacks and difficulty recovering from TBI or battlefield trauma.

The 4F Responses: Engraving Persistent Survival Patterns. Those automatic responses — freeze, fight, flight, and fawn — get etched into habit under chronic childhood threat. On the line, they meant survival. At home, they can sabotage trust and intimacy, cause sudden outbursts, or produce long spells of emotional withdrawal. Families pay a price too: partners and kids may pick up secondary trauma symptoms from living with someone whose default is one of these hardwired modes. Understanding these patterns is just the first step; the next is to translate that knowledge into concrete family education and practical strategies:

- Education: Provide basic, practical trauma-informed education for family members—simple neuroscience, what emotional flashbacks can look like, and why reactions are not personal. This reduces misunderstandings and lowers secondary PTSD risk.

- Boundaries and signals: Set clear boundaries and a brief, agreed signal for "I need a timeout" so everyone knows when to step back without escalation.

- Emergency plan: Create a short emergency plan that includes who calls whom, a designated safe room or place, and a simple grounding object or step to reach for in crisis.

- Grounding tools: Learn two short grounding lines or grounding steps to offer (never force). Keep them concise and practiced so they can be used calmly in the moment.

- Routine and predictability: Maintain basic, small predictable structures—regular meals, sleep schedules, and brief daily rhythms—to help the nervous system settle.

- Check-ins and naming sensations: Hold a weekly family check-in where members can name sensations or emotions without judgment and update the emergency plan as needed.

- Caregiver support: Schedule regular check-ins for caregivers, set limits to prevent burnout, and seek family-focused resources or professional guidance when reactions become overwhelming.

Emotional Flashbacks: Names and Recognitions

Emotional flashbacks, as defined earlier, are sudden, intense emotional reactions that feel like an unexpected explosion—you feel the blast before you see it. For soldiers and their families, these events can resemble combat reactions: disorientation, panic, anger, or withdrawal that emerge out of nowhere. The key difference is that the enemy is a memory, and the battlefield is the present.

Familyfocused tactics to manage emotional flashbacks:

- Identify triggers by keeping a shared diary or journal.

- Use grounding techniques such as the 54321 sensory focus exercise.

- Encourage open communication: a brief "checkin" before meals or bedtime.

- Establish a safe word or signal that family members can use when a flashback surfaces.
- Seek professional help or support groups tailored to military families.
- Practice memory reframing in a calm setting with a trusted therapist or counselor.

The following body signals can indicate the onset of the condition:

- Dizziness

First tactical order: scan your body. Before the story in your head fires up, the body often radios in. Make a short list of your personal signals and train with them like a premission checklist. Common calls include:

- Headache
- Nausea
- Dizziness
- Tightness in the chest or throat
- A knot in the gut
- Sudden heat or cold
- Tunnel vision, dizzy lightheadedness
- Numbing or detachment from limbs

When those signals pop, call them out aloud or in your head—"tight chest," "hot face," "numb hands." Naming sensation interrupts the automatic relay between limbic hijack (the rapid takeover of the limbic system that triggers intense emotional responses) and fullscale flashback. Think of it as throwing on ear protection before the next round.

Triggers and Contextual Cues: Map the Ambush Points Triggers are rarely dramatic booms; they're more like tripwires. Smells, certain tones of voice, crowded spaces, or feeling penned in can all cue a memory. Keep a trigger log for a week: note the stimulus, what you were doing, the bodily signal, and how long the reaction lasted. That afteraction snapshot helps you spot patterns so your team—therapist, partner, squad—can plan responses.

4F Responses in the Flashback Firefight: When an emotional flashback ignites, one of the 4F responses kicks in:

These survival protocols are not moral shortcomings; they are instinctual defenses. By recognizing which 4F response is running on repeat, you can apply targeted strategies: if you tend to freeze, practice gentle, smallmovement exercises; if you fawn, rehearse assertive oneliners; if you fight, use breathing techniques to calm before speaking; and if you flee, create safespace cues that remind you of grounding practices. This tailored approach turns passive patterns into active, empowering tools for emotional resilience.

Finding Safety and Integration: Tactical Tools for the Ground

This section outlines the core aims: establishing immediate safety, down-regulating physiological alarm, and linking traumatic memories to presentday safety. The detailed, stepbystep frontline techniques (breathing cadences, grounding drills, and practical safeenvironment scripts) have been moved to the book's practical healing sections so they can be used as handson tools during daily practice. Here we focus on the principles that guide those interventions: simplicity, sensory anchoring, rehearsed response, and coordination with therapeutic support.

Longer-term integration requires therapeutic processing. Therapies that combine somatic regulation with memory work (EMDR, sensorimotor approaches, trauma-informed CBT) help link the old alarm system to present safety. Think of this work as routine maintenance on gear: regular therapeutic check-ins, practiced regulation skills, and gradual memory processing reduce the risk of reactivation and support durable safety.

Supporting families: Complex secondary PTSD refers to the traumatic stress that family members of a person with PTSD or TBI may experience when they repeatedly encounter threat signals. Symptoms include hypervigilance, avoidance, emotional numbing, irritability, and cognitive fog.

If there is a history of TBI or concussion, begin with a comprehensive neuroassessment and medical readout. Brain injury can alter trigger thresholds and delay recovery from flashbacks, so a coordinated plan that brings together neurology, mentalhealth professionals, and family caregivers is essential for clarity and rapid stabilization. Tailored rehabilitation and grounding techniques—brief, repeatable practices that help maintain identity when the brain activates old alarms—are especially effective during stressful moments. When medications are needed, start at low doses, titrate slowly, and keep the neuroteam involved to monitor seizure thresholds, cognitive side effects, and sleep patterns.

Flashbacks aren't failures in will—they're alarm bells from an overworked system. With clear detection, immediate ground tactics, and sustained therapeutic work, those bells can be quieted and rewired so present-day life no longer feels like combat.

The 4F Responses: Fight, Flight, Freeze, Fawn

Picture this: you're clearing a dark hallway on a training op and your radio squawks. Old wiring, wrong sound, and suddenly your body acts like it's back in Kandahar. That same automatic response—meant for survival in combat—can stick around after the tour and show up in day-to-day life when the true danger is a raised voice or a slammed door. For many veterans, and for folks whose CPTSD began in childhood, the 4F responses become the brain's default combat orders. Learning to read those orders is the start of taking back control.

The 4F Responses — automatic survival patterns formed in early threat — are useful in life-or-death moments. Trouble is, they weren't designed for grocery stores, boardrooms, or family dinners. When triggered in safe settings they look like this:

Fight is the active, confrontational stress response that prepares a person to defend themselves or remove a threat through aggression, resistance, or assertion. Physiologically it involves adrenaline release, increased heart rate, muscle tension, and a surge of energy directed toward taking action. Behaviorally it can show up as anger, verbal or physical confrontation, boundary-setting, or lashing out; psychologically it may feel like righteous fury or overwhelming irritation. Evolutionarily, fight can neutralize immediate danger, but when triggered in nonlifethreatening situations it may lead to relationship problems, reactive aggression, or internalized shame. Therapeutic approaches often focus on safety planning, emotional regulation skills, somatic work to release tension, and learning constructive ways to assert needs.

Flight is the escapeoriented stress response in which the organism withdraws from perceived danger to seek safety. It is marked by physiological arousal geared toward rapid movement—fast breathing, elevated heart rate, and mobilized muscles—and by behaviors such as running away, avoiding people or places, emotional withdrawal, or procrastination. Functionally, flight removes the person from harm, but in modern contexts it can become chronic avoidance, social isolation, or difficulty engaging with important tasks. Treatment typically includes paced exposure to feared situations, grounding and breathwork to reduce immediate arousal, and skills to tolerate distress while increasing approach behaviors.

Freeze is a defensive response characterized by immobility, dissociation, or paralysis when neither fighting nor fleeing is possible or safe. Physiological signs can include a sudden drop in motor activity, numbness, slowed or shallow breathing, and a sense of detachment or unreality. Behaviorally it may present as being unable to move, speak, or make decisions, blank staring, or emotional numbing. Freeze can reduce detection or limit harm in some situations but often results in later feelings of helplessness, shame, or confusion about one's reactions. Therapeutic work emphasizes gentle reengagement with the body, titrated trauma processing, grounding techniques, and practices that restore a sense of agency and safety.

Fawn is an appeasement response in which a person adapts to threat by pleasing, placating, or complying with others to avoid conflict or harm. It often appears as excessive peoplepleasing, prioritizing others' needs over one's own, difficulty saying no, scant boundaries, and anxious caretaking. While fawning can temporarily reduce immediate danger by calming an aggressor, it frequently leads to burnout, loss of identity, chronic resentment, and problems asserting needs. Treatment focuses on rebuilding boundaries, developing assertiveness and selfvalidation skills, exploring underlying beliefs that drive appeasement, and creating safety around expressing authentic feelings.

Why these old orders keep kicking in? In highthreat moments the amygdala and brainstem fire first, the PFC steps back, and the body and old survival circuits replay a stored response—producing an emotional flashback that feels like combat even when the kitchen is safe.

Traumainformed awareness changes that pattern by viewing these responses as tactical indicators, not moral failings. A field guide you can carry in your head:

- Run a quick reconnaissance: name the feeling ("anger," "numb," "I need out," "I'll agree")—one-line intel shuts down spirals faster than moralizing.
- Use an on-the-ground anchor: carry a physical cue (dog tag, coin, textured patch). Touch it, slow the breath, and issue a two-sentence reality check: "This is 2025. I'm not on patrol. I am safe." Short, concrete, and repeatable under stress.
- Box in triggers: keep a log for two weeks—what time, who, where, what body sign. That's tactical data for therapy and for family planning.

First, use the 54321 grounding technique to anchor yourself.

- 5 things you see – say "I see present."
- 4 things you touch – part of the 54321 grounding technique; say "I feel present."

2 scents you smell – say "I smell present."

As part of the grounding practice, identify one flavor you taste – say "I taste present."

Do it standing, practicing a soft stance you use in everyday life so the body learns the pattern.

No single drill fixes everything, but treating 4F responses like operational alerts—collecting intel, using a simple protocol, and rehearsing new moves—gives you options where automatic reactions used to rule. Think of it as retraining the unit: the body keeps the memory, but you can rewrite the orders it follows. Detailed, stepbystep drills and protocols are available in the book's daily healing practices and practical healing planning sections.

Neurobiology of Trauma: Brain and Body

The amygdala is the brain's alarm bell. In CPTSD it rings loudly for harmless sounds, turning a BBQ moment into a battlefield in seconds. To counter this overreactivity, name the alarm aloud—"amygdala alarm"—and take three slow breaths. Naming lowers the immediate surge and gives the PFC a split second to intervene.

The hippocampus links events to time and place. Prolonged stress breaks this link, leaving memories in shards. Blast exposure or mild TBI can damage hippocampal circuits, worsening contextual recall. Keep a short trauma log—date, trigger, sensations—to give the hippocampus practice in reordering events.

The Autonomic Nervous System: When the Body Stays at Red Alert. The autonomic nervous system is the brain's messenger to the rest of the body. In CPTSD it can stay in hyperarousal mode: high heart rate, sweating, jumpiness, sleep disruption. This is the physiological side of fight, flight, freeze, fawn. Combattrained vigilance can harden into chronic scanning — useful in theater, hazardous at home. Families can learn quick interventions: a threepart grounding (feet on floor, 5 things you can see, two slow breaths) interrupts the cascade. For dissociation, sensory anchors — a textured object in your hand, cold water on the face — can bring someone back from the drift.

Physical Symptoms of Hyperarousal

Hyperarousal shows up physically: palpitations, tremors, sweating, tunnel time perception, numbness. Those are not signs of moral failing; they're violations of the ANS's operating protocol. If you're clocking repeated chest spikes or blackout episodes, get a medical workup that includes TBI screening — blast injuries and repeated concussive events can mimic or magnify CPTSD symptoms.

The Prefrontal Cortex (PFC) calms the rest of the brain and coordinates responses. Chronic stress blunts its function, but PFC skills can be trained.

Useful drills include: see the earlier section on PFC training for the full list.

- Short, frequent executive breaks: five minutes of focused breathing or a brief cognitive task (simple arithmetic or a memory game) to engage working memory.
- Physical exercise with coordination (boxing pads, ruck marches with variable pace) to connect body regulation with frontal control.
- Sleep hygiene and consistent sleep windows — PFC repair happens on the clock during good sleep.

Trauma-focused therapy and cognitive work that practice reappraisal and delayed response.

Complex secondary PTSD: Families in the Blast Radius. When a soldier's nervous system stays on high, spouses and kids pick up the slack. Children can develop Complex secondary PTSD patterns that mirror parental hypervigilance or withdrawal. Tactical family moves: set predictable routines, create "safe signal" words for grounding help, and hold short weekly check-ins where each person names one trigger and one coping action. These small habits reduce household uncertainty and strengthen collective regulation.

Closing field note: brains adapt to survive. That adaptation becomes the problem in safe environments. The task is to retrain alarm systems, rebuild context, and sharpen command-and-control functions — with small, repeatable drills, medical checks for TBI, and family-level tactics that keep everyone mission-capable.

Shame, Silence, and the Silence Breaks

Building on the circuitry map established earlier, shame and silence lock the system into place. They keep the amygdala primed for threat, dampen the prefrontal cortex's regulatory influence, and prevent the hippocampus from recontextualizing events. The result is a body that stays in hypervigilance, with tense muscles, a racing pulse, and spontaneous emotional flashbacks that flare up without clear triggers. These automatic fightflightfreezefawn responses maintain the nervous system in constant readiness, prolonging distress even after the original threat has passed.

Shame isn't just an ugly feeling. It programs the body. A corporal who was bullied in childhood and then survived an IED might find their chest tightening before any conscious thought arrives. That's the body acting on stored shame: hypervigilance, tense muscles, rapid pulse.

Silence can feel tactical—keep your mouth shut, don't make waves. A platoon leader once told me, "You keep your head down, you survive."

How to break the cycle: safe, paced disclosure

You don't have to spill everything in one debriefing. The right way is gradual and controlled. Here are combat-tested steps:

- Pick your target: a trusted therapist, chaplain, or peer who has command presence and won't panic.
- For families, choose a counselor skilled in secondary trauma.
- Identify the goal of your disclosure: what do you want to achieve?
- Choose a safe, private setting where interruptions are unlikely.
- Use short, simple sentences; pause to gauge the listener's reaction.
- Offer the listener an out: "If you need a break, just say so."
- Monitor your own stress signals and adjust the pace accordingly.

- After the conversation, debrief with the professional or peer.
- Start small: practice telling a short, factual piece of the story—date, place, what happened—without trying to make it mean anything. Keep it to two minutes.
- Build trust in increments: increase time and emotional detail only when your nervous system stays steady afterward.
- Use safety checks: end each sharing with a grounding ritual—breathwork, hand on knee, or a short walk. If dissociation spikes, pause and return later.

Structured sharing: unit cohesion for healing

Building on the individual grounding practices, the next phase is structured sharing groups. Structured sharing groups give veterans and families a controlled setting to metabolize trauma. A facilitator keeps timing and tone disciplined so each person can tell, get witnessed, and be returned to calm. For families dealing with complex secondary PTSD, structured sessions teach how to listen without fixing, set boundaries, and share care duties so no single member burns out.

Shame and silence can keep a soldier's mind on red alert. The countermeasure is deliberate: small disclosures, body-based practice, and disciplined group witnessing. That combination pulls traumatic memories out of the bunker and gives them less power over daily life.

Building Safety: First Steps for Healing

If you asked any squad leader what comes first on a patrol brief, they'd say "security." Healing from trauma follows the same rule: safety first. Without a secure baseline, everything else—therapy, exposure work, relationship repair—risks collapse. Think of safety as the perimeter wire you put up before you sleep: boring, repetitive, but it keeps you alive.

When danger is sensed, the brain triggers the 4F responses—fight, flight, freeze, fawn—via a fast, chemical alarm. Emotional flashbacks are essentially false alarms: the amygdala activates, the body enters a survival mode that mirrors the original threat, and the prefrontal cortex is suppressed. Building safety means quieting the amygdala so the prefrontal cortex can resume control.

Predictable daily routines act as a steady mooring for the nervous system, keeping the mind from drifting and reducing hypervigilance. A consistent schedule functions like a regular curfew and a clear field order, laying out simple, lowthreat steps that let the fightflightfreeze response recede and sleep deepen without surprise flashbacks.

A practical way to start the day is a morning stack: two minutes of breathing; five minutes of writing one line, "Today I need…."; tenminute walk. This microroutine signals the prefrontal cortex that the world is not in chaos. A daily plan that names wake time, meals, a short physical task, and a calming checkin is missionessential for CPTSD survivors, especially when childhood wounds mix with combat scars.

After the day's activities, a quick afteraction check—each person naming one win and one need—helps reinforce gains and identify support areas.

To wind down, stick to fixed sleepwake times and an evening ritual that eases the transition. Designate a quiet corner of the house for downtime, reduce clutter, soften lighting, and create a "reload" space that signals safety. These steps lower baseline arousal and create a predictable environment that quiets the sentry.

Meeting basic needs

Basic needs are not optional in trauma recovery. Sleep restores the brain's threat-processing systems. Food and hydration keep the body from escalating stress hormones. Families often miss these signals—partner exhaustion, skipped meals, or kids going unsupervised are signs of secondary strain. Put reminders in place: shared grocery lists, sleep-shift swaps for partners, and a "hydration bottle" rule for the kitchen table. Treat these like mission-essential whiteboard notes.

Meeting basic needs: Evening winddown rituals help reset the nervous system after a day of stress. Start by turning off bright screens an hour before bed and dimming the lights. Sip a warm, caffeinefree drink like chamomile tea. Spend five minutes in mindful breathing or gentle yoga stretches. Write three things you're grateful for or note a positive moment in a journal. End the routine with a soft playlist or nature sounds, then settle into a dark, cool room to encourage melatonin production. Consistency turns these actions into a nonnegotiable selfcare habit that supports recovery. The fulfillment of basic needs such as safety, belonging, and autonomy is vital for emotional resilience. Creating a personal safety plan further anchors your sense of security and empowers you to take proactive steps toward safety.

Addressing sleep, nutrition, hydration, and gentle movement is foundational to trauma recovery; these basics create the stability that allows other healing work to proceed.

Meeting basic needs

The fulfillment of basic needs such as safety, belonging, and autonomy is vital for emotional resilience.

Evening winddown rituals help reset the nervous system after a day of stress. Start by turning off bright screens an hour before bed and dimming the lights. Sip a warm, caffeinefree drink like chamomile tea. Spend five minutes in mindful breathing or gentle yoga stretches. Write three things you're grateful for or note a positive moment in a journal. End the routine with a soft playlist or nature sounds, then settle into a dark, cool room to encourage melatonin production. Consistency turns these actions into a nonnegotiable selfcare habit that supports recovery.

Creating a personal safety plan

- Identify your warning signs and common triggers.
- List coping strategies you can use in the moment (grounding techniques, breathing, movement).
- Name safe people to contact and safe places to go.
- Include crisis contacts (hotlines, local emergency numbers) and clear steps to take if risk escalates.
- Make sure your environment reduces harm (secure medications, remove potential means).
- Review and update the plan regularly; keep a copy in an accessible place.

Together, meeting basic needs, a predictable evening routine, and a well-prepared personal safety plan strengthen emotional resilience and support ongoing recovery.

Meeting basic needs: Every service member should carry a simple, rehearsed safety plan. Write it down and post it where the family sees it. Include:

Here are three calming options you can incorporate into your safety plan:

- Call a specific friend
- Go to a preagreed room
- Use breathwork
- Who will take over childcare or household tasks if you need space.
- Emergency steps if thoughts get dark (hotline numbers, crisis contact).

Practice the plan so it feels like muscle memory; when the alarm goes off, muscle memory wins.

Grounding techniques

When an emotional flashback hits, anchor yourself to the present with the 54321 grounding technique.

5 things you see – say "I see present."

4 things you touch – say "I feel present."

3 sounds you hear – say "I hear present."

2 scents you smell – say "I smell present."

1 flavor you taste – say "I taste present."

Carry a small object—a smooth river stone or a worn challenge coin—to focus tactile attention during the touch step.

If you have TBI or prefer a simpler drill, start with feeling your feet on the floor and naming three colors in the room; then gradually add the full 54321 steps.

Breathwork and calming spaces

Tactical breathing (inhale for four, hold for four, exhale for four, hold for four) lowers heart rate and brings the thinking brain back. Create a calm corner with a blanket, noisecancelling headphones, or a mental image rehearsed like a hand signal. Families should map these spots and agree on boundaries so everyone knows when someone is retreating to recharge. Safety is ongoing: regular checks, rehearsals, and routine actions reassure the brain that the perimeter is secure, allowing real healing to proceed.

Tactical breathing — inhale for four, hold for four, exhale for four, hold for four — is evidence-based: it lowers heart rate and helps bring the thinking brain back online. Build a calming space nearby—this could be a physical corner with a blanket and noisecancelling headphones, a simple mental image, or a handsignal rehearsed in advance. Families should map these spots and agree on boundaries so everyone knows when someone is retreating to recharge. Treat safety as ongoing maintenance: regular checks, rehearsals, and routine actions reassure the brain that the perimeter is secure and allow real healing to proceed.

Veterans and Civilians: Shared Pathways

Shared Neurobiology: Same Warroom, Different Fronts

If you picture the brain as a command post, soldiers and civilians who carry complex trauma often end up with many of the same damaged wiring. Combat scars and childhood scars may look different on the surface, but the circuits that run threat detection, memory, and regulation are shared. That shared neurobiology helps explain why a Marine snapping at a car backfire and a parent flinching at a raised voice are often fighting the same internal battle.

Emotional Flashbacks: When the Past Pops Up Like an Uninvited Patrol

Emotional flashbacks are wholebody recalls that thrust a person back into a feeling of threat. The amygdala fires an alarm, the prefrontal cortex is weakened, and repeated trauma can impair the hippocampus's ability to contextualize memories, so a scent or sound can transport someone to a past danger without a clear timestamp.

The 4F Responses: Flight, Fight, Freeze, Fawn — Old Orders, Poor Timing

The 4F responses are hard-wired survival moves. They were brilliant when we needed them: run, fight, play possum, or drop. In CPTSD, those responses can be on autopilot. A service member might default to fight in crowded public spaces. A civilian might freeze at a family dinner when a raised voice echoes a childhood moment. Both are using the same system—hypervigilant, primed for threat, but misreading current safety. The more the brain has been trained by early or repeated trauma, the quicker it flips into those modes.

Childhood Trauma and the Regulation of Safety

Early life trauma programs the nervous system. Think of it as field training that never ended: constant alerts, over-readiness, and a lowered tolerance for uncertainty. Research on adverse childhood experiences shows how these early patterns increase the risk of later CPTSD. For veterans who also had rough starts, military trauma layers on top of an already sensitized system; the combined effect can magnify dysregulation. That's why safety—predictable routines, known people, clear boundaries—matters more than pep talks.

Shared Healing Tools — Tactical Adjustments for Soldiers and Families

The toolbox is shared. Techniques like grounding, containment, and pacing work across the board, but tactics change by role.

- For soldiers: build a pre-trigger plan—identify likely triggers (locations, sounds), rehearse a brief self-script to regain orientation, and use a trusted "battle buddy" for quick debriefs after an event. Keep a two-minute breathing protocol you can do in the prone position or while standing watch; practice until it's as automatic as checking your gear.
- For families: learn containment language—short, non-judgmental phrases that signal safety ("You're home; you're safe") and set predictable check-in times so Complex secondary PTSD doesn't sneak in. Create pacing agreements: low-stim evenings, clear advance warnings before big conversations, and an agreed signal if someone needs to pause.

Recognize Complex secondary PTSD as defined earlier. Those are not moral failures; they're learned responses to living with chronic threat signals. Tactical family interventions—scheduled decompression time, shared routines, and access to family-focused therapy—interrupt that pattern.

A Developmentally Shared Pathway

Think of trauma as a path cut through the woods early in life. Later exposures simply widen that track. When childhood adversity is present, later military trauma often follows the same path with bigger consequences. Understanding that developmentally shared pathway helps clinicians and commanders design interventions that target the root wiring, not just the surface behavior.

The practical take-away: training, therapy, and family strategies that honor the shared neurobiology will be more effective across populations. Treat the wiring, include the family, and drill the new skills until they become the default response.

A Roadmap for Healing

Building on the understanding of the nervous system's adaptations and initial steps for stabilizing it, the next phase of healing of hidden scars requires careful construction. It begins with establishing safe, respectful boundaries for sharing personal stories, ensuring explicit consent and careful pacing to reduce re-traumatization. We ground our approach in the overlap between military trauma and civilian CPTSD, making familiar concepts relevant to veteran experiences and contextualizing symptoms.

See the definition of emotional flashbacks in 'Emotional Flashbacks: Names and Recognitions', and the 4F responses in 'The 4F Responses: Fight, Flight, Freeze, Fawn'.

A Personal Story Assessment provides the foundation for healing, linking past events to present reactions and guiding treatment.

This involves identifying recurring patterns from childhood trauma, pinpointing triggers, and charting the cycles of coping, including emotional flashbacks and 4F responses.

We will consider how fear, frustration, helplessness, and aggression appear in thoughts, feelings, and actions.

This assessment extends to current functioning across daily life—work, connections, health, and routines—and lists personal strengths and existing support networks that bolster resilience.

Healing then moves to clarifying goals, setting concrete, outcomefocused steps, and considering a structured 12month path emphasizing gradual progress.

This path builds foundational safety, regulates arousal, establishes daily routines including sleep, nutrition, and trusted supports to calm the nervous system, and develops skills in movement, mindfulness, and social connection.

See the definition of 4F responses in "The 4F Responses: Fight, Flight, Freeze, Fawn" and emotional flashbacks in "Emotional Flashbacks: Names and Recognitions". While labels assist in understanding patterns without confining a person's unfolding story, we prioritize mechanismbased terms like hyperarousal or emotional flashback, which reduce blame and guide effective approaches.

The personal narrative remains central, honoring childhood origins and giving meaning and context to healing.

Safety, boundaries, and selfcompassion establish the bedrock, outlining core skills and the mindset needed. We establish predictable routines, create personal boundaries to protect emotional safety, and practice grounding techniques for immediate calm.

Selfcompassion, gentle selftalk, and selfcare mitigate distress.

An introductory selfassessment framework provides ethical guidelines for its use, including symptom checklists, 4F stressresponse prompts, and trigger mapping.

Journaling begins the healing conversation, offering a private space to document experiences, label emotions, connect mind and body through sensations, and map responses to triggers, ending with gratitude or grounding.

Readers will also gain a boundary toolkit—identifying personal needs, communicating limits clearly, practicing conversations, choosing supportive connections, and recognizing violations without selfblame—all at a moderate pace to prevent overwhelm. Through these careful steps, we begin to build the secure ground required for true recovery.

Personal Story Assessment

Setting Safe and Respectful Storytelling Boundaries

If you've sat in a clinic chair, on a base, or on a couch with a veteran who's carrying combat memory plus old childhood wounds, you know storytelling about trauma isn't casual chit-chat. Treat disclosure like a premission brief: set rules of engagement, run a safety check, and establish signals for immediate ceasefire. That's how you keep the person in the present instead of accidentally hauling them back into a firefight or a kitchen where childhood terror started.

Explicit Consent and Pacing: Rules of Engagement

Before requesting details, obtain explicit consent. Use short, clear language: "I'm going to ask some questions about what happened. Are you okay with that right now? If you want me to stop at any time, say 'pause'." Offer options for pacing — shorter sessions, breaks every 10–15 minutes, or writing instead of speaking. Create a clear pause/stop signal and rehearse it once: it's the therapeutic equivalent of a red card. If the person has TBI, slow the tempo, repeat key points, and use written reminders.

Grounding the Session in Military Trauma and CPTSD

Frame the interview so clinical labels and combat language meet. Say something like, 'Some symptoms after combat overlap with longterm patterns from childhood; we'll look at both.' Cite practical frameworks veterans recognize. Emphasize how emotional flashbacks and the 4F responses (flight, fight, freeze, fawn) can look the same whether the trigger is mortar fire or a parent's door slam.

The Personal Story Assessment: How to Run One

Run the Personal Story Assessment like an afteraction report with a narrative map:

- Identify early-life patterns that echo in current reactions.
- List recurring triggers and describe typical emotional flashbacks.
- Chart which 4F responses show up and in what situations.

Use concrete prompts: "Tell me about a time you felt suddenly overwhelmed — what happened right before, and what did you do?" Record findings with the individual's permission and keep entries brief and dated.

Assess Current Functioning and Strengths

Measure functioning across duty areas: work, relationships, sleep, medical issues, daily routines. Ask for three strengths — they can be small (keeps appointments) or large (protects others). Map supports: who's reliable in a crisis, what community groups are within reach, online forums for caregivers. This helps families see the network around the veteran and flags Complex secondary PTSD risks for spouses and children (see 63).

Creating a Path Forward: Tactical Steps

Turn assessment into an operational plan:

- Set one short-term goal (e.g., attend one peer-support meeting within two weeks).
- Set a mid-term goal (e.g., learn two grounding skills to use during flashbacks).
- Assign responsibilities and a realistic timeframe.

Include a safety plan and contacts for crises. Recommend specific community resources and therapy types, and schedule a reassessment.

Takeaways

- Obtain clear, verbal consent and set a pause/stop signal.
- Pace sessions to match cognitive load and TBI limits.
- Ground storytelling in both combat trauma and CPTSD frameworks.
- Use the Personal Story Assessment to connect past events to present reactions.
- Evaluate functioning across life areas and list personal strengths/ supports.
- Create concrete, timed steps with supports and a safety plan.

Keep the tone straightforward, keep the breaks frequent, and treat storytelling like a mission where safety comes first.

Month Healing Plan Overview

A 12Month Roadmap for Recovery: the Lay of the Land

Think of this as mission planning for the long haul. Recovery from Complex PTSD after childhood trauma or combat is a marathon, not a sprint—and like any good operation, it needs phases, objectives, and realistic patrols. Below is a fourphase, monthbymonth roadmap you can use with a clinician, a battle buddy, or family members.

Phase 1 — Months 1–3: Establish Safety and Regulate Arousal

Objective: Calm the nervous system and build steady basics.

Sleep: Put sleep on the priority list like weapons checks. Fix wake and sleep times, darken the room, cut screens an hour before bed, and use a short winddown ritual (breathing, light stretching). Tiny, steady adjustments pave the way for lasting rest.

- Nutrition: Aim for regular meals with whole foods—vegetables, whole grains, lean proteins. Avoid heavy caffeine after noon if nightmares are an issue. Think fuel that steadies the body and mood.

Trusted Supports: Build a quickreaction team. That might be a therapist, a veteran peer, a spouse, or a close friend who knows the plan for latenight flareups. Set checkin times and an agreed script for what helps when someone's system flips into 4F (see foundational definition in 1013).

Phase 2 — Months 4–6: Begin Trauma Processing at a Comfortable Pace

Objective: Start memory work without tipping the system.

Pacing is everything. Processing should only begin when Phase 1 yields consistent stability. Use short, scripted exposures and clinicianguided techniques.

- Grounding Techniques: Drill these like a piece of kit. Box breathing (inhale 4 counts, hold 4, exhale 4, hold 4), progressive muscle relaxation, and the 54321 sensory exercise are reliable. Carry a tactile anchor—coin, smooth stone, or small patch—that brings you back to the present.

- Memory Integration: Work with a trained clinician using methods such as narrative work, EMDR, or somatic approaches. The aim is to reduce the amygdala's hyperalert response and strengthen the prefrontal cortex's regulatory control, making memories less triggering.

Phase 3 — Months 7–9: SkillBuilding for Resilience

Objective: Fortify the body and mind to handle stressors.

- Continued Sleep and Nutrition maintenance.
- Movement: Daily movement—walks, swimming, strength training, or yoga—helps downregulate arousal. Treat exercise as regular maintenance, not punishment.
- Mindfulness: Short, consistent practice (5–15 minutes) reduces reactivity over time. Use guided meditations if concentration is tough.
- Social Connection: Rebuild trusted networks. Small group activities with fellow veterans or family therapy sessions reduce isolation and the risk of Complex secondary PTSD among loved ones.

Phase 4 — Months 10–12: Integration and Civilian Roles

Objective: Reestablish meaningful roles and community ties.

- Social Supports: Deepen peer connections—mentoring newer vets, joining a unit reunion, or attending a veteran support group. Shared experience is stabilizing.
- Meaningful Roles: Find a role that fits current capacity—volunteer, coach, advocate, or work that provides structure and purpose without overwhelming stress.
- Community Engagement: Regular, lowpressure civic involvement—volunteering at a shelter, helping at a local VA event—helps rebuild identity outside of trauma.

This overview introduces the phenomenon of emotional flashbacks as intense, automatic emotional relivings rooted in the brain's threat system. It summarizes the concept; practical recognition cues, grounding techniques, and stepbystep containment practices are presented in the sections dedicated to daily practices and healing work.

See "Emotional Flashbacks: Names and Recognitions" for a definition of emotional flashbacks and "The 4F Responses: Fight, Flight, Freeze, Fawn" for the 4F framework.

Final Tactical Notes for Families and Clinicians

Teach family members the difference between primary PTSD and Complex secondary PTSD—how caregiving stress and repeated exposure can traumatize loved ones. Create clear boundaries, shared safety scripts, and scheduled debriefs so families don't become collateral damage. With steady phases, practical skills, and supportive peers, progress is measured in increased calm, better sleep, and more days where life feels manageable rather than overwhelming.

Diagnosis vs. Narrative: Reconciling Labels

We just covered emotional flashbacks and the 4F alarm system—now let's talk about the tag you pin on that problem. Labels in clinical work are like dog tags: they give useful information under stress, but they don't tell the whole person story. Used well, they help you and your clinician aim treatment; used poorly, they turn into a single-line ID that follows you off the base.

Labels: tool, not tattoo

Imagine a sergeant reading a situation report. The words "enemy contact" tell the unit what to do next. Mechanism-based labels work the same way for trauma: terms like "hyperarousal" or "emotional flashback". That specificity reduces blame — it's easier to work a problem when you can point to a malfunctioning circuit instead of blaming character. But a diagnosis that becomes the only story a person hears can lock them into a role: patient, casualty, broken. The goal is to keep the language tactical and time-limited, not identity-defining.

Why precision matters in the brain

Naming that automatic shift as an "emotional flashback" lets you plan—breathe, ground, reorient—because you know, per its definition in 1, it's a circuit firing, not personal failure.

A short field story: after a patrol, the Marine apologized for feeling weak after repeatedly reliving a convoy hit. His clinician changed the phrasing to "you had an emotional flashback to the convoy." The Marine didn't become a label overnight, but hearing a biological explanation reduced shame and opened him up to practical drills.

Putting narrative back in command

Labels should sit under the larger story of a person's life. A narrative-aware approach lets clinicians map how childhood trauma plus combat experiences produced the current pattern. For veterans with childhood

CPTSD, symptoms often mirror combat-related PTSD—heightened startle, mistrust, shutdown—but the origins and triggers differ. Therapy that stitches those threads together gives meaning and helps people re-author their past actions as survival strategies, not character defects.

Tactical steps for soldiers and families

- When talking with a loved one: use specific, short phrases. "You're having an emotional flashback" beats "you're overreacting." It signals response over judgment.
- For families: learn signs of complex secondary PTSD. Treat your responses as reactions to prolonged stress, not personal failures.
- In treatment planning: ask for mechanism-focused goals (reduce hyperarousal episodes by X% over Y months) and periodic narrative sessions to integrate history and meaning.
- At home: set short, concrete protocols for flare-ups — a brief safe-room step, a code word, or a timeout plan — so labels trigger action, not labels-alone.

Flexible labels for ongoing recovery

Think of labels as mission orders that can be updated. As therapy progresses, a diagnosis may shrink, change, or be replaced by new descriptors that fit current functioning. That shift signals progress, not erasure of past struggle. Clinicians and families should use language that tracks change and preserves dignity: specific, temporary, and attached to a plan.

When labels are held lightly and used precisely, they become navigation tools for treatment and family support — not shackles defining who someone is.

Safety, Boundaries, and Self-Compassion

Safety and Stability: Setting the Perimeter

Predictable daily routines anchor the nervous system and create the predictable perimeter needed for early recovery. For people with CPTSD—when childhood wounds combine with combat or other traumatic histories—reliable structure reduces hypervigilance, lets the fightflightfreeze response recede, and gives the prefrontal cortex a cue that the world is not chaos right now.

Why routines help

- They act like a steady mooring for attention and arousal, lowering baseline tension and making sleep deeper and less reactive.
- Clear, lowthreat steps reduce decision fatigue and provide repeated signals of safety.
- Small, consistent sequences re-engage executive function so people can move from survival responses into problem-solving and rest.

Practical elements to build

- Morning stacks (short, repeatable sequences): for example, two minutes of breathing, five minutes of writing one line ("Today I need…"), and a ten-minute walk. That compact stack cues the brain and sets a predictable tone for the day.
- Micro-routines for transitions: one-minute handwashing ritual before meals, a three-breath pause before starting a task, or a 60second tidy of a workspace. Tiny, frequent rituals are easier to complete and reinforce stability.
- Evening wind-down rituals: fixed sleep-wake times, 30–60 minutes of low-stimulation activities (reading, gentle stretching, warm beverage), dimmed lighting, and a brief "shutdown" checklist that names tomorrow's first simple task.
- Environmental cues: designate a corner of the house for downtime, reduce clutter, soften lighting, and create a "reload" space that signals safety for veterans with sensory sensitivity.
- After-action checks: Regular, low-stakes debriefs where each person names one win and one need. These short reviews close the day and normalize reflection without pressure.

How to implement

- Start tiny and repeat: pick one morning stack and one wind-down element for two weeks, then add another micro-routine once the first feels automatic.

- Keep plans visible and simple: a written daily plan that names wake time, meals, one short physical task, and an evening calming check-in reduces ambiguity.
- Make adjustments sensorywise: if certain lights, sounds, or clutter raise arousal, adapt the space and the timing of routines to lower stimulation.
- Use consistency, not perfection: missed routines are expected. Return to the next cue rather than judging or abandoning the sequence.

The goal is stabilization through predictability: consistent, low-effort sequences give the nervous system repeated evidence of safety and practical scaffolding for recovery.

For definitions of emotional flashbacks and the 4F responses, see "Emotional Flashbacks: Names and Recognitions" and "The 4F Responses: Fight, Flight, Freeze, Fawn".

When a veteran collapses into overwhelming shame or terror, it's the limbic circuitry lighting up, not a character flaw. Emotional flashbacks arise when the amygdala sounds the alarm, the hippocampus and frontal cortex go offline, and the body reengages the classic 4F pattern from past danger. Recognizing this mechanism turns blame into targeted work.

Grounding Techniques: Battlefield First Aid for the Nervous System

When the alarm goes off, use simple grounding drills that orient the senses and slow the system:

- Plantfeet grounding drill: notice three points of contact between each foot and the ground; press each point into the floor and count to ten. This technique focuses on physical grounding only. If you wish to combine it with breathing, inhale as you press and exhale as you release.
- Auditory anchor: carry a two-minute playlist of one song that steadies you; play it on repeat when needed.
- Tactile kit: keep a small object—smooth stone, knit square, or a stress ball—in a pocket for immediate sensory input.

- Weighted cover: use a heavy blanket or vest for short intervals to calm hyperarousal.

Boundaries: Rules of Engagement

Boundaries are the rules that prevent repeated hits. Treat them like ROE (rules of engagement): clear, repeatable, and nonnegotiable when needed. Short scripts work under stress — for example: "I'm not available for that right now," or "I'll respond when I can." Train them like radio calls: practice, then use them without apology. Families can back this up by recognizing and respecting those declarations as enforcement, not rejection.

Self-Compassion: R&R for the Fighter

Self-compassion is the field medic who keeps you in the fight. It's brief and tactical: when a flashback hits, say a short, grounding phrase—"I'm safe now, I'm doing what I can"—and follow with a small care action (water, sitting down, adjusting clothing). These mini-acts interrupt the internal critic and re-establish a basic level of safety.

Complex Secondary PTSD: The Unit Catches Fire Too

Families often carry secondary wounds—partners and children can show hypervigilance, withdrawal, or caregiving burnout. Teach the unit basic psychoeducation: explain emotional flashbacks and 4F responses in plain terms, run shared routines (meals at the same time), and set a simple signal for when someone needs space (a hat on the chair, a text code). Couples and family tactics that respect boundaries and offer consistent safety reduce re-traumatization and improve cooperation.

Final Drill

Safety, boundaries, and self-compassion are not soft options; they are tactical priorities. Start small, practice the scripts and grounding drills until they become reflex, and bring the family into the plan. That converts isolated survival behaviors into unit procedures that hold when the alarms go off.

Self-Assessment Tools for CPTSD

If the previous pages built your base camp—safety, boundaries, and the soft skills of self-compassion—this next phase hands you a field manual: an introductory self-assessment framework to run regular after-action reports on your nervous system. Think of it as SOP for your emotional operations: simple, repeatable, and honest.

Emotional flashbacks are sudden, intense re-experiences of a traumatic event, often triggered by sensory cues. They can feel as vivid as the original trauma and may involve distressing emotions, physical sensations, and intrusive memories. The 4F response framework refers to four instinctive reactions—fight, flight, freeze, and fawn—that people may exhibit when facing threat. Understanding these helps identify coping patterns. Traumatic brain injury (TBI) results from a blow or jolt to the head and can alter cognition, emotion, and physical functioning, often cooccurring with PTSD symptoms.

Why self-assess? Because without regular checks you won't know whether your coping plan is working or if you're still marching into the same ambush. A short, disciplined check-in helps you spot triggers, track emotional flashbacks, and spot patterns in the 4F responses (fight, flight, freeze, fawn). For veterans, these patterns often overlap with combatrelated responses and with residues from childhood experiences; for families, assessing changes in household stress can reveal signs of complex secondary PTSD.

Ethics first: run your assessments with compassion and plain honesty. Treat your inner report like you'd treat a wounded buddy—no ridicule, no ducking. Be honest about limitations: this framework is an operational tool, not a diagnosis. If answers point to severe symptoms or suicidal thinking, call a clinician or crisis line immediately.

Framework overview — purpose, scope, timing, limits, and engagement:

- Purpose: to map symptoms, triggers, and stress-responses so you can set realistic treatment targets.

Emotional flashbacks are sudden, intense re-experiences of trauma. The 4F responses—fight, flight, freeze, and fawn—are instinctive reactions to threat. Traumatic brain injury (TBI) can cause physical and cognitive changes such as headaches, sleep disturbances, and impaired concentration, and it often cooccurs with PTSD.

- Scope: emotional flashback frequency/intensity and the 4F profiles, plus common physical and cognitive signs (sleep, concentration, headaches associated with TBI).
- Timing: run a quick check weekly and a deeper review monthly; after major events, do an immediate short assessment.
- Limitations: not a substitute for professional assessment; TBI can muddy some cognitive signals—bring any concerns to a neuropsychologist or military medical team.
- Engagement: keep it low-friction—five minutes for a weekly check; 20–30 minutes for a monthly debrief.

Practical tools

- Symptom checklist (quick): rate on 0–10 scales for last week — emotional flashback intensity, number of flashbacks, nights of poor sleep, days with strong 4F reactions, concentration dips, muscle tension. Use the same scale each time.
- Reflective scale (vulnerability vs. strength): mark where you felt resilient and where you felt exposed. Short comments next to ratings are gold.

4F prompts (use as guided questions in your log)

- Fight: When did I feel an urge to push back or lash out? What triggered that feeling?
- Flight: When did I want to withdraw or avoid? Where did I go—physically or mentally?
- Freeze: When did I feel stuck or numb? What sensations accompanied it?
- Fawn: When did I people-please or override my needs to keep peace? Who was present?

Trigger mapping and diary practice

Keep a trigger map and one-line diary entries after notable incidents. Map: cue → bodily sign → emotion → behavior. Example: loud truck backfire → heart racing, stomach knot → terror → bolted for the truck bay. From that map, write a two-step safety plan: immediate grounding tactic and a post-incident recovery action (call a buddy, 10-minute breathing, rest).

Quantify impact

Track frequency (times per week), intensity (0–10), and functional impact (days avoided, work missed). Graphing a simple weekly table shows trends faster than gut feeling. For families, run couple or household AARs: short, non-blaming check-ins that surface Complex Secondary PTSD (CSPT) and allow shared safety plans.

Final tactical reminder: keep records short, honest, and routine. The goal is clear intel on your internal battlefield so your treatment team, family, and you can plan effective moves.

Journaling as a Healing Practice

Journaling Begins the Healing Conversation

Emotional flashbacks are brief, intense episodes in which memories of a past trauma are relived with the same physiological arousal and emotional intensity as when it originally happened. They are often triggered by sensory cues and can overwhelm the present moment. The 4F responses are the four basic instinctual reactions to perceived threat that the brain can trigger automatically: Fight, Flight, Freeze, and Fawn (or Fade). Recognizing these patterns helps in understanding the body's reactions and guiding calm strategies. Think of a journal as a quiet field notebook — it's not a parade report, it's where you log what happened inside you when no one else was watching. For service members and veterans dealing with CPTSD, putting thoughts to paper starts a private conversation that can calm a hypervigilant nervous system and make emotional flashbacks less mysterious and less dangerous. Journaling gives you a simple, factual, honest record of patterns—your triggers, bodily reactions, and emotional responses—so you can spot the signals that once seemed chaotic. By recording what you feel and how it shows up in the body, you connect mind and body, reduce the amygdala hijack, and create a roadmap for handling flashbacks safely.

Actionable steps

- Name the dominant feeling first (anger, shame, hollow, etc.).
- Rate its intensity on a scale of 1–10.
- Ask yourself: "What part of the body is talking?"
- Note any memory content that appears.
- Keep entries tactical: four short lines—feelings, trigger, body, thought—avoiding long essays when the brain is fogged from TBI or exhaustion.
- Use prompts such as:
- What happened today that triggered a response?
- Which bodily sensations came up?
- What thought accompanied the sensation?

- How intense was the feeling?

These steps engage the prefrontal cortex, calm the nervous system, and turn chaotic flashbacks into recognizable signals you can manage.

Creating a Safe Space

Write where it feels secure: a bedside table drawer, a locked app, a metal locker. The point is predictable privacy. If a combat veteran told me once that his helmet still feels safer than his living room, that's a cue — pick a space that lowers tension and commit to it. Safety also means rules: no editing drafts during a flashback, no sending entries in the heat of the moment, and using a short grounding checklist at the top of each page (date, time, one breathing exercise).

Establishing a Reliable Rhythm

Military life runs on routine because it reduces surprises. Use daily prompts to build the same predictability into your writing. Keep entries short on hard days: a line or two counts. For those with TBI or concentration limits, use voice notes or bullet points. Sample prompts: "What tension do I feel in my body right now?" "What small thing went right today?" Set an alarm or pair journaling with a stable habit — coffee, PT cooldown, or before lights out.

Labeling Emotions Before Memories

Emotional flashbacks are brief, intense episodes in which memories of a past trauma are relived with the same physiological arousal and emotional intensity as when it originally happened. They are often triggered by sensory cues and can overwhelm the present moment. The 4F responses are the four basic instinctual reactions to perceived threat that the brain can trigger automatically: Fight, Flight, Freeze, and Fawn (or Fade). Recognizing these patterns helps in understanding the body's reactions and guiding calm strategies. One tactical trick: name the feeling first — anger, shame, hollow — then note any memory content that shows up. Labeling reduces amygdala hijack by engaging the prefrontal cortex. When an emotional flashback hits, pause, write the dominant feeling, rate its intensity (1–10), then ask: "What part of the body is talking?" Add a short note of any memory images or phrases that surface and one small grounding action you can do now. This sequence moves the experience into language and calms the brain enough to handle the memory with less overwhelm.

Connecting Mind and Body

A brief, deliberate link between sensations and words is what makes journaling effective. Use a short body scan before or during an entry: notice where a feeling lives, describe its quality (tight, hot, heavy), and write that description down. Naming bodily sensations pulls the experience out of automatic reactivity and into conscious awareness, which helps regulatory systems settle.

Add a sensory line to every entry: pulse, breath depth, stomach tightness, jaw clench. These small observations teach the nervous system it can be checked and recorded rather than obeyed immediately. Try a one-minute body-scan entry: list the top three sensations, then do a grounding drill (5-4-3-2-1) and note the change.

Mapping Responses and Creating a Path Forward

Use your journal as an after-action report. Track triggers, your 4F responses, and what workably reduced reactivity. Over weeks you'll see patterns — times of day, certain family comments, or loud noises. Convert patterns into tactics: pre-planned exits, code words with a partner, breathing routines, or a 10-minute distraction protocol. For families dealing with Complex secondary PTSD, encourage separate journals to process vicarious trauma and a shared, brief "what helps me now" page to reduce cross-triggering during conflicts.

Ending on a Positive Note

Close each entry with a tiny win: a gratitude line, a grounding sentence, or a safety affirmation. Even a single line — "I breathed through it" — consolidates a safety signal. Veterans report that ending this way feels like re-raising the unit flag after contact: small, tactical, and morale-boosting.

The Power of Journaling

For soldiers and families, writing isn't soft — it's an operational tool you can use every day to reduce 4F reactivity, map triggers, and keep the lines of communication open between clinic and home.

Boundaries in Relationships

Boundaries: The Protective Shield for Safety and Healing

If your trauma recovery had a field manual, boundaries would be the first section: how to set the perimeter, post a sentry, and mark no-go zones. For combat vets and veterans of rough childhoods, boundaries are not a nicety — they're a mission-essential system that reduces surprise triggers and gives the nervous system a chance to stand down.

Identifying Personal Needs and Nonnegotiables

Start like an intelligence brief: list the conditions that keep you safe. Quiet corners, predictable plans, physical distance, limits on topics, or no touch without consent—these are your nonnegotiables. CPTSD from childhood and combat often produces overlapping triggers: sudden loud noises, unexpected closeness, or emotional pressure. Note which of these trigger your 4F system (fight, flight, freeze, fawn) or spark emotional flashbacks—sudden, intense reliving of old feelings, behaving like incoming fire. Once identified, these needs become the coordinates for your perimeter.

Communicating Boundaries Early and Clearly

Think of this as rules of engagement. Say your limit plainly, with minimal drama and an "I" line: for example, 'I feel unsafe when plans change without warning; I need a headsup.' Short, factual, and repeatable statements reduce pushback. If someone pushes back, you don't have to win an argument; you just need to maintain the perimeter.

Building Confidence: Drill and Role-Play

Before you call in an airstrike of confrontation, train on the range. Role-play boundary conversations with a trusted ally or therapist. Run the script, practice the pause, rehearse the exit. Confidence comes from repetition: after a few dry runs, real interactions feel less like live fire. Families can run these drills too — it helps partners learn what a healthy limit feels like, and stitches the fabric of trust back together.

Surrounding Yourself with Respectful People

People who consistently honor your limits are like good squad members; they keep you alive. When connections repeatedly cross your lines, it drains readiness. That may mean stepping back from old contacts or reassigning certain people to different roles in your life. Your safety comes first.

Maintaining Boundaries and Re-asserting After Breaches

Boundaries need maintenance. When someone breaches your limit, treat it like an after-action report: note what happened, avoid self-blame, and state the next step. A simple script: 'You crossed my boundary when X happened. I'm asking you to stop, and here's what will change if it continues.' Consequences should be realistic and enforceable — not theatrical.

The Boundary Toolkit: Scripts, Grounding, Pause Strategies

Carry a pocket kit:

- Two short scripts: one for first contact, one for repeat violations.

Use the primary threebreath grounding drill described in the breathwork section; it integrates breathing with grounding by focusing on bodily sensations.

- A pause phrase: "I need a timeout" — gives permission to exit.
- A safe word with family members for urgent shutdowns.

Gradual Exposure: Small Patrols, Not Full Assaults

If a situation feels like enemy territory, approach in small patrols. Test it with low-stakes interactions, increase exposure slowly, and debrief each step. This pacing reduces overwhelm and trains the brain to know that not every trigger equals total collapse.

Families and Complex secondary PTSD

Households with a veteran with CPTSD often experience secondary wounds. Setting clear household boundaries protects everyone and models healthy limits for children who grew up in chaos. Teach family members the toolkit and run regular checkins — small, scheduled briefings that cut down on surprises and recalibrate expectations.

Boundaries are not walls meant to isolate; they're a defensive system that lets you engage from a place of strength. Set the perimeter, practice the drills, and keep your toolkit within reach — safety is a skill, and you can train for it.

What to Expect from This Book

What to Expect from This Book: A Field Manual for Healing Hidden Scars

Think of this book as a field manual handed to you after a long operation: clear, practical, and written with the kind of plain talk soldiers trust. It will cover what CPTSD is, how childhood wounds shape adult behavior, the brain science that explains why feelings hijack you, and hands-on tools that work in real life — for veterans, active-duty, and the families who carry the fallout.

Foundational Concepts You Can Trust

In this book we'll explore the core features often associated with CPTSD — emotional dysregulation, negative selfconception, relational difficulties, and altered threat perception. The foundational neuroscience in this book explains how prolonged threat alters threatdetection, regulation, and attachment circuits, making reactions feel like reflexes rather than choices.

Emotional Flashbacks and the 4F Response

The 4F responses—fight, flight, freeze, and fawn—have already been defined earlier in this book. In this section, we focus on their practical application.

- Fight: further explored in later chapters, detailing its manifestations and strategies for working with it.
- Flight: further explored later, describing patterns of avoidance and approaches to regulation.
- Freeze: further examined later, covering shutdown responses and paths to recovery.
- Fawn: further examined later, exploring peoplepleasing dynamics and healthier alternatives.

Knowing which response is your default matters. It lets you design tactics to interrupt the automatic response and replace it with safer, chosen action.

Practical, Daily Healing Steps — Tactical Edition

- Regulation drills: short, repeatable exercises you can run in the mess hall or at your desk. A 60second body scan; or a simple 54321 grounding checklist. Make these habitual.
- Safety perimeter: Create routines and physical cues that signal safety — a dedicated chair, a low-light lamp, a family "standdown" ritual before bed. Consistency flags the nervous system that danger is lower.
- Controlled exposure: Move toward difficult memories in small, planned rehearsals with a clinician or trusted wingman. Think of it as progressive training: short, structured, and reviewed afteraction.

Veterans, Childhood Trauma, and Shared Pathways

Combat trauma and childhood harm can end up with the same symptoms: hypervigilance, dissociation, emotional flashbacks, relationship problems. For a veteran whose baseline teaches constant alertness, childhood-derived CPTSD can amplify reactions; for someone raised in chaos, military stressors can reactivate old systems. Treatment that recognizes both sources — the combat scar and the earlier wound — produces better outcomes.

Families are not neutral ground. Secondary effects show up as caregiver burnout, child behavior changes, and relational drift. Spouses may develop anxiety or hypervigilance from longterm exposure to a partner's symptoms. Tactical recommendations for families:

- Brief the family: Simple, compassionate education about symptoms reduces blame.
- Set clear roles: Use shift—like schedules for emotional labor (who handles morning routines, paperwork, sleep checks).

Closing the Brief

This book will blend research, veteran stories, and actionable drills you can put into play tomorrow. Read it like a field manual: pick one regulation drill, run it daily, and report back to your team — small, consistent moves win the campaign.

The Body Speaks: Trauma in the Nervous System

Trauma doesn't just happen to you; it fundamentally changes how your internal systems operate. This shift leaves the nervous system perpetually primed for danger. Hyperarousal becomes the default, keeping the body vigilant even when safe. The brain's capacity for planning and judgment falters, giving way to persistent rumination and the unbidden return of past emotions as visceral, presentday sensations—emotional flashbacks. Your body, now a sentinel, misreads safety cues, anchoring traumatic memory in physical signals and keeping the primal fight, flight, freeze, or fawn responses on constant alert.

Yet, understanding these deep-seated adjustments offers a path to recalibration. This section lays out practical, science-informed strategies to restore a sense of safety from the inside out. We will examine how intentional breathing, grounding practices, and structured routines can stabilize arousal, quiet hypervigilance, and rebuild connection to the present moment. We will see how tending to sleep, nourishment, movement, and self-compassion are not secondary measures, but direct methods to calm the nervous system and cultivate a lasting internal peace.

How Trauma Rewires the Nervous System

I was on a chow line in garrison when a truck backfired like a mortar. Everyone flinched. My buddy tossed his tray, went rigid, and his face tightened into a gaunt expression—into a corner where a different war was being fought. That splitsecond collapse was not weakness. It was a nervous system doing what it was built to do: protect the body at any cost. This is the operational reality of trauma. Trauma rewires the nervous system, and that rewiring changes how you think, feel, and act.

Trauma Rewires the Nervous System

Highpressure events trigger neuroplastic changes. The foundational concept explains how the PFC goes on defensive, impairing executive function and leaving individuals stuck replaying events or struggling with simple tasks.

Neuroplastic Changes and Executive Function

Imagine your brain as a forward operating base. When the base is under repeated attack, command nodes can get cut off, and the troops default to immediate survival moves. In brain terms, stress strengthens fast threat pathways and weakens prefrontal control. Rumination—replaying incidents on loop—runs on those strong threat circuits. Tactical tip: re-establish command. Short, predictable routines and written checklists reduce the load on the prefrontal cortex and make planning manageable while the brain heals.

Hyperarousal and Constant Vigilance

PTSD often sets a new baseline: hyperarousal. The body lives with fight-or-flight dialed up, scanning for danger in safe places. Picture walking a quiet town but feeling like you're on overwatch, eyes sweeping for enemy movement. That constant vigilance is exhausting and degrades sleep, concentration, and trust. Field drill: breathing and movement reset. Box breathing (inhale 4, hold 4, exhale 4, hold 4) paired with a 2minute walk lowers arousal fast enough to reengage executive control during routine tasks.

The 4F Responses: Fight, Flight, Freeze, Fawn

Trauma keeps the 4F responses on call. These were meant for seconds, not years. Soldiers and survivors can snap to fight or flight, lock down into freeze, or go limp into faint reactions when no immediate threat exists. Family-facing tactic: create a trigger script. When a flashpoint shows up, a partner can say, "I've got you—let's do 2 minutes of breathing," which signals safety and interrupts the old survival loop.

Survival Patterns and Emotional Flashbacks

Those survival patterns that worked under fire stick around. For a comprehensive understanding of emotional flashbacks, refer to the foundational definitions earlier in this text. A smell, tone, or touch can send the system back into old modes. Skill to practice: name and ground. Saying out loud, "This is an emotional flashback; I am safe here" while orienting to five facts in the room brings the body back to now.

Body Memory and Interoception

Traumatic memories are often felt first as bodily sensations—tension, nausea, a tight chest—rather than as explicit story details. Our interoceptive system, which senses internal states, can misfire as a false alarm, flagging even tiny cues as threats. This is especially true after TBI or battle fatigue, where the signals are louder and more confusing.

Families carry this too: partners and children can develop Complex secondary PTSD from repeated exposure to a veteran's symptoms. Practical orders for families—set structure, practice calm response scripts, maintain safe escape plans for intense episodes—reduce re-triggering and protect caregivers.

The brain changes after trauma are real, stubborn, and measurable. But knowing what's happening—how the prefrontal cortex, neuroplasticity, hyperarousal, the 4F suite, emotional flashbacks, and body memory interact—gives you tactical options. The next pages lay out field-tested methods to reclaim control, rebuild planning muscles, and restore safety for veterans and the families who stand watch with them.

Neuroception and Perceived Safety

Neuroception — the body's automatic assessment

If your body had a sergeant, neuroception would be the one staring into the dark with night-vision goggles and a hair-trigger. You walk into a room and your gut tightens before your brain has time to jot down a mental report. That pre-verbal alarm is neuroception: an unconscious scan by the nervous system that decides, fast and quietly, whether the situation is safe for a chow line or requires taking cover.

This scan is aimed at both physical and social threats. A calm voice, open posture, and predictable timing send "all clear" signals. A sudden tone, a cluttered room, or an ambiguous stare can throw the system back to red. For troops, that split-second read is lifesaving in combat; for veterans and people with CPTSD, it can keep firing long after the battle ends.

How trauma rewires the sentry

Trauma lowers the threshold for danger, causing the 4F responses to fire on autopilot. This is the same mechanism detailed in the foundational explanation, where repeated threats keep the sentry overalert and the brain wired for heightened vigilance.

TBI and childhood-origin CPTSD raise similar symptoms: misreads of safety cues, poor tolerance for sensory load, and quick flips into survival modes. The mechanisms are shared: altered neural circuits that bias toward threat detection and away from social engagement.

Social engagement and co-regulation: the human reset button

Our species didn't evolve to fight alone. Facial expressions, tone, and touch are part of how the nervous system judges safety. That's where co-regulation comes in: a trusted person helps downshift arousal. Think of a battle buddy who knows when you need a slow breath and when to shut up.

Complex secondary PTSD is a form of PTSD that develops in close relatives of trauma survivors; it is characterized by chronic anxiety, intrusive memories, and hyperarousal triggered by cues reminiscent of the veteran's experiences. Traumatic Brain Injury (TBI), often a concussion or mild brain injury from blast, impact, or whiplash, can impair cognition, emotion, and arousal regulation. Families carry a double burden. Partners and children can develop complex secondary PTSD from the constant highalert environment, and they, too, remain on watch. Training families to coregulate reduces strain for everyone. A practical set of drills combines a prearranged "pause" signal, a 60second joint breathing exercise, a short grounding phrase, and a twominute partner routine: sit facing each other, match a slow breath for six cycles, and exchange one sentence of groundtruth without judgment. These short, predictable practices widen the sense of safety for both the veteran and the family member, and break automatic escalation cycles that fuel secondary trauma. For vets with TBI or battle fatigue, keep sensory input low when possible and keep the drills brief. Simple shared cues—such as a family signal that means "pause and breathe," a brief grounding before meals, or a daily minute where everyone places a hand on their chest and breathes together—serve as a medic for the nervous system, promoting mutual regulation and reducing household hypervigilance.

Emotional flashbacks and distorted safety

Refer to the foundational definition of emotional flashbacks provided earlier; this section focuses on how those flashbacks can produce distorted senses of safety and influence behavior and decision-making.

Grounding tactics to interrupt the hijack:

- Slow, paced breathing: inhale 4, hold 2, exhale 6 — three rounds.
- Sensory anchor: name five things you can see, four you can touch, three you can hear.
- Body check: plant feet, feel chair under you, relax jaw.

Environmental control and routines.

Maintaining a consistent environment is key to the wellbeing of patients. This involves regulating temperature, humidity, and light to create a soothing atmosphere. Routine checks, such as monitoring air quality and ensuring proper ventilation, support both staff and patients in achieving optimal health.

Practical interventions to recalibrate neuroception

Start with felt safety before you chase insight. Tactical approach:

- Daily micro-practices: 2–3 short breathing sets per day.
- Gradual exposure: map triggers, rank them, expose for short, controlled periods with a buddy present.
- Sensory anchors: chewable necklace, textured patch, or a specific song that reliably calms.
- For TBI: shorten exercises, use tactile anchors, and repeat often.

Families often face complex secondary PTSD and, when caring for veterans with TBI, must understand that these conditions can amplify stress. Families: learn to coregulate and protect your own reserve. Set limits on debriefs, schedule checkins, and keep a private "afteraction" plan so caregiving doesn't become constant hypervigilance.

In the next chapter we'll put these pieces into a field manual: a weekbyweek program for soldiers and families to retrain neuroception and restore the sense of safety in ordinary rooms, not just on the line.

Breath, Heart Rate, and State Regulation

Calming the Storm Within: Breath, Heart Rate, and Nervous System Regulation

If you've ever been told to "just breathe" in the middle of a firefight (no one said that—don't be ridiculous), you know the look that comes back at you—a mixture of suspicion and the silent question, "Is this a trick?" It's not a trick. Breath is a frontline tool: cheap, portable, and surprisingly effective at turning down the volume on a panicked nervous system.

For a detailed definition of an emotional flashback, see Emotional Flashbacks: Names and Recognitions. How breath helps: slow, diaphragmatic breathing engages the vagus nerve, the key pathway that tells your heart to calm down and your stomach to stop doing acrobatics. This lowers sympathetic drive and increases parasympathetic tone, which makes emotional processing feel less chaotic. Veterans who trained simple breath routines report fewer hijacks from emotional flashbacks and an easier time staying present during stressful triggers.

Heart Rate Variability: the quiet indicator of flexibility

Think of heart rate variability (HRV) as how well your heart can play followtheleader with the moment.

Think of heart rate variability (HRV) as how well your heart can play follow-the-leader with the moment. High HRV means your autonomic system shifts gears smoothly—useful when a loud noise is a truck backfiring and not incoming fire. Low HRV looks like rigid, stuck responses: fight, freeze, or flee on autopilot.

The 4F reflex – freeze, fight, flight, fawn – is essentially the same set of responses described in The 4F Responses: Fight, Flight, Freeze, Fawn. For a detailed explanation, see that section. Interoception—feeling what's going on inside—lets you catch warning signs before the 4F reflex slams the door. By tuning into physical cues—tightening in the throat, quickening pulse, shallow breathing—you activate heartrate variability (HRV) pathways that help regulate the sympathetic–parasympathetic balance. Practice improves detection: noticing these signals gives you options other than reacting. A simple, evidencebased technique is structured box breathing: inhale for 4 counts, hold for 4, exhale for 4. One round can shift you from freezing to focused action. Build up to five rounds while sitting or standing to strengthen autonomic regulation.

Concrete drills you can run

- Grounding cues: pick a reliable physical anchor — touch the heel of your hand against your thigh, feeling the contact, feel the roughness of your boot, or press your fingertips together. Train it during calm moments so it works under pressure.

- Body scan: run a quick six-point check (feet, calves, hips, chest, shoulders, jaw). Stop where there's tightness, breathe into that spot, and let it loosen.

- Micro-practices for deployment life: at checkpoint, spend the ten seconds you're doing equipment checks to run one breath cycle and a toe press; it's discipline with a purpose.

Shifting the 4Fs in the field and at home

Regulation isn't about making the 4Fs disappear. It's about interrupting instinct long enough to choose a more effective response. Treat it like a battle drill: detect the sign, label the sensation, execute your breath routine, and re-assess. Repeat until the nervous system learns new patterns.

TBI and modifications

If a traumatic brain injury affects concentration or memory, simplify routines: one-count inhale, two-count exhale, repeat five times. Use tactile anchors (a coin in the pocket, a bracelet) and practice the action until it becomes automatic.

Putting it into regular PT

An emotional flashback is an involuntary, vivid reexperiencing of a traumatic event that feels as real as the original moment, often accompanied by intense physiological arousal. Treat these techniques like weapons maintenance: ten minutes a day, mixed into PT or morning prep. Track

HRV with whatever device you already use or just note resting pulse trends. Small, steady practice shifts baseline physiology, raises resilience, and reduces the number of times emotional flashbacks hijack a mission or family dinner.

This is not woo-woo. It's practical conditioning for a nervous system that's been through combat or childhood trauma. Run the drills, teach the family, and keep your tool kit close. The storm quiets faster with training and a pocketful of practiced breaths.

Grounding Techniques that Work

Grounding Techniques: A Bridge to Present Safety

If breath and heart rate are your internal field manual, grounding techniques are the quick-response kit you pull out when the situation goes hot. Think of them as immediate, low-tech tools that anchor you to now — not to the past—so the body and brain can stop treating an old fight like current combat. For veterans and their families coping with complex PTSD, these techniques can stabilize arousal in the moment and build a habit of returning to safety faster.

Presence in the Here-and-Now

Trauma-trained brains are pros at time travel: one smell, one tone of voice, and suddenly you're back in a childhood basement or an ambush. That split-second dissociation is survival by default, but it's a poor fit for daily life. Grounding works by directing attention outward or to neutral internal cues so the brain can reclassify the environment as non-dangerous. Practically: orient your senses — what you can see, feel, hear — and state simple facts out loud. Short, factual sentences cut through panic like headlights through fog. This tactic is equally useful for a soldier having a flashback at a family dinner and for a spouse who's absorbed secondary trauma after years of caregiving.

Regulating the Nervous System with the Senses

Senses are reliable anchors. Tactile cues are simple and immediate: feel the weight of your boots on the floor, press your palms together, run your fingers over a textured object. Sound can steady you — hum a few bars of a calming song, tune in to ambient noise and name it ("air conditioner, distant traffic, spoon clinking"). Smell ties strongly to memory; a small bottle of a calming scent can function like a personal ceasefire. These inputs tell the nervous system, "I'm here. I'm alive. This is now."

Practical Sensory Exercises

- Tactile anchor: carry a smooth stone or fabric square. When alarm rises, hold it, describe its texture, temperature, and shape.

- Auditory anchor: list five sounds you can hear, then three you can focus on.
- Olfactory anchor: inhale a calming scent for three slow breaths while naming the scent.

Body Checking without Judgment

Body checking isn't a CHECKLIST for panic — it's neutral reconnaissance. Scan your body top to toe and label sensations without judgment: "jaw tight," "shoulders heavy," "butterflies in stomach." Replace catastrophic thoughts with descriptive statements: swap "I'm losing it" for "my hands are trembling." This quiet, factual reporting reduces escalation because the brain accepts neutral data better than alarmed interpretation.

Reducing Emotional Flashbacks

Grounding interrupts that loop by shifting sensory weighting back to current input. The faster you can reorient attention to the present, the fewer resources the flashback consumes. Train this like clearing a bad comms channel: detect early signs (sensory dissociation, racing pulse), deploy grounding (tactile + breath + naming), then reassess. Earlier foundational definitions describe emotional flashbacks in detail.

Breathwork as a Grounding Tool

Traumatic brain injury (TBI) is a disruption of brain function caused by an external force, often leading to cognitive and emotional changes. Gently breathe diaphragmatically: inhale to a comfortable count, pause a beat if desired, then exhale about 1.5 times as long as the inhale. Repeat 2–4 slow cycles with a tactile anchor to reduce arousal—this rhythm is safe and effective for people with TBI.

Creating a Portable Grounding Kit

Complex secondary PTSD is a chronic stress response that can develop in caregivers who are repeatedly exposed to the traumarelated symptoms of their loved ones. A compact kit turns improvisation into routine. Suggested items: a smooth stone or stress ball, a small scented vial, a laminated cue card with 3–5 grounding steps, a playlist on a thumb drive or phone, and a tactile fabric. Train with the kit weekly so using it under stress feels like a practiced drill. Families should build complementary kits for kids and partners—when the caregiver has tools, Complex secondary PTSD is less likely to cascade.

Final drill: pick three grounding tools you'll use tomorrow, practice them for five minutes, and run a short after-action: what worked, what didn't, and what you'll change. Small, consistent practice turns emergency skills into muscle memory — and that muscle memory is survival in civilian clothes.

Somatic Awareness without Overwhelm

Beginning with Gentle, Science-Informed Somatic Awareness

Picture this: a squad on a long patrol stops at a creek. The commander asks everyone to check kit, then checks in—no shouting, just a two-minute pause so the men and women can breathe and reset. That tiny interruption—slow, simple, intentional—is exactly what somatic awareness looks like when it works well for trauma. For soldiers and families dealing with combat stress, childhood wounds, or the muddled symptoms of TBI, the body often speaks louder than words. We can learn to listen without getting dragged into full combat with our own nervous systems.

Set a Slow Pace Like a Tactical Halt

Fight, flight, freeze, and fawn—the four primary responses of the autonomic nervous system—are instinctive reactions that the brain triggers when it perceives threat. Start small. Big drills and intense movement can trigger these 4F responses, especially when childhood trauma is layered under combat memory. If the brain or brainstem is already overtaxed from a blast or repeated deployments, abrupt stimulation will backfire. Use micro-actions: slow breaths, soft shoulder rolls, and a two-minute standing still. Think of it as a tactical halt for your nervous system: no fireworks, no sprint, just controlled minimalism that lets the autonomic system downshift.

Notice the Boundary between Body Signals and Thoughts

One of the most useful skills is separating a raw physical sensation from the story your mind immediately attaches to it. The body might tighten—that's a signal. The mind will usually add a narrative: "I'm under attack," or "I'm a failure." Train to pause and label each independently. A practical drill:

- Stop for one breath.
- Identify the first thing you feel physically ("tight chest," "cold hands").
- Name the thought separately ("That sound means danger," "I'm not good enough").

See Emotional Flashbacks: Names and Recognitions for a detailed definition. Grounding tools can address the physical signal without escalating catastrophic thinking, preventing emotional flashbacks from snowballing.

Use Breath Rhythms to Modulate Arousal

Breath is the quickest manual control we have over the autonomic system. For most folks, slow, diaphragmatic breathing lowers heart rate, calms the vagus nerve, and decreases 4F activation. For those with TBI, keep it gentler: inhale for a count that feels easy, pause a beat if comfortable, exhale a little longer. Try this in the field or at home:

- Feet planted, hands on belly.
- Inhale slowly through the nose (count to whatever feels steady).
- Exhale through the mouth or nose, a touch longer.

Repeat three to five times, and check for a drop in tension.

Briefly Name Sensations and Return to a Neutral Pose

Long analysis is for therapy, not for a roadside check. When a sensation surfaces, use a one-line label—"tight chest," "buzzing hands," "empty stomach"—then move to a neutral posture: shoulders down, jaw soft, even weight on both feet. That neutral pose tells the body it's allowed to stop scanning for danger. The script might be: "Tight chest—soften shoulders—breathe." Say it in your head, out loud, or use a partner for a prompt.

Tactical Notes for Families and Teams

Brief, action-focused guidance for caregivers and professional teams managing acute behavioral episodes. These notes collect simple, evidence-informed tactics designed for quick use: clear steps you can practice, adapt, and rely on when plans and patience are under pressure.

These are not magic fixes. They are tools—small, science-informed, and field-ready—that stop a bad episode from becoming a full mission failure. Use them like you would any standard operating procedure: simple, practiced, and ready when needed.

Sleep, Resetting, and Restoration

Sleep is the unsung logistics commander of nervous system recovery. If your system is stuck on red alert after combat or childhood trauma, getting sleep to behave like a dependable NCO can make everything easier to manage. Think of sleep not as an indulgence but as a field repair shop for the brain and body.

Predictability Lowers Hyperarousal

See The 4F Responses: Fight, Flight, Freeze, Fawn for a comprehensive description. A predictable routine anchors the nervous system, reduces hypervigilance, and keeps emotional flashbacks from breaching the perimeter at night, enabling restorative sleep.

Structured Routines to Regulate the 4Fs

The four primary threat responses—Fight, Flight, Freeze, and Fawn—are collectively called the 4Fs. They are automatic coping strategies that can become hyperactive after trauma.

Treat sleep like a pre-mission check: make it a nonnegotiable priority and build a simple, repeatable routine to prepare for rest.

- Fix wake and sleep times and keep them consistent daily to anchor your circadian rhythm.
- Darken the room and remove or power down screens at least one hour before bed.
- Use a short, repeatable winddown ritual — breathing exercises, light stretching, or a quick reflection — to signal the body and mind it's time to sleep.

Small, consistent wins matter.

See The 4F Responses: Fight, Flight, Freeze, Fawn for details on these reactions. A daily plan with fixed sleep windows, scheduled movement, and windingdown rituals regulates the 4Fs. When behaviors follow a predictable cadence, the body is less likely to default to emergency mode. Practical move: choose a 30–60 minute presleep window—light out, quiet task, comfortable position—treated like mission prep.

Light Exposure and Circadian Signals

Your internal clock reads light like an operational brief. Morning natural light is a briefing: start patrol mode. Evening screens are like false alarms—blue light tells the brain it's still daytime and delays the sleep command. Tactical steps: get sunlight within the first hour after waking; dim overhead lights and remove screens at least an hour before bed. For TBI cases, light regulation can be awkward—work with medical staff on timing and intensity.

Sleep Duration and Emotion Processing

See Emotional Flashbacks: Names and Recognitions for a definition of emotional flashbacks and The 4F Responses: Fight, Flight, Freeze, Fawn for the body's automatic reactions. Adequate sleep allows the prefrontal cortex to regain topdown control over the amygdala, reducing emotional reactivity. Shortened sleep or nighttime disturbances—such as sweats, awakenings, or nightmares—indicate unresolved emotional flashbacks and interrupt restorative processes, hampering regulation.

Stabilizing Cortisol Rhythms

See The 4F Responses: Fight, Flight, Freeze, Fawn for how cortisol rhythm influences these reactions. Cortisol should peak in the morning and taper toward night; disruption can hyperactivate the 4Fs. Consistent sleep and regular wake times reduce cortisol chaos and lower 4F flareups.

Sleep and Memory Reconsolidation

During deep sleep the brain reprocesses memories—what used to be a hair-trigger memory can get re-stored with less charge. That's vital for healing from trauma: restful sleep supports this reconsolidation, making traumatic memories less explosive over time.

When Sleep Reflects Unresolved Flashbacks Addressing Nightly Reactivity

If you wake in a panic, use brief, efficient steps: ground with 5–10 slow breaths, press feet flat to the mattress, name three safe things in the room, then employ a steady breathing pattern or lowvolume sound machine to reestablish calm. Complex secondary PTSD—when family members experience chronic arousal due to a loved one's trauma—can perpetuate sleep disturbances. For families experiencing this, shared household predictability—lightsoff rules, agreed wake times, and quiet hours—reduces nightly reactivity and improves sleep.

Traumatic brain injury (TBI) is a disruption of brain function caused by an external force, often leading to cognitive, emotional, and sleep-related changes. Complex posttraumatic stress disorder (CPTSD) involves prolonged exposure to trauma, resulting in pervasive emotional dysregulation and intrusive memories. If you've had TBI or longstanding CPTSD, consult your provider about sleep medications, targeted therapies, and the possibility of a sleep study to evaluate altered architecture. Sleep is not a luxury or a weakness; it's a frontline tool. Treat it like equipment: maintain it, stick to a regular schedule, and use it to repair the system so you can show up for the mission of life.

Nutrition, Movement, and Recovery

If sleep opened the door to nervous system repair, think of stable nourishment and regular movement as the floorboards and handrails that keep you from falling through the house. In combat, you learned quick fixes: a Cration bar, a sip of water, a tenminute stretch before pushing on. In recovery, those same basic moves stack up into real regulation – the kind that calms the 4F responses and tames emotional flashbacks that can show up like phantom firefights from childhood or combat. See "The 4F Responses: Fight, Flight, Freeze, Fawn" for details.

Regular meals: a low-tech, high-impact tactic

A brief order: eat at regular times. When glucose dips low, the amygdala— a brain structure that detects threat and triggers fight/flight responses— lights up and the body goes into threat mode — that's when intrusive memories (unwanted, vivid recollections that surface spontaneously) and hypervigilance (a state of heightened alertness to potential danger) spike. Eating at consistent intervals stabilizes energy and mood, reduces blood sugar shocks, and buys your prefrontal cortex time to work. Practical order: set three main meal times and one or two proteinrich snacks. If you're a nightshift veteran or parenting a kid with CPTSD, anchor meals to clock times rather than feelings — it's less drama and more discipline.

Protein and timing: load the front line

Protein supplies amino acids that are raw material for neurotransmitters. Make protein the first thing in the morning — eggs, Greek yogurt, canned tuna, a scoop of nut butter — and again in mid-afternoon so you don't crash into a flashback. Smaller, frequent portions blunt adrenaline spikes better than one massive plate. Field rule: protein within an hour of waking and a protein-plus-carb snack mid-shift (or mid-afternoon) reduces the odds of a crash that looks like panic.

Hydration and sleep support brain repair

After a TBI, the brain's metabolic pathways are altered and it is especially vulnerable to oxidative stress and inflammation. Adequate hydration supports neuronal membrane fluidity, facilitates the removal of metabolic waste through the glymphatic system, and helps maintain electrolyte balance—all of which are crucial for functional recovery. Water keeps neurons firing cleanly. Dehydration amplifies fatigue and anxiety; sip regularly rather than chug. Aim for steady intake through the day — two liters is a rough baseline, adjusted for heat, size, and workload. Paired with solid sleep routines, good hydration helps the brain clear metabolic waste and supports recovery processes that are vital after trauma or TBI. See "Traumatic Brain Injury" for details.

The hypothalamicpituitaryadrenal (HPA) axis is the body's hormonal stress response system that releases cortisol and other glucocorticoids. Nutrient timing—when you eat—and micronutrients—tiny vitamins and minerals—can help steady this axis and reduce the overactivation that fuels the 4Fs and emotional flashbacks.

Timing meals around your daily rhythm influences cortisol pulses and the 4F balance. Foods rich in omega-3s, vitamin C, B-complex, magnesium, and potassium moderate stress responses. Think salmon, citrus, leafy greens, nuts, bananas. Before starting supplements, run it by your medical provider — pills aren't the same as chow. Tactical tip: add a handful of mixed nuts or a piece of fruit to your kit for quick nutrient hits.

Movement that calms the system

Not every movement needs to be a ruck march. Lowimpact activities — walking, swimming, cycling, tai chi, yoga — soothe fight/flight reactions—rapid bodily responses to perceived danger that trigger the 4Fs—and reduce the frequency of emotional flashbacks—vivid, intrusive memories of past trauma that feel as if they are happening in the present. Start with ten minutes: a brisk walk with diaphragmatic breathing, or a short tai chi flow. Mindful movement sharpens interoception: scan the chest, belly, hands, and feet; name one sensation in each spot. That naming pulls a person out of dissociation and into presentmoment control.

Orders for families and partners

Complex secondary PTSD refers to the condition where individuals in a traumaexposed household develop PTSDlike symptoms not only because of direct exposure, but also through repeated indirect exposure to the primary trauma or ongoing stressors. In these households, the nervous systems of multiple members are dysregulated, making daily routines critical for emotional stability. Set shared meal times, keep proteinand nutrientrich snacks visible, and plan gentle movement together – a twentyminute afterdinner walk can reset the household's nervous system. Create nonjudgmental checkins: "How's your energy?" is better than "Are you okay?" because it targets physiological regulation. Encourage each family member to keep their own water bottle and a small stash of protein. See "Complex secondary PTSD" for details.

Treat these steps like basic kit maintenance. They won't fix everything overnight, but consistent meals, regular hydration, and gentle, mindful movement strengthen the nervous system so the therapies and hard memory work have a fighting chance.

Self-Compassion as a Daily NervousSystem Practice

Selfcompassion feels like stepping into fire when your training has left you hypervigilant. Treat it instead as a quiet, ondemand lifeline that signals safety to a nervous system stuck in 4F mode (see "The 4F Responses: Fight, Flight, Freeze, Fawn") and helps break emotional flashbacks (see "Emotional Flashbacks: Names and Recognitions").

Noticing the Inner Critic

The inner critic is often louder in people with CPTSD (Complex PostTraumatic Stress Disorder, a chronic condition marked by emotional dysregulation, negative selfimage, and relational challenges). In combat terms, it's like a hostile radio channel that broadcasts worstcase intel 24/7. First mission: notice that signal without engaging. Field exercise: when you hear the critic ("You're weak," "You should've handled it"), mentally mark it as "incoming trauma memory" instead of truth. Short script to use: "That's the critic talking. I'm safe now." Say it out loud or under your breath. This small reappraisal helps the brain reclassify the noise and reduces hypervigilant firing, allowing the prefrontal cortex (the brain region that governs executive control and regulates the amygdala) to step in.

Naming and Labeling Emotions

Emotional labeling is a frontline tactic for calming overactive circuits. When a surge hits, pull out the oneline report: "I'm feeling scared," or "I'm tense and angry." Labeling shifts activity from emotional centers such as the amygdala to the prefrontal cortex, lowering arousal. Practice in noncombat moments: pause, take two breaths, then name the feeling. Families can teach kids the same move—short language reduces overwhelm and cuts down on complex secondary PTSD symptoms that spread through the household.

Brief Soothing Rituals

Small rituals are dependable safety signals. They don't need to be poetic. Examples: a twominute tea check, rubbing a fingertip to thumb for thirty seconds, or a threecount inhaleholdexhale before getting out of bed. Consistency matters more than duration. These microrituals create predictable cues the nervous system learns to trust, reducing sudden spikes and calming the 4F response.

Grounding with Breath and Body Awareness

During a flashback or a 4F surge, try a breathandbody routine: inhale slowly for four counts, pause for two, exhale for six, and repeat three times. Then perform a quick scan—feet on the floor, shoulders down, jaw relaxed—to release a single tight spot. This couples interoceptive grounding with paced breathing, quickly lowering arousal. The extended exhale activates the parasympathetic brake—think of it as a manual override.

Extending Compassionate Intent to Parts

CPTSD (see "What CPTSD Really Means") often includes damaged, frightened inner parts—think of them as crew members who need care. Invite those parts in with a brief, neutral script: "I see you. You're tired. I'll help." Visualize offering water or shelter to the scared child part. This practice reduces shame and integrates fragmented memory networks. Partners and families can join by learning compassionate phrases they can offer during high arousal: short, concrete, and calming.

Tactical Checklist for Daily Use

- Notice the critic: label it "trauma memory" and say one-line counter.
- Name the emotion in one sentence.
- Do a one- to two-minute soothing ritual twice daily.
- Use the 4-2-6 breathing drill during spikes.
- Offer a compassionate phrase to a distressed part once a day.

These are low-tech, high-impact tools. Soldiers and their families can practice them anywhere—bunker, kitchen, or living room—and, over time, they rewiring the nervous system to read safety where it once read threat.

Daily Healing Practices

The path to recalibration begins with tangible actions. This section offers a direct approach to managing the persistent vigilance trauma leaves behind, providing a practical arsenal of self-regulation techniques. We will discover how to stabilize the nervous system during moments of intense arousal, using quick, body-centered strategies to reduce emotional flashbacks and quiet the 4F responses. From immediate grounding tactics and focused breathwork to intentional movement and daily routines, these methods build a framework for internal safety. We also look at how regular mindfulness practice, protective boundaries, and structured sleep rituals reinforce a steady sense of calm, transforming internal chaos into predictable peace. These are not passive concepts; they are active tools designed to be deployed in daily life, allowing you to regain command over your internal state.

Grounding Toolkit for Everyday Life

Grounding Toolkit for Everyday Life

Think of grounding like a fieldexpedient kit for the nervous system — small, portable, and useful when the situation goes sideways. Emotional flashbacks are intense, involuntary reexperiences of past trauma that hijack the body's stress circuitry (see Emotional Flashbacks: Names and Recognitions). The 4F responses—Fight, Flight, Freeze, and Fawn—are automatic nervoussystem reactions that can become stuck during a flashback (see The 4F Responses: Fight, Flight, Freeze, Fawn). For veterans coping with combatrelated PTSD, battle fatigue, or TBI, the kit also works when CPTSD traces back to childhood (see What CPTSD Really Means). Grounding seeks to bring the body and mind back into the present so emotional flashbacks lose their fuel and the 4F responses quiet down.

Bodily Awareness Anchors for Daily Routines

Use the body as an anchor. Use simple checks woven into your day to cut dissociation in its tracks.

- Feet on the floor: pause for a breath and state mentally, "Feet on the ground." It's blunt and it works — like putting a patrol on the ground to hold a position.
- Back against the chair: during briefings, meals, or phone calls, feel the contact where your spine meets the seat. That physical pressure sends a signal to the brain that you're here and not back in a firefight or a childhood kitchen that felt unsafe.
- Hands in lap or gripping the steering wheel: notice the texture of clothing, the tension in fingers. These sensations tether attention to now.

Make these anchors routine: at wakeup, before stepping out the door, and after any trigger. Drill them like PT until they're automatic.

Breathing and Heartbeat Grounding

When the body goes into 4F mode, breath and heart feed it. Reverse that flow. A practical drill: Breathe in for a count of four, hold for two, exhale for six. The slightly longer exhale nudges the vagus nerve toward calm, helping to shift the nervous system from the FightFlightFreezeFawn cascade back to a state of regulation.

- Find a seated position that feels secure.
- Repeat the breathing pattern.

Shift attention to the heartbeat — place a hand on the chest or the carotid pulse if you need to. Tell yourself the rhythm: "Onetwo, onetwo." Matching attention to steady beats interrupts the runaway alarm cascade that drives emotional flashbacks, which are the sudden, vivid reliving of traumatic memories (see Emotional Flashbacks: Names and Recognitions) and the limbic hijack that keeps the brain in a hyperalert state.

If you've got TBI and counting is tricky, use a softer version: breathe slowly and feel the pulse, no numbers required. This is about calming sensors, not passing a test.

Sensory Grounding Tools

A compact sensory kit can be a frontline resource. Keep a small pouch in your vehicle, rucksack, or nightstand:

- Textures: a stress ball, a swatch of cordura, or a soft scarf to rub between fingers.
- Scents: a dab of peppermint or lavender on a cotton square (carry in a sealed bag).
- Temperature: a sealed ice pack or a warm pack — brief cold or warmth snaps attention to sensation and away from the memory loop.

These items give the nervous system new data to process. For families, give kids their own kit so caregivers don't have to be the only anchor during a meltdown.

Micro-Pauses During Daily Tasks

Micro-pauses are three- to ten-second interventions that reset arousal. Use them:

- Before stepping into a meeting, doorway, or crowded space.
- Between tasks at work or home.
- During transitions: end of shift, after a call with a loved one, while swapping childcare duties.

A micro-pause can be as simple as noticing breath, pressing feet into the floor, and choosing one grounding object to touch. Teach battle buddies and family members to cue you: a discreet tap on the shoulder or a text message that says "Ground?" helps when speech is hard.

These tools soften flashbacks and help you live with CPTSD. Practice them regularly, preferably with a partner, and watch how family stress drops as primary PTSD steadies, easing secondary PTSD in the wider system. Primary PTSD refers to the core symptoms directly stemming from the traumatic event, while secondary PTSD describes additional stress reactions that arise in people closely connected to the trauma survivor.

Breathwork for Regulation

Breathwork: a daily regulation tool for calming the nervous system

If you ever thought breathing was automatic and not worth training, think again. In deployed life we polished rifles and boots; in recovery, breath is the tool you polish every morning. Proper breathwork gives you a steady baseline so an emotional flashback doesn't feel like incoming mortar fire.

How it quiets the body

Stress pins the autonomic nervous system to the fight/flight position—a rapid, involuntary response that mobilizes energy, increases heart rate, and readies the body for action. Breathwork nudges the system back toward restanddigest by changing the rhythm your body expects. Slow, paced breathing increases parasympathetic tone (the "put the rifle down and eat" system) and lowers the adrenaline spike. Parasympathetic tone is the nervous system's calming branch that slows the heart, promotes digestion, and supports recovery. That shift isn't magic—it's physiology you can control with practice. One effective routine that harnesses this is Combat Calm: inhale for 4 counts, hold for 1, exhale for 6. The long exhale biases the vagus nerve toward calming, helping you reset between briefs or after a tense encounter.

Build interoceptive awareness

Daily breath practice trains you to notice internal cues before they blow up into a fullblown reaction. An emotional flashback, as defined in "Emotional Flashbacks: Names and Recognitions", is an involuntary reexperience of a past traumatic event that triggers the same fight/flight physiology and can feel like a new threat. You begin to detect subtle rises in heart rate, tightness in the ribs, or a hollowfeeling in the gut—early warning signs of an emotional flashback. Once you can spot them, you can act: slow the breath, ground with touch, or use a short sensory anchor to stop escalation.

Tactical breathing routines (field-ready)

- Combat Calm (simple, quick): Inhale for 4 counts, hold for 1, exhale for 6. Repeat 4–6 times. Long exhale biases the vagus nerve toward calming. Use this between briefs or after a tense encounter.

- Buddy Sync (co-regulation): Sit or stand shoulder-to-shoulder.

Leader breathes at a calm pace; partner matches. Shared rhythm pulls both autonomic states toward safety — useful after an after-action or during family debriefs.

- Up-Shift for Freeze/Collapse: If someone goes flat or dissociates, avoid overly slow breathing alone. Pair the breath with gentle movement (march in place for 30 seconds) and breathe steadily, 3–4 counts in/out, to bring nervous-system tone back up without panic.

Match technique to the 4F responses, as described in "The 4F Responses: Fight, Flight, Freeze, Fawn". Each response engages distinct physiological patterns—fight elevates heart rate and muscle tension; flight increases heart rate and hyperalertness; freeze can slow heart rate and induce dissociation; fawn suppresses threat signals and can lead to exhaustion. When choosing a technique, align it with the specific F that matches the person's current state. For example, a calming long exhale is effective for Fight or Flight, gentle rocking can help Freeze, and a brief grounding cue can support Fawn.

Your breathing choice should reflect which 4F state you're in. Hyperarousal (fight/flight) benefits from slower, extended-exhale patterns. Hypoarousal (freeze/collapse) needs careful stimulation — gentle movement, sensory input, and regulated breathing that avoids deep, emptying breaths which can deepen disconnection. Fawning shows up as hypervigilant, short-breathing; coaxing longer inhalations with a comforting tone can shift that pattern.

Ritualize practice—make it small and daily

Soldiers run drills until movements are reflex. Treat breathwork the same way. Five minutes in the morning, a two-minute reset mid-shift, and three minutes before bed builds predictable neural circuits that respond more reliably under stress. Call it a morning "stand-to" for your autonomic system.

Flexible implementation for real life

No fancy room required. Do it in your rack, in the convoy, at a kitchen table, or in the ER waiting area. Keep instructions short and portable: a written cue card, a text reminder, or a shared family rhythm after a difficult talk. For families dealing with Complex secondary PTSD, co-regulating breath practices can reduce escalation in the household and create a steadying pattern everyone can follow.

Cautions and next steps

Start small. If you have a history of TBI, chest injury, or breathing-related panic, check with a clinician before pushing limits. Track what patterns help and which ones trigger more alarm; adjust accordingly. With consistent practice, breathwork becomes a reliable tool in your kit — free, always with you, and effective when used like a well-drilled procedure.

Mindfulness for CPTSD

If breathwork is the field-expedient tool in your kit, mindfulness is the tactical plan that gives the unit a routine to follow under fire. Think of it as training your attention so the brain stops running on autopilot when a threat cue shows up. For veterans and people with CPTSD rooted in childhood, the same alarm system gets tripped by different things: a slammed door, a sudden touch, a raised voice, or an old smell. Mindfulness trains an alternate response so the alarm doesn't send everyone into chaos.

The practical effect is simple: short, regular practices teach the brain to come off automatic reactivity and return to deliberate response. This looks like:

- retraining attention to reduce mind-wandering,
- strengthening prefrontal circuits that downshift amygdala hijacks, and
- boosting interoceptive awareness so bodily signals are noticed and managed before they escalate.

From a neurological standpoint, an emotional flashback is a sudden, vivid reexperience of past trauma that feels like the present moment—see Emotional Flashbacks: Names and Recognitions for a full definition. Mindfulness reduces the intensity by creating a brief pause between sensation and reaction. During that pause you can label the emotion, recognize which of the four primary defensive reactions—fight, flight, freeze, or fawn—has taken over, and choose a conscious containment strategy instead of a reflexive action. For details on the 4F activation, see The 4F Responses: Fight, Flight, Freeze, Fawn. This process strengthens prefrontal circuits, enhancing topdown regulation. In combat terms: instead of firing on the wrong target, you check your sights.

Body awareness is the bridge from noticing to acting. Scan quickly for muscle tension, posture shifts, throat tightness, or shallow breathing—these are hardware clues your brain follows, each pointing to a different 4F response: tight jaw or clenched fists signal fight; a tense back and rapid heartbeat point to flight; a rigid spine and shallow breath suggest freeze; a constricted throat or feeling of needing to please indicate fawn. Use those cues to manage the 4F responses: soften clenched areas to calm the fight response, widen the breath to counter flight, ground your feet and release tension to break freeze, or give yourself a short internal command to hold a boundary when fawning impulses show up. This somatic check keeps your reactions in check and supports mindful choice.

Safety-first adjustments are crucial. Combat trauma and early abuse histories mean some practices can trigger rather than help. Avoid long guided visualizations at first; start open-eyed and upright. One-minute cycles are the standard-issue drill: a focused breath, a single sensory anchor, or a quick body check. Increase duration only when the practice is clearly tolerable.

Field-ready mindfulness options:

- Breath awareness: observe inhales and exhales without forcing them; more surveillance than control.
- Fast grounding: name five things you see, four you can touch, three you hear, two you smell, one you taste or feel — do it briskly.
- Compact body scan: a head-to-toe check for tension, pausing to release any locked-up areas.

Starter mission plan:

- Pick one cue (a watch buzz, a doorway, a spoon clink). When the cue occurs, do one minute of mindfulness.
- When it happens, do one minute of mindfulness.
- After, name one word that sums up the feeling.
- If it stays manageable, extend to 3–5 minutes over weeks.

Short, consistent practice wires new regulation into the nervous system. Think of mindfulness as command presence: when alarms sound, it gives you a procedure to keep the post intact.

Evening Rituals for Wind-Down

Winding Down: Essential Evening Routines for PTSD Recovery

Why a predictable wind-down matters

Think of your evening as a field order for sleep: a steady anchor that steadies the nervous system, a regular curfew that signals the perimeter is safe, and a simple sequence of lowthreat cues. By keeping the routine predictable, you dampen the 4F response—a rapid, automatic pattern the body uses to protect itself when it feels threatened—see The 4F Responses: Fight, Flight, Freeze, Fawn for details. This eases hypervigilance and keeps emotional flashbacks—see Emotional Flashbacks: Names and Recognitions—in check, allowing deeper, more restful sleep.

Dim the lights, calm the senses

Start with the easiest command: lights low. Bright overhead bulbs and glowing screens are like flares at bedtime—they push up alertness and suppress melatonin. Run a blackout on screens at least 30–60 minutes before lights-out. Swap the phone for a paper book or an audiobook on low volume. If you must check something, use a red-tinted flashlight or set devices to their lowest blue-light setting. Think of it as tactical light discipline for your brain.

Grounding objects: a simple field tool

Grounding objects—physical items that provide a tangible connection to the present moment—work like a gobag for the nervous system, the network that controls bodily functions. Pick one item that carries comfort and stability—a dog tag, a worn band, a small patch of fabric—and keep it on the nightstand or under your pillow. When a flashback occurs—see Emotional Flashbacks: Names and Recognitions for its definition—or a hypervigilant spike—an abrupt surge of heightened alertness—shows up, touch the item slowly and name three things in the room: texture, color, sound. That brief contact shifts attention from threat to hereandnow. Combat vets often report that a small, meaningful object can stop a panic climb before it starts.

Breath-centered routines: slow the engine

Use diaphragmatic breathing—a breathing technique that engages the diaphragm to produce slow, deep breaths—as a core method to calm arousal, the heightened physiological and psychological state the body enters during stress. Place a hand on the belly to confirm deep belly movement. Then try these variations: 44 breathing—inhale for 4 counts, pause for 1 count, exhale for 4 counts. If it feels too strenuous, shorten to 33 breathing—inhale 3, pause 1, exhale 3. For a slower rhythm, use 46 second slow inhales followed by longer exhales; this pattern calms the heart rate and signals safety. Perform three to six cycles while seated, then repeat the same pattern lying down. The goal is to coax the parasympathetic system—part of the autonomic nervous system that promotes relaxation and recovery—back to base.

Gentle movement and somatic resets

If your body is still running drills, give it a brief cool-down: two to five minutes of neck rolls, shoulder shrugs, and hip openings, or a slow walk around the block. Rocking slowly in a chair or doing light cat–cow stretches can dissipate stored tension. Avoid intense workouts close to bedtime—those are like combat PT right before lights-out.

Body scans and reflective journaling

A short body scan shifts attention from thought to sensation, easing hypervigilance. Scan from toes to jaw, noting tight spots, softening muscles as you go. Follow with two quick journal items: one thing that tired you today, one small thing that went okay. The point is not problem-solving; it's offloading and closing the day's file.

Putting it together: a tactical checklist

- 60 minutes before bed: dim lights, switch devices to airplane mode or stash them away.
- 45 minutes: pull out grounding object, set a small lamp with warm light.
- 30 minutes: light breath routine (3–6 cycles), gentle stretching.
- 15 minutes: body scan; if needed, journal two lines.

- Bedtime: hold grounding object for a pause, breathe, lights out.

Families and secondhand wounds

Partners and children feel the ripple effects of sleepless nights. Create shared wind-down cues: a low-volume playlist, a specific blanket for kids, or a short family circle where everyone names one neutral fact about their day. For households where family members carry Complex Secondary PTSD, schedule separate wind-down spaces when needed—one habitat for the veteran, another for others—so everyone can execute routines without triggering one another.

A final field note

Consistency is the operational advantage here. Like any tactic, these elements work best when drilled regularly. Try the checklist for a week, tweak it to fit your life, and keep the items small and predictable. Nighttime can become a safe sector again—one low-light, slow breath, grounding object at a time.

Movement to Release Tension

Gentle movement is where fieldcraft meets bodywork. Think of it as a slow, deliberate patrol through your own muscles—no sprinting, no heroics, just reconnaissance. For veterans who carry the hyperalert brain of combat and the wounded wiring of childhood trauma, this kind of movement restores a feeling that the body can be trusted again.

Invite safety and stability first. Use physical supports: sit in a chair with your back against the wall, loop a strap around your foot while lying down, or brace a hand on a table. These props act like a buddy on watch—quiet reassurance that you're not alone if the system freaks out. The aim is to keep intensity low so the nervous system doesn't flip into the 4F response (the body's rapid, automatic protective mechanism—fight, flight, freeze, fawn) — that hardwired triage mechanism that saved lives in combat but misfires in daily life.

Paced movement is the essential tactic. Move in small arcs: rotate the shoulders four to six degrees, rock the pelvis from side to side, flex the spine one vertebra at a time. Slow is not slow for laziness; it's slow for safety. Pay attention to sensations—tightness, pins-and-needles, warmth—and treat them like markers on a map, not red alerts demanding immediate action. This practice builds interoception: the skill of noticing inner signals without automatically reacting.

Sync movement with breath to anchor attention. Breathe in as you open or lengthen; breathe out as you close or soften. This breathsynced pattern calms heart rate and reduces adrenaline spikes. An emotional flashback—an instant, bodyfirst reexperience of trauma that can be triggered by a cue—hits; breathsynced movement turns it into a manageable physiological signal. Slow movement plus steady breathing gives you a hand on the wheel.

Expect surges. The prefrontal cortex, the part of the brain that manages executive functions and decisionmaking, can be reengaged through pausing. If tension spikes or fear surfaces, stop. Name it: "Tension spike—pausing." Shift to a supported posture, squeeze a grounding object, and lengthen the exhale until the body steadies. These pauses train the nervous system that distress can be tolerated and resolved rather than escalating into full 4F mode. Over time, those pauses become the prefrontal cortex's cue to re-enter command.

Finish every session with consolidation and a compact somatic checklist: posture upright, feet on floor, breath even, five senses noted, one supportive thought. Families, here's how you help without turning into a clinician: offer predictable practical support (make tea, hold a blanket), learn a chosen grounding cue, and honor boundaries when a pause is requested. Complex secondary PTSD can affect partners and children. Practicing these rituals together reduces household tension and teaches co-regulation.

A final field order: do this short sequence daily for three weeks, scale slowly, and log what changes. The body remembers competence; with paced movement and breath as allies, many veterans reclaim a quiet base from which recovery can proceed.

Artful Self-Soothing Techniques

Artful Self-Soothing Techniques

See Emotional Flashbacks: Names and Recognitions for a definition of emotional flashback. See The 4F Responses: Fight, Flight, Freeze, Fawn for the 4F cascade. If gentle movement is the patrol that keeps you steady, consider these selfsoothing techniques your field kit: compact, reliable, and ready to deploy when the body or mind goes into alarm. They give clear sensory information to the brain when old wiring (amygdalaled alarm circuits) drags you back into a prior threat. When an emotional flashback occurs, these practices offer presentoriented sensory signals that calm the system and give you time to reengage the thinking brain.

Sensory Grounding Routines

- 54321: Name five things you can see, four you can touch, three you can hear, two you can smell, one you can taste. When arousal spikes, grip a small item—soft cloth, smooth stone, stress ball—and note its texture, weight, temperature. This tactile input talks directly to the brainstem and helps downshift the fightflightfreezefawn cascade.
- Mindful Walking: Walk for two minutes at patrol pace and track each footfall—the heel, the roll, the toe. Pair it with steady breathing. Even short steps anchor the nervous system by giving continuous, predictable input.

Breathwork and Micro-Movements

Breath is the simplest lever we've got. Diaphragmatic breathing expands the belly and signals safety through the vagus nerve. The 4F cascade—Fight, Flight, Freeze, Fawn—represents the four core threat responses that the body can automatically enact; modulating these responses helps restore calm. Practice it standing in formation or sitting at the kitchen table: inhale slowly for a count that's comfortable (three to five), let the belly fill, then exhale longer. Pair each breath with a tiny movement—shoulder roll, wrist flex, a gentle neck stretch. These micromovements reduce muscle bracing and modulate the 4F responses by restoring sensory predictability.

Art-Based Soothing Modalities

Creativity doesn't require galleries—think scribbles in a notebook between briefings. Drawing or painting translates raw affect into a visible object you can handle and modify. Journaling, even five minutes of streamofconsciousness, externalizes the inner alarm and helps identify triggers. Music and dance provide rhythmic input that organizes the nervous system; play a track you can move to and allow a simple sway. For those with TBI, choose lowstimulation formats (soft music, large brushstrokes) that respect sensory thresholds.

Self-Compassion and Safe-Space Rituals

Complex secondary PTSD is a condition that develops in caregivers or family members who repeatedly witness or learn about a loved one's trauma, leading to intrusive memories, hyperarousal, and avoidance. Soldiers perform rituals all the time—kit checks, premission briefs. Use similar predictable cues at home. Guided selftalk can be tactical: short, calm phrases like "This is a memory, I'm here now," or "My body is reacting; I will slow my breath." Designate a small safe area—a chair with a blanket, a low lamp, a familiar scent. Families can create parallel rituals: a fiveminute checkin, a signal for when someone needs space, a shared calming playlist. These predictable actions help contain complex secondary PTSD by giving family members clear, repeatable responses instead of chaotic emotional guessing.

Put a few of these tools into daily practice—pick one sensory routine, one breath/movement drill, and a small creative task. Run them like drills: brief, regular, and practical. Over time the nervous system gets retrained to accept that the present is not always a threat, and that's the tactical advantage most of us are after.

Sleep Hygiene and Sleep Rituals

Establishing a Calming Nightly Routine

Think of your pre-sleep routine as pre-mission checks before lights out. The brain likes predictable cues — they quiet the amygdala and invite the prefrontal cortex back to the table. Pick a three- to five-step sequence you can run every night: dim lights, change into comfy gear, thirty minutes of low-stimulation activity (reading or calming music), a warm wash or soak, then thirty seconds of deep belly breathing. Keep it the same. Repeatable routines train the body to drop alert levels on cue.

Tactical options that work in tight quarters:

- Read a non-political, non-combat manual — fiction or calming essays will do.
- Take a warm bath or shower to lower core temperature afterward; it's like telling your internal alarm system to stand down.
- Sip herbal tea or a sleep-friendly drink (decaf, low sugar) while doing gentle stretches.

Reducing Nighttime Arousal: Short Drills for the Limbic System

The limbic system is the part of the brain that processes emotions and memories. When it becomes overactive at night, it can trigger heightened arousal, emotional flashbacks, and the 4F response. The drills below target these pathways to calm the limbic system, reduce arousal, and help you fall into deeper, restorative sleep.

Nighttime is prime real estate for emotional flashbacks and 4F activation. Handle them with three quick moves, using the routine outlined in the previous section. For details on the 4F response, see The 4F Responses: Fight, Flight, Freeze, Fawn.

- Clear the field: keep a bedside notebook. Dump the intrusive thoughts onto paper for five minutes — the act of externalizing interrupts rumination.
- Reset the breath: diaphragmatic breathing calms heart rate and

signals safety. Use the core belly-breathing technique and choose a variation that fits the moment—4-4 (inhale 4, pause 1, exhale 4), 3-3 for a shorter rhythm, or slow 4–6 second inhales with longer exhales (exhale longer than the inhale) to increase parasympathetic activation.

- Ground the body: press feet into the mattress and note three solid sensations — pressure, warmth, pulse. Low-tech, immediate, effective.

Consistency Is a Non-Negotiable

Sleep timing seven nights per week stabilizes circadian rhythm. If shift work or training disrupts that, pick an anchor: a fixed wake time or fixed wind-down start. On days off, keep the same wind-down window; weekend "sleep-ins" trick the circadian system and ramp up anxiety.

Pre-Sleep Worry Management for Combat-Brain and Family-Brain

For service members and partners coping with complex secondary stress, a short family ritual helps. Ten minutes of shared jotting or a calm check-in before the routine can offload worry and prevent late-night spillovers. For solo use, a structured worry journal with a "worry parking lot" section—write it, close the book, shelve it—reduces nocturnal rehearsal.

Limit Stimulants and Screens — Apply With Precision

Caffeine and nicotine: stop consumption at least four to six hours before lights out. Electronics: institute a hard cutoff about an hour before bed; if that feels impossible, use blue light filters and shift content toward low-stimulation audio (podcasts without adrenaline). Treat the phone as a piece of kit that's powered down during the final phase.

Creating a Trauma-Informed Sleep Space

Make the bedroom a safe perimeter. Soft, cool colors; blackout curtains; a mattress and pillow that support spines and brains; weighted blankets if they decrease hyperarousal. Earplugs or whitenoise machines mask sudden sounds that trigger hypervigilance.

Soothing Sensory Cues and Rituals

Assign one scent (lavender or vanilla) and one sound cue (nature loop, low-volume guitar) to the wind-down. Use the same cues so the nervous system learns to link them with safety.

When to Call for Backup

If nightmares, insomnia, or night sweats persist, bring in a clinician. Cognitive Behavioral Therapy for Insomnia (CBTI), traumafocused therapies, medication review, and sleep studies are standardissue tools. Families experiencing complex secondary PTSD should seek familyfocused therapy to stop nocturnal stress from cycling through the household.

Night operations shift with environment, training, and equipment condition — yet clear drills, sensory cues, and timely professional support turn sleep into a wellplanned, highchance endeavor.

Daily Boundaries and Routine

You did the intel-gathering on sleep; now it's time to secure the perimeter for the rest of the day. Sleep strategies are essential, but for many of us the daily grind — meetings, crowds, family duties — is where the nervous system takes incoming fire. Establishing clear daily boundaries is the field manual for protecting that system from overload and emotional flashbacks.

Boundaries are the clear, intentional limits we set in our daily interactions to protect our physiological and psychological wellbeing. They serve as a first line of defense against triggers that can spark emotional flashbacks—intense, involuntary reexperiences of past trauma that manifest as sudden panic, dissociation, or a sense of reliving the event. By mapping out safe spaces, time limits, and communication norms, we create a predictable environment that calms the autonomic nervous system, keeps the sympathetic and parasympathetic branches in balance, and reduces the likelihood of a flashback. A practical routine might include setting a "nophone" period in the morning, scheduling short breaks to scan the body for tension, and establishing a firm "I am safe" mantra before entering potentially stressful situations. Consistent boundarysetting also nurtures the four foundational facets—Physical, Emotional, Cognitive, and Spiritual—ensuring each receives attention, which is essential for maintaining overall equilibrium.

Think of boundaries as your personal force field: blunt, practical, and nonnegotiable when necessary. For a veteran, that might mean announcing a "novisit" window after a heavy shift or walking out when a conversation turns into a baited line. For someone whose CPTSD traces back to childhood, those same rules stop old scripts from hijacking the present.

Creating a Morning Grounding Routine

Morning routines are low-tech mission prep. Ten minutes can change a day. Try this drill:

- 2 minutes: three deep abdominal breaths, slow in, slow out.
- 5 minutes: purposeful movement — a short walk, slow stretches, or marching on the spot while counting cadence.
- 3 minutes: a brief intention statement — one sentence about how you want to show up.

A missionessential practice: start each day with a brief, repeatable grounding routine that calms the autonomic nervous system and lowers the odds that a seemingly small trigger will turn into an emotional flashback. Treat it like preops—brief, repeatable, and nonnegotiable. To make this work, block out dedicated time in your schedule each morning for selfregulation, ensuring the routine is protected and practiced consistently.

Schedule blocks like you would a patrol. Self-regulation is mission-essential. Examples that actually work in the field:

- 30-minute afternoon break for quiet reading, listening to steady-tempo music, or mindful breathing.
- Short "reset" slots mid-morning and mid-afternoon (5–10 minutes) for grounding drills.

Make these blocks visible on your calendar and announce them to your housemates or unit so they're less likely to be violated.

Limiting High-Stimulus Environments

Crowds, loud spaces, and endless scrolling are good ways to trip fight, flight, freeze, or fawn reactions. Reduce exposure with tactics that fit the mission:

- Use noise-cancelling headphones or steady-beat playlists during shopping or transit.
- Take alternate routes or quieter times for errands.
- Set strict social-media windows; treat feeds like hostile terrain unless you're on a recon mission.

The Importance of Regular Practice for 4F Balance

4F Balance is a holistic framework that organizes personal growth into four interrelated fields: Physical, Emotional, Cognitive, and Spiritual. Each field supports the nervous system's capacity to regulate stress, sustain resilience, and foster wellbeing. Regular practice—whether through movement, breathwork, journaling, or quiet reflection—creates a rhythm that strengthens the parasympathetic nervous system, lowers baseline cortisol, and embeds adaptive habits. For example, a daily 10minute mindful walk nourishes the Physical field; a brief gratitude reflection activates the Emotional field; a focused breathing session trains the Cognitive field; and a silent meditation cultivates the Spiritual field. When all four are practiced consistently, the nervous system operates in a state of calm readiness, and the likelihood of an emotional flashback is markedly diminished.

The nervous system learns by repetition. Regular practice strengthens the ability to shift out of fight/flight/freeze/fawn and back into a regulated state. Short, consistent drills beat irregular marathon efforts every time. Keep a log of what works — which cues calm you, which environments spike you — and adjust.

Making Boundaries Stick

Consistency plus self-compassion is the protocol. Start with small, enforceable rules and praise yourself for adherence. When a boundary is breached, debrief like a unit: what happened, what triggered it, what's the next tweak? For families and partners dealing with Complex secondary

PTSD, teach the same tactics: clear windows for respite, signals for when someone needs space, and scheduled caregiver breaks.

Closing Tactical Note

Boundaries are not punishment; they are strategy. Protecting the nervous system keeps you operational — for missions, for family, for life outside the wire. Implement the drills, clock the practice, and treat nervous-system safety as a daily assignment that earns real returns in calm and stability.

Invisible Scars Across Identities

Trauma's deep impact is never isolated; it is etched into the intricate design of our identities. Our racial background, gender, sexual orientation, physical ability, economic standing, and the language that shapes our thoughts all profoundly alter how we experience harm. What is seen as danger, how we express distress, or where we seek comfort, often stems from deeply rooted expectations and common understandings within our groups. A dismissive glance, a silent judgment, a denied access – these moments are not neutral. They can reignite old wounds, triggering familiar surges of fear or detachment, making the present echo with prior harms. This means our sense of belonging, the stigma we face, and the protective frameworks of our heritage are integral to our sense of safety. True healing acknowledges these interwoven layers, making them central to every step of recovery.

Racial and Cultural Layers

They told me combat teaches you to read the room. It also teaches you how a whispered insult can sound like incoming mortar. In plain terms: where you come from — your racial background, your shared values and traditions, the rules you grew up with — shapes how you perceive danger, report pain, and ask for backup. For many troops from racial and ethnic minority groups, that means trauma often comes with a second wound: the worry that no one will believe them or that they'll be judged for speaking up.

Cultural norms shape what gets said and what gets swallowed. In some units and families silence is treated like discipline—a sign of toughness—while in others speaking out is honored. These norms steer disclosure and shape fear responses. CPTSD, defined elsewhere (see the section "What CPTSD Really Means"), overlaps with combat PTSD because the same neurobiological wiring that protected a child from family chaos can snap under the intense stress of battle, turning internalized fear into constant hypervigilance.

Microaggressions are not small to a nervous system already primed for threat. A throwaway comment, a dismissive look, an offhand stereotype, can trigger emotional flashbacks—nonverbal, visceral reliving episodes where past harm is reexperienced without a tidy memory. The brain treats the present slight like past harm; heart rate spikes, breath shortens, the world narrows.

That's where the 4F stress responses show up: fight, flight, freeze, and fawn. These are automatic nervous system modes that can dominate a veteran's reaction to perceived threat. When racialized safety cues appear—a tone, a gesture, a setting—some veterans go into freeze—numb, detached, unable to move. Others fawn: appeasing to avoid escalation. Families feel this secondhand. Partners and kids can develop complex secondary PTSD from living with a veteran whose nervous system is on hairtrigger alert.

Intergenerational trauma complicates things. Family loyalty, silence about past abuse, and handeddown rules about honor can intensify CPTSD; see the section "What CPTSD Really Means". Secrets become reactive triggers. complex secondary PTSD is the chronic, layered trauma that family members, especially partners and children, experience by living with a veteran whose nervous system is on constant alert; see the section "complex secondary PTSD".

Practical ground rules for soldiers and families: name the response (freeze/fawn/etc.), use twominute grounding (feet, breath, five objects), establish a safetyfirst signal with your partner, and seek clinicians who understand racial and cultural backgrounds — safety matters more than ideology. Family therapy must address both primary PTSD and the secondary trauma that follows it. This book will show how the brain pulls the trigger and how to put the weapon down, with tactics you can use on the line and at home.

Gender Identity and Expression

This section outlines key concepts of complex posttraumatic stress disorder (CPTSD) and associated phenomena. For a detailed definition, see What CPTSD Really Means. Emotional flashbacks are described under Emotional Flashbacks: Names and Recognitions, and the 4F responses—Freeze, Fight, Flight, and Fawn—are explained in The 4F Responses: Fight, Flight, Freeze, Fawn.

The next front to hold: gender identity under fire. For veterans and service members with CPTSD rooted in childhood harm, gender expression can become a minefield—not because identity itself is broken, but because the nervous system has been trained to expect danger when personal truth peeks out. Emotional flashbacks and the 4F responses can slam the brakes on anyone trying to act on their gender instincts, turning simple choices—what to wear, how to speak, who to trust—into tactical problems.

How trauma scrambles gender signaling

Trauma rewires the brain's circuits that mark signals as safe or unsafe. The amygdala, a key structure for threat detection, becomes hypersensitive; prefrontal control, which normally regulates impulses, thins out; and the insula's sense of body ownership can become inactive without notice. These biological shifts make gender enactment feel exposed; hypervigilance—an overawareness of potential danger—watches for threats, and emotional flashbacks can detach someone from their body or flood them with shame. Add a history of relational harm from family or units that punished difference, and dysphoria (persistent discomfort with one's gender identity), anxiety, or depression can follow like bad weather on a polar route.

Family and community expectations as compounding forces

When families or tightknit communities demand conformity, the pressure compounds the internal alarm system. Relational trauma—disapproval, secrecy, punishment—teaches survival strategies: hide, perform, placate. These strategies may have kept you alive then, but they also block authentic selfexpression now. For military families, that can mean partners and children picking up Complex Secondary PTSD symptoms. Complex Secondary PTSD is a distinct pattern of distress that emerges in close family members who repeatedly witness or are indirectly exposed to a loved one's PTSD. It manifests as chronic hyperalertness, excessive caretaking, emotional numbing, and a persistent sense of personal threat. These symptoms—hypervigilance, overresponsibility, or walking on eggshells—are not just secondary reactions; they are themselves debilitating disorders that can erode the family's sense of safety and cohesion.

For background on CPTSD, see What CPTSD Really Means; for emotional flashbacks, see Emotional Flashbacks: Names and Recognitions; and the 4F responses are described in The 4F Responses: Fight, Flight, Freeze, Fawn.

Tactical safe-space strategies

Think like mission planning. Create validated spaces where expression is low-risk and rehearsable. Practical steps:

- Establish a clear signal (a word, gesture, or routine) that says "I'm safe to be myself here."
- Run short rehearsals in low-stakes settings: one trusted friend, a support group, a therapist who affirms gender.
- Use grounding drills before and after tests of expression: breath counts, sensory checks, 5-4-3-2-1 naming.
- For families: hold a debrief after disclosures without interrupting, set boundaries both ways, and rotate care so no one takes on all the emotional load.

Neurobiological anchor points for clinicians and loved ones

Explain gently that identity and emotion share neural highways. Therapy that combines skill training for emotional regulation with identityaffirming work helps rebuild safety in the body. For veterans with TBI, add targeted cognitive supports: shorter sessions, written plans, and repetition to compensate for processing gaps. traumatic brain injury (TBI) is damage to the brain caused by an external force—such as a blow, whiplash, or blast—that disrupts normal brain function. It can result in cognitive deficits (memory, attention, executive function), emotional lability, and physical symptoms that interfere with daily life. By acknowledging these neurological underpinnings, therapy can be tailored to meet veterans' unique needs, ensuring that interventions respect both the brain's altered capacity and the person's sense of self.

Final order: validate first, train second, and protect the unit. When service members and families apply these fieldtested steps, the body can stop treating authenticity like a combat zone — one small step at a time.

Sexual Orientation and Intimacy

Sexual Orientation, Intimacy, and Trauma: Unraveling the Complexities

You've been trained in rules of engagement; apply the same discipline to closeness. For veterans carrying CPTSD from childhood plus combat wounds, intimacy can trigger old alarms — not just combat memory. CPTSD (Complex PostTraumatic Stress Disorder) arises from repeated or prolonged trauma, often beginning in childhood and compounded by combat experiences, and it manifests as chronic emotional dysregulation, intrusive memories, and a hypervigilant state. Emotional flashbacks, which are involuntary, intense reexperiences of past trauma that can appear as sudden fear, shame, or freezing, often feel out of proportion to the present. These reactions typically fall into the 4F framework: Fear, Fight, Freeze, and Fawn, each representing an automatic defensive response. Adding traumatic brain injury (TBI) to the mix means the brain's arousal systems can misfire or lose their signals entirely, leaving confusion for both partners as they navigate a minefield of misfired alarms.

Attachment Disruptions and Intimacy

Early attachment damage sets faulty expectations for safety. Some folks swing hard toward isolation to avoid getting hit emotionally; others run straight into intense, clinging partnerships that burn out fast. Think of it as old wiring: the brain defaults to whatever kept you alive as a child. For troops, the overlap with battle-broken trust—where watchfulness kept you alive—compounds the problem.

The Impact of Early Trauma

If a child learned that closeness equals danger, adult closeness still smells like danger. That history rewrites what "safe" looks like, so vulnerability feels like surrender. Clinically, that shows up as avoidance, explosive closeness, or alternating cycles that exhaust everyone involved.

Stigma, Identity Complexity, and Compounding Stress

Sexual orientation and minority stress pile extra weight on top of CPTSD. Internalized shame can erode sexual self-concept and make asking for what you need feel impossible. Families and partners can unintentionally trigger this shame, producing Complex secondary PTSD in caregivers who carry guilt and hypervigilance.

Communication, Consent, and Dissociation

Dissociation can mute arousal cues and scramble consent. Practical fix: set up a pre-contact briefing — a brief, explicit check-in script that covers comfort, hard limits, and a verbal or nonverbal safe-word. Practice the script sober; rehearse it like a brief before a mission. Use a single-word "pause" or a hand signal for dissociation. If an emotional flashback hits, stop. Grounding drills (5-4-3-2-1 senses, paced breathing, bilateral tapping) are field-expedient tools.

4F Responses and Boundary Setting

4F responses refer to the four core traumabased reactions—Fear, Fight, Freeze, and Fawn—that can surface in any highstress situation, including moments of intimacy. Understanding each response helps couples recognize when one partner is slipping into automatic defense rather than genuine engagement.

- Fear: heightened alertness, avoidance, or hypervigilance.
- Fight: aggression, anger, or argumentation.
- Freeze: numbness, dissociation, or paralysis.
- Fawn: excessive compliance, peoplepleasing, or selfneglect.

Boundary setting involves clearly articulating personal limits, communicating them consistently, and honoring each other's boundaries to prevent retraumatization. Techniques include: using "I" statements, establishing safe words or signals, and scheduling checkins to review how boundaries are functioning.

- Identify your default 4F pattern—fight, flight, freeze, or fawn—and tell your partner.
- Fawners often overaccommodate; fighters may escape.
- Translate defense into directives: "When I freeze, I need a tenminute

quiet timeout with a glass of water." Those are boundary orders, not punishments.

- Use consentcentric, traumaaware routines: preintimacy checklists, slow exposure to touch, partner coaching by a traumaliterate clinician, and family education to reduce secondary CPTSD.

- Small wins matter—practiced checkin, one successful grounding during closeness, a mutual pause respected without shame.

- Healing isn't erasing the past; it's learning to carry it without letting it drive the present. For soldiers and families, that's a strategy worth training on.

Healing and Relational Practices

- Identify your default 4F pattern—fight, flight, freeze, or fawn—and tell your partner. Fawners often overaccommodate; fighters may escape. Translate defense into directives: "When I freeze, I need a tenminute quiet timeout with a glass of water." Those are boundary orders, not punishments.

- Use consent-centric, trauma-aware routines: pre-intimacy checklists, slow exposure to touch, partner coaching by a trauma-literate clinician, and family education to reduce secondary CPTSD.

- Focus on small, concrete wins — a practiced check-in, one successful grounding during closeness, a mutual pause respected without shame.

- A survivor put it plainly: healing isn't erasing the past; it's learning to carry it without letting it drive the present. For soldiers and families, that's a strategy worth training on.

- Accessibility Is Central to Recovery: ensure services are reachable and inclusive — flexible scheduling, remote options, transport assistance, clear communication, sensory accommodations, trauma-informed physical spaces, and staff trained in both accessibility and trauma care.

Disability and Accessibility

Think of accessibility like mission planning: skip it and you get friendly fire on progress. For folks with CPTSD—whether a childhood-trauma survivor sitting in a therapy room or a combat vet with a TBI being assessed at the VA—accessibility is not an add-on. It's the basic gear that keeps someone in the fight for healing.

How Disability Identities and Trauma Stories Cross Paths (unique ID: 683)

In military units we talk about "fit" and "fit checks." Outside, people carry labels—TBI (definition elsewhere), sensory sensitivities, chronic pain, neurodivergence—that change how trauma shows up and how a person asks for help. A veteran with a brain injury may have trouble with paperwork, memory, or tolerating crowded waiting rooms; a childhoodtrauma survivor may shut down when deadlines or rigid rules pop up. Emotional flashbacks (definition elsewhere) can also surface. Stigma makes both less likely to raise their hand. That silence feeds shame and intensifies emotional flashbacks and 4F responses—freeze, fight, flight, and fawn—the basic adaptive reactions to threat that can derail care. A cluttered clinic can trigger a freeze, a surprise phone call can shove someone into flight.

Make Accessibility Part of Care Planning

Start care plans at intake like you'd plan an operation: map risks, list environmental triggers, and build options. Practical moves include written session agendas, predictable calendars, plainlanguage summaries, cognitive breaks, and quiet rooms onsite. For those with TBI, slow down processing demands: allow extra time for forms, offer audio recordings of sessions, and use simple visual cues. Honor 4F responses—give choices, allow a timeout signal, and outline an exit plan before a session begins so hypervigilance doesn't hijack treatment. By understanding that a freeze can feel like paralysis, a fight response can surface as irritability, a flight reaction as avoidance, and a fawn reaction as peoplepleasing, clinicians can design interventions that meet each response type without triggering the next.

Design Healing Spaces That Reduce Load

Physical design matters: lowstim lighting, sound buffering, clear wayfinding, and seating that offers both support and a quick path to leave. Sensory tools—noisecancelling headphones, fidget objects, weighted lap pads—work like field kit items; small, portable, and missioncritical when an emotional flashback hits. These tools help modulate sensory input, providing the calming anchor needed when the brain's fightflight circuitry is activated.

Accessibility as a Tactical Therapy Tool

Treat accommodations as clinical interventions. Flexible scheduling reduces hypervigilance; quiet pre-briefs limit surprises; written consent and stop-words protect agency. Families get briefings too—Complex secondary PTSD is real, and caregivers need boundaries, respite plans, and backup. Teach families a two-line debrief script, set an agreed signal for "pause," and rotate roles to limit burnout.

When accessibility is built in from the first contact, safety and control are restored. That's not soft support—that's smart strategy for long-term recovery.

Class, Poverty, and Economic Stress

Economic Stress and Invisible Scars

Accessibility gets you into the door; money keeps you in the room. For a detailed definition of CPTSD, see What CPTSD Really Means. For a detailed description of emotional flashbacks, see Emotional Flashbacks: Names and Recognitions. For a detailed explanation of the four primary survival responses, see The 4F Responses: Fight, Flight, Freeze, Fawn. Economic insecurity is not an external problem—it's a recurring trigger that punches the nervous system's weak spot. Picture a combat vet who grew up with unpredictable meals: a bounced check can replay that helplessness faster than a flashbang. That replay often looks like an emotional flashback—sudden, overwhelming feelings that drop you back into earlier fear—and slides straight into the 4F responses. Hypervigilance, the heightened state of alertness that keeps the brain on guard for danger, is amplified by such financial stress.

The Vicious Cycle of Poverty and Trauma

Poverty increases everyday unpredictability: late rent, skipped meds, food scarcity. Those threats act as safetyviolations for a brain wired to watch for danger. In this context hypervigilance—an almost constant state of heightened alertness—spikes, leading the nervous system to cycle through the four primary survival responses: fight, flight, freeze, or fawn. The result is a loop—economic stress heightens hypervigilance and avoidance, which then undermines work, careseeking, and benefit navigation. A veteran avoiding the VA phone because the hold music triggers panic won't get the paperwork done; no paperwork means no benefits; no benefits deepen the crisis.

The Physical Toll of Economic Stress

Chronic money anxiety disturbs sleep, appetite, and mood regulation. Sleepless nights look a lot like a long patrol: exhausted, reactive, short on judgment. Over time, this wear-and-tear worsens PTSD symptoms and increases medical visits — the exact opposite of "getting stable."

The Impact on Safety Cues

Financial chaos erodes the small safety markers we rely on—a steady paycheck, a functioning car, a fridge stocked with food—while also creating gaps in benefits and mounting debt. When those cues wobble, hypervigilance rises, the brain scans ordinary places for threats, and the constant alert state leaves families strained. The loss of stability triggers shame, as individuals feel they have failed to provide, and it can manifest as emotional flashbacks that worsen PTSD symptoms in caregivers.

Gaps in benefits and mounting debt are powerful shame triggers. Shame fuels isolation and avoidance—people skip calls, stall appointments, and sit with flashbacks instead of filing claims. Debt collectors' calls can mimic the tone of past abusers for some survivors, instantly shifting the nervous system into 4F mode, where fight, flight, freeze, or fawn responses dominate. For a detailed description of emotional flashbacks, see Emotional Flashbacks: Names and Recognitions. For a detailed explanation of the four primary survival responses, see The 4F Responses: Fight, Flight, Freeze, Fawn. Hypervigilance is amplified, preventing the person from engaging in necessary steps to resolve debt or claim benefits.

Tactical Steps to Break the Cycle

- Financial assistance: Locate emergency grant programs (VA claims fast-tracks, vet-specific charities, local hardship funds). Keep a short list of three places to call when the bottom drops out.

- Access to resources: Use sliding-scale clinics, food pantries, and pharmacy assistance programs. Put key contacts in one phone note labeled "Safety Net."

- Support networks: Build a crew — a buddy, a caseworker, a family member — who can stand in when triggers block action. Give them clear roles: one handles calls, another watches finances, one checks in after appointments.

- Financial education: Enroll in nonprofit credit counseling, basic budgeting classes at community centers, or veteran financial-literacy workshops. Small practical drills (weekly bill-checks, emergency-savings goals of $500) beat theory.

Quick field tactics for families

- When bills trigger panic, use a two-line script: "I'm overwhelmed; can you call X for me?" Keep one person as the designated caller to reduce repeated triggers.

- Break tasks into 15-minute missions: complete one form, schedule one appointment. Celebrate small wins.

- If debt collectors cause freeze or fight responses, ask for written verification and pause communication until a caseworker or counselor can intervene.

Addressing money problems isn't just about cash. It quiets the alarms in the nervous system, reducing hypervigilance and the intensity of emotional flashbacks—sudden, overwhelming reexperiencing of past trauma that can hijack the present moment—allowing people the breathing room to engage in therapy and rebuild functioning. Treat economic stress like an operational vulnerability: identify it, allocate resources, and train teams—families and clinicians—to respond when it flares, recognizing that such stress can trigger the four primary survival responses: fight, flight, freeze, or fawn.

Language, Immigration, Belonging, and Trauma

Immigration and the attempt to belong can leave scars the eye doesn't see. For combat veterans who leave one homeland and land in another, old wounds can flare when language, customs, and daily cues change. I once talked with a sergeant who laughed about learning local slang — then admitted the laugh came with an edge: missing phrases would trigger a flashback mid-conversation, like a radio popping into static.

The amygdala is the brain's alarm system, detecting threat and triggering rapid physiological responses. The prefrontal cortex governs higherlevel reasoning, decision making, and emotional regulation. For a detailed definition of emotional flashbacks, see "Emotional Flashbacks: Names and Recognitions". The 4F response model—fight, flight, freeze, and fawn—is explained in "The 4F Responses: Fight, Flight, Freeze, Fawn".

How does this happen? Two brain facts: trauma tightens the amygdala's grip and blunts the prefrontal cortex's reasoning under stress, making emotional flashbacks more likely— a smell, phrase, or accent can catapult someone into the emotions of a past event without the autobiographical memory tagging along. Add traumatic brain injury or battle fatigue and the wiring that helps translate feeling into words becomes frayed. Enter the 4F responses: fight, flight, freeze, fawn. Language gaps can push a veteran straight into freeze or flight because the safer option is silence. For an immigrant veteran, saying "I'm scared" in the wrong tongue can feel impossible. Practical fixes: find a therapist who works in the veteran's preferred language or uses trained interpreters; create symptom sheets with pictures or simple phrases; practice short scripts for common interactions (clinic visits, school meetings); use roleplay at home so family members recognize trigger signs and know a calm response plan.

Secondary CPTSD, also called vicarious or secondary posttraumatic stress disorder, occurs when a person close to someone with PTSD experiences trauma symptoms through exposure to the primary trauma and its aftermath.

Belonging is medicine. Build networks of people who share background and service experience — local veteran groups, community centers, or online forums where a broken joke about drill life lands without explanation. Families matter. Secondary CPTSD can show up as partners imitating hypervigilance or children taking on caregiving roles. Tactics for families: set clear boundaries, schedule respite, get family therapy that teaches grounding exercises, and map triggers together so everyone knows the routes out of escalation.

Childhoodorigin CPTSD develops from chronic earlylife trauma—such as abuse, neglect, or inconsistent caregiving—and produces lasting emotional, relational, and physiological dysregulation. Attachment wounds arise when early caregiving relationships fail to provide consistent, secure support, leaving a lingering sense of insecurity that amplifies later stressors. For veterans, military service adds another layer to this story: it becomes a major stripe on the selfuniform, interwoven with other stripes of gender, race, class, and ability. These intersecting identities shape how CPTSD presents itself, how it manifests in daily life, and how easily or hard it is to seek help. CPTSD rarely appears as a single, onesizefitsall problem; instead, belonging feels like the anchor, while identity is the rigging that holds the whole thing together—ropes that twist in complicated ways as combat trauma compounds the early wounds.

Linking childhood-origin CPTSD to combat trauma helps explain why some veterans react more intensely to displacement. When early attachment wounds meet battlefield trauma, emotional flashbacks amplify and the manual for belonging gets dogeared. The remedy isn't instant, but languageaffirming care, concrete routines, and community that accepts both the combat patch and the accent create steady, practical steps toward healing — the kind you can measure in calmer nights and fewer sudden alarms in the middle of a family dinner.

Intersections: Complex Identities

Where trauma and identity meet, symptoms shift. A woman who fought and returned home carrying both combat scars and the weight of being a minority in the ranks may face different barriers than a white male veteran. Add a physical disability or invisible injuries like TBI, or traumatic brain injury, an ofteninvisible injury that can disrupt cognition and emotion, and access to services and understanding can shrink. Stigma within communities and family groups often muffles reports of distress — in some backgrounds, speaking about fear or crying is labeled weak, so survivors learn to shut down. That shutdown is fertile ground for emotional flashbacks, sudden, intense waves of feeling that feel like reexperiencing a traumatic memory but are experienced as if the past is now.

Let's get tactical about the brain mechanics. Emotional flashbacks—sudden, intense waves of feeling that feel like reexperiencing a traumatic memory—trigger the 4F set of responses (fight, flight, freeze, fawn). When a veteran also carries childhood harm, these alarms can be triggered by a wide range of cues. For a comprehensive definition of emotional flashbacks and the 4F responses, refer to "Emotional Flashbacks: Names and Recognitions" and "The 4F Responses: Fight, Flight, Freeze, Fawn".

Here's how to act, for service members and families:

- Recognize multiple identity layers: list the roles that apply (service member, parent, immigrant, person with a disability) and note how each changes triggers and supports.

- Push back on stigma and local scripts: create a nonjudgmental phrase family members can use when they see a flashback (e.g., "Check-in code: five breaths").

- Make care reachable: short-term steps like clear referrals, transportation options, and therapists who respect language and background.

For families dealing with complex secondary PTSD, or PTSD that arises in family members due to another person's trauma, practical moves work: set simple boundaries, build predictable routines, insist on respite, and get psychoeducation about emotional flashbacks and the 4F response. Clinicians and comrades will see the same lesson: treatment that ignores identity layers misses the target. Healing looks different for different people — tactical plans should too.

Culturally Informed Healing Practices

Healing that honors background and lived experience

You wouldn't hand an arctic parka to a Marine returning from the desert and call it support. The same logic applies to mental-health care: treatments that ignore a person's upbringing, faith, language, or local practices often miss the mark. In the case of CPTSD, old childhood wounds and combat trauma can overlap, so a veteran might be dealing with a lifetime of learned survival strategies on top of battle stress. That stack matters.

Why sensitivity to background matters neurologically and practically

For a detailed explanation of the 4F responses, emotional flashbacks, and Complex secondary PTSD, see "The 4F Responses: Fight, Flight, Freeze, Fawn" and "Emotional Flashbacks: Names and Recognitions".

Tactical actions for clinicians, leaders, and families

- Do a quick cultural inventory in intake: ask about home practices, spiritual supports, language, and who the person trusts. Treat that like mission planning.

Grounding drill for flashbacks: 54321 senses, paired with paced breathing (4 counts in, 6 out). For more on emotional flashbacks, see "Emotional Flashbacks: Names and Recognitions". Have family practice this together so they're not guessing when an emotional flashback occurs.

- Scripted responses: train families to say short validating lines—"I see you're triggered. I'll stay with you for five minutes"—then follow the plan. Consistency beats advice.

- Use trusted community anchors: chaplains, elders, veteran-run groups, sports teams, or traditional healers. Invite them into care as co-pilots when the patient wants that.

Programs that work, in the field

Real-world examples: horseback programs that link horsemanship and ceremony with therapy; language-specific PTSD groups that run sessions in the veteran's first language; drum or music sessions that let memory and emotion come out nonverbally. These aren't soft options— they lower arousal, build trust, and give the limbic system safer script options.

Addressing families and complex secondary PTSD

Families carry battle fatigue too. In complex secondary PTSD, caregivers can internalize the veteran's traumatic responses, experiencing their own emotional flashbacks and 4F reactions—fight, flight, freeze, fawn—without recognizing them as part of the trauma system. Teach family members about emotional flashbacks and the 4F responses so they stop taking triggering behavior personally. Encourage boundarysetting and separate recovery goals: one plan for the veteran, one for family members' mental health. Support groups for spouses and kids are missioncritical.

Validation and identity integration

Respecting multiple self-frames—soldier, child survivor, parent, member of a faith or tribe—helps stitch a coherent self back together. Validation is simple and powerful: acknowledge what the veteran lived through, name the protective strategy they used, and work together to replacc old scripts with safer, chosen responses. That shifts the brain from default survival mode toward deliberate living—and that's the objective every operator and family deserves.

Survivor Voices: First-Person Vignettes

The path from enduring past harms to finding steady ground is marked by subtle, persistent work.

Where earlier we considered the intricate layers of identity in how trauma settles, here we focus on the practical, often quiet, shifts that signal deep repair.

These are not grand gestures, but small, embodied gains that slowly recalibrate a nervous system once dominated by distress.

We witness the gradual emergence of a survivor's authentic voice, reshaping their personal narrative even as memory intrudes through emotional flashbacks. The intentional introduction of safety cues helps calm internal alarms, reducing the grip of 4F responses and constant vigilance. Nurturing connections and consistent care builds trust, laying the foundation for emotional steadiness, especially when dealing with complex trauma. This process involves reframing fear as a chance for learning, which naturally lowers threat perception and invites growth.

Through deliberate sensory integration, practiced grounding techniques, and routines that create predictability, the body and mind learn new responses. For those facing specific challenges—be it queer individuals redefining boundaries against invisibility, parents reclaiming nightly rest after trauma, veterans grappling with battlefield echoes, or individuals finding stability amid chronic pain and disability—these practices offer concrete ways to restore a sense of self. They reveal how community and cultural anchors strengthen resilience, helping to integrate past distress into present-day, values-driven choices. Ultimately, this work fosters a quiet arrival, where identity fragments fuse, gratitude for small freedoms blooms, and hope gently whispers of an unfolding path to sustained safety.

Vignette: A Child's Quiet Breakthrough

When cultural and community anchors are in place, you can start watching for small breakthroughs in the children in our lives—tiny shifts that seem unremarkable until you realize they are hardwon gains of trauma work. Think of them as reconnaissance, where a child clears the way back into curiosity. For service members used to reading terrain, this is crucial intel.

How safety cues flip the script. Kids respond to cues such as a calm voice, a predictable bedtime, or a particular chair where you read together—signals that lower the threat dial.

See the definition of 4F action in "The 4F Responses: Fight, Flight, Freeze, Fawn".

Kids operate on cues. A calm voice, a predictable bedtime, a particular chair where you read together — those are signals that lower the threat dial. Neurologically, those cues tell the amygdala it's safe enough to stop screaming for 4F action (fight, flight, freeze, fawn). In practice: pick one consistent safety cue (a worn blanket, a low lamp, a phrase) and use it when the child is calm so it becomes associated with safety. That's environmentbased regulation in action.

A caregiver's field manual: nurture and secure attachment

Consistent presence and attuned responses deepen trust. For parents or partners who are veterans, that means showing up without needing to fix everything — hold, reflect the feeling, and label it. Quick tactic: the five-minute check-in — uninterrupted time where you mirror the child's emotion and name one strength you saw that day. Repeat. Reliability rewrites threat expectations.

Reframing fear, stepwise

Tiny exposures — a short walk past a dog, a brief story about trying something new — lower threat perception. Use play to let the child test outcomes. Celebrate attempts like mission milestones: a nod, a sticker, a fivesecond highfive. The brain learns from nonthreatening repetitions.

Sensory integration: practical drills

Create a sensory kit—chewy tube, weighted lap pad, textured ball, soft music—to provide predictable grounding.

Refer to Emotional Flashbacks: Names and Recognitions for a detailed explanation.

Create a sensory kit: chewy tube, weighted lap pad, textured ball, soft music. Use heavy work (pushing a cart, carrying groceries) to calm the nervous system. Fivesenses grounding (name five things you see, four you touch…) is a combatproven way to break an emotional flashback — those sudden adultsized feelings that are really childhood memories hijacking the limbic system.

Use heavy work, such as pushing a cart or carrying groceries, to calm the nervous system.

When a child's trauma triggers a partner who is a veteran, complex secondary PTSD can emerge. Have a prearranged safety phrase and a pause plan: step outside, three slow breaths, sip water, then reengage. Seek peer support and family therapy early; treating the household reduces spillover.

Let the child's voice matter

Validation rewrites invisibility into agency. ask open questions, mirror feelings, and honor small wins. If a kid says, "I wasn't scared this time," treat it like earned ground. Small gains stack. They add up, and for veterans and families used to missionfocused progress, those stacks are how real recovery moves forward.

Vignette: A Veteran's Emotional Flashback

The small wins we just talked about in kids show up again in veterans, but the battlefield leaves different marks. Combat-related PTSD often arrives with flashbacks that feel less like memories and more like time travel. One moment you're in your living room, the next you're back under fire — sights, smells, and sounds dragging you into a past that your body thinks is still present.

When a flashback hits, the body automatically shifts into the 4F mode (fight, flight, freeze, or fawn) described in earlier foundational sections. In civilian life this response can look maladaptive, with a racing heart, tightened muscles, and tunnel vision. Traumatic brain injury can slow the reset of these reactions, making them harder to read and more confusing for the veteran and their family.

So what works in the wire-tight moments? Grounding techniques are practical and tactical. Try these field-ready options:

Use the Grounding Technique—Naming Sensations—by naming three sensations you feel in your body, such as the weight of your boots on the floor, the pressure of your palms, or the breeze on your face; keep it blunt, as labeling interrupts the replay and drags the brain back to the present.

Grounding Technique – Paced Breathing: Inhale for four counts, hold one, exhale for six. Repeat. Slow breath downshifts the autonomic system so you stop acting like you're still in a firefight.

- Carry a small object (coin, patch, textured cloth). Touch it, describe it. The tactile detail snaps attention to now.
- Check in with a trusted person: a short conversation with someone trained to keep you safe can prevent escalation. Families can keep a simple script to use in calls: calm tone, steady prompts, and permission to sit with silence.
- Practice family grounding: learn the signs of Complex Secondary

PTSD, create a lowstimulus safe space, practice the same grounding drills together, and seek professional support when patterns repeat.

If TBI is involved, add formal neuro-assessment and tailored rehab: cognitive pacing, visual-vestibular therapy, and slow exposure work. Veterans who combine grounding skills, supportive relationships, and targeted clinical care often regain a larger share of daily life. It doesn't erase the past, but it downgrades the alarms so you spend more hours in the present where real living happens.

Vignette: A Queer Journey to Boundaries

Framing Queer Boundary Work: A Trauma-Informed Context

Think of boundary work like premission checks. For queer survivors with combat stress or childhood CPTSD, clear limits act as a defensive posture—not rigid fortification, but a map of safe approaches that protects what matters. CPTSD—complex posttraumatic stress disorder—arises from prolonged or repeated trauma, especially in childhood, and manifests as difficulties with emotional regulation, selfimage, and trust. By mapping safe approaches, survivors can navigate daily life with fewer internal alarms and more agency.

Why boundaries matter for trauma recovery

Boundaries restore agency after events that stole it. For veterans who also carry childhood harm, symptoms overlap—persistent hypervigilance, shamedriven peoplepleasing, and emotional flashbacks. Hypervigilance is an elevated, continuous state of alertness that keeps the nervous system on high alert, while emotional flashbacks are intense, involuntary reexperiences of traumatic scenes that feel as though they are happening in the present. Setting limits reduces exposure to triggers that can reawaken those recordings, giving the nervous system fewer false alarms and the person more control over daily choices.

Invisibility as an obstacle

When identity has been erased or minimized—by units, family, or civilian systems—it undercuts the ability to name needs. That silence looks like weakness to some, but it is a survival tactic honed under threat. Breaking that pattern takes practice and small wins: one clear boundary at a time, starting where the risk is lowest.

Trauma-informed boundary practice (tactical steps)

- Conduct a quick afteraction review: note a recent moment when you felt violated or unsafe. What signaled danger? Which bodily cue showed up first? Use that cue as an early warning.

- Draft two-line scripts for common scenarios ("I'm not discussing my past right now" or "I need space for X hours"). Rehearse in the mirror or with a trusted comrade.
- Test a micro-boundary. decline one social ask that drains you. Track the outcome; give yourself credit for the rehearsal.

Turning emotional flashbacks into action

An emotional flashback is a sudden, intense reliving of a traumatic event that feels as if it is happening now. Emotional flashbacks can be treated like alarms: don't fight the sound—use it. Pause, identify the feltsense, consult your values checklist, and select the smallest protective act available (step aside, call a support person, or invoke a preagreed signal). Over time, those splitsecond choices build predictability and trust in yourself.

Family impact and complex secondary PTSD

Families absorb shocks too. When a veteran's boundaries change, partners and children may react with confusion or hurt. Communicate brief rationale and offer concrete alternatives (e.g., "I can't do that tonight, but I can sit and listen on Sunday"). Encourage family members to learn basic ground rules and safety signals; couples or family therapy that understands complex secondary PTSD provides practical role-plays.

Values-driven choices

Identify three non-negotiables—safety, honesty, rest—and let them guide responses. Values act as mission orders when the field gets noisy: they convert panic into consistent, small acts that protect dignity and keep forward motion.

A short field story: a queer corporal was repeatedly subjected to late-night barracks hazing. He started answering the first insult with a canned line and left the room. At first it felt awkward; after three reps, the squad recognized the boundary and incidents dropped. The corporal gained more than quiet—he gained predictability.

Boundaries are practical tools.

They reduce retrauma, protect identity, and create the conditions where healing strategies—therapies, support groups, rehearsed breathing—can actually take hold.

Vignette: A Parent Reclaiming Sleep

Reclaiming Sleep After Trauma: A Parent's Field Manual

CPTSD (Complex PostTraumatic Stress Disorder) develops after repeated or prolonged exposure to traumatic events such as childhood abuse, neglect, or combat. People with CPTSD often experience a chronic state of hyperarousal—an ongoing physiological readiness for danger. The 4F response—fight, flight, freeze, fawn—summarizes the four instinctive reactions the nervous system deploys when a threat is perceived. Emotional flashbacks are vivid, intrusive memories that feel as intense and present as current danger, and they can hijack the senses with the same urgency as a combat alarm.

Night shifts at home feel like guard duty gone wrong: the perimeter never feels secure and the brain scans for threats. For parents whose CPTSD stems from both childhood trauma and combat, darkness becomes a possible engagement zone. The 4F response—fight, flight, freeze, fawn—activates when nighttime cues mirror past danger, and emotional flashbacks hijack the senses with the same urgency as a combat alarm. This hyperarousal spills over to the household: the parent's jittery breathing, tightened jaw, or distracted voice act as microsignals that a child picks up on, turning a routine bedtime into mutual stress and a shared state of hypervigilance.

CPTSD can keep the nervous system in a 4F state—fight, flight, freeze, fawn—where the body is constantly preparing to respond to perceived threats. Hyperarousal describes the ongoing physiological hyperalertness that makes relaxation difficult. Emotional flashbacks are intense, intrusive memories that feel immediate and real.

Impact on parentchild hyperarousal: The parent's heightened 4F state creates a feedback loop that keeps both parent and child in a state of hyperarousal, disrupting sleep and reinforcing each other's anxiety.

Hyperarousal reduces tolerance for normal child noises, lowers patience, and makes consistent routines hard to maintain. Complex secondary PTSD

(C-PTSD) can ripple through the family: partners and children learn to anticipate the parent's triggers and either withdraw or overcompensate, creating a cycle that reinforces sleep disruption.

Practical tactics for the nights

- Pre-sleep SOP: set a predictable schedule and a short, calming pre-sleep ritual—two pages of a book, five minutes of guided breathwork, or a quiet hymn—so the nervous system gets repeated signals that it's safe to downshift.
- Environment ops: darken the room, cut ambient noise or use white noise at low volume, and remove screens at least 45 minutes before lights-out.
- Grounding drills with your kiddo present: paced diaphragmatic breaths (4–6 counts), a palm-to-heart pause, or a simple sensory check—name three things you can see, two you can touch, one steady inhale. These drills soothe both bodies and create attachment-safe signals.
- Physical reassurance: a hand on a shoulder, a brief cuddle, or a whispered, factual phrase—"You're safe here"—bluntly counters threat logic.

Self-compassion as field care

Treat your limits like supply constraints: acknowledge them, call for support when needed (partner nights, family, clinician), and rebuild trust with small, repeatable actions. Sleep won't flip on overnight; consistent tactics, patience, and occasional outside support (therapy, medication consult) are the logistics that win this campaign. Reclaiming rest improves parenting capacity and shrinks the battlefield atmosphere at home—one disciplined night at a time.

Vignette: A Person with Disability Finds Ground

When disability arrives, it doesn't simply check in and move to the guest room; it takes the bed, rearranges the furniture, and starts issuing orders. For veterans who carry battle scars and service histories, chronic pain or a new injury can reactivate the brain's ancient protective circuitry, the 4F responses—fight, flight, freeze, and fawn—designed to keep us alive in immediate danger. When these circuits flare, they can trigger emotional flashbacks: vivid, presentcentered feelings of threat that feel like reliving a dangerous event, even though the specific memories are fuzzy or missing. Grounding, the field manual for staying present, helps counteract the pull back into these old survival modes by anchoring attention in the here and now.

Sensory Grounding: touch, rhythm, breath

Start small and tactical. Pick one comforting object — a worn dog tag, a soft scarf, a weighted lap blanket — and make holding it part of your nightly routine. Pair that with rhythm: playlists of steadytempo songs, recorded nature sounds, or the metronome on your phone. Then add breath: box breathing, slow counts, or a simple 46 inhaleexhale pattern will downshift sympathetic arousal. This threepart combo interrupts dissociation and emotional flashbacks by giving the nervous system predictable input it can process safely. Visible reminders and physical anchors further stabilize your presence. Hang a small photo or a quote that reminds you of calm on your bedside table, or place a tactile object—like a smooth stone or a textured mug—on your nightstand so you can touch it when anxiety rises.

Create visible markers that say, "You are here, you are okay." A photo clipped to your nightstand, a small ritual before bed (lighting a candle, scribbling two lines in a journal), or an adaptive device that feels personal — a favorite cane, a contoured pillow — become physical evidence that you still exist the same person inside a changed body. These anchors validate experience and make it easier to ask for help when needed.

Community Support and Connection

This is not a solo operation. Peer groups, clinicians who specialize in combat trauma and childhood complex posttraumatic stress disorder (CPTSD), and family members trained in calm, grounding responses work together to recalibrate the brain's threat systems. Combat trauma refers to the psychological wounds sustained during war, while childhood CPTSD describes chronic, repeated exposure to traumatic events during early development that disrupts emotional regulation. Families can create simple scripts and safetouch cues to deescalate a 4F spike—a sudden surge in fight, flight, freeze, or fawn reactions—by using a prearranged phrase, a gentle hand on the shoulder, or a short, shared grounding drill of about five minutes.

Actionable checklist

- Choose one tactile anchor and use it nightly.
- Build a 3-step sensory routine: touch, rhythm, breath.
- Place two visible reminders where you'll see them at night.
- Identify a peer group or clinician and set one small contact goal.
- Teach one family member a short grounding script.

Vignette: An Immigrant Family's Safe Return

Re-entry as a Cohesive Sequence: an Immigrant Family Returns to Safety

Think of coming home after displacement like a platoon returning to base: there's the initial securing of the perimeter, the accounting of personnel, and the slow, awkward unpacking of what you carried out of the field. For immigrant families who survived war or forced moves, that sequence—arrival, assessment, settling—can actually be the scaffolding for healing. When safety becomes predictable, the brain's alarm system calms down.

Safe Arrival and Reducing Hypervigilance

The amygdala is a small almondshaped cluster of nuclei deep in the temporal lobe that signals threat and initiates the fightorflight response. The prefrontal cortex, located in the front of the brain, evaluates risk and modulates the amygdala's output, helping to keep emotions in check. For a definition of emotional flashbacks, see Emotional Flashbacks: Names and Recognitions.

On the neurological level, predictable cues lower amygdala firing and let the prefrontal cortex do its job again. That's the clinical way of saying a calm, familiar kitchen can stop your body from treating every passing truck like a mortar round. Emotional flashbacks—sudden reliving of past terror—are less likely when routines and visible safety markers are in place, especially when shared family narratives are woven into these cues, externalizing trauma and reducing shame. Tactical tip: create a brief "safe arrival checklist" the family runs through together—lights on, favorite chair accessible, phone numbers in a visible spot. Short, repeatable steps give the nervous system something reliable to latch onto.

Shared Family Narratives and Intergenerational Dialogue

Storytelling works like a squad debrief that includes grandma and the kids. When older relatives recount what happened in measured pieces, it externalizes trauma and reduces shame. Younger members can question, correct, or add context—this shared narrative rewrites isolation into a team report. Practical move: set a weekly "story time" where each person shares one memory, one value, and one small victory. Keep it short and grounded so arousal patterns don't spike—if voices get loud or someone freezes, pause and use a breathing anchor.

By weaving trauma stories into daily rituals, families externalize painful memories, turning them into shared knowledge that reduces shame and reinforces predictable cues. When the prefrontal cortex is engaged in recounting safe, familiar moments—like the routine of the safe arrival checklist—amygdala firing drops, emotional flashbacks are mitigated (see Emotional Flashbacks: Names and Recognitions), and healing flows across generations.

Heritage, Identity, and Ritual Anchors

Language, food, songs, and rituals reconnect people to their background and to each other. These are not just sentimental; they send consistent signals of safety to a nervous system scarred by chaos. Actionable step: pick two rituals to do every week—a meal, a song, a holiday practice—and protect that slot like duty time.

Community Support and Integration: Tactical Steps

Community programs act like support fire: they reduce isolation and give families practical resources. For veterans and their relatives at risk of Complex secondary PTSD, seek groups that understand both combat trauma and childhood-based Complex secondary PTSD patterns. Do this: identify one local peer group, one culturally informed therapist, and one social activity to attend monthly. Assign responsibilities—who calls, who brings a dish—to keep engagement predictable.

The 4F scrambling refers to the rapid, overlapping surge of Fear, Fatigue, Frustration, and the instinct to Flight that can overwhelm a displaced family when coping mechanisms are not in place.

Final note: recovery after displacement isn't a single event; it's a sequence of small, repeatable actions that retrain the nervous system. Treat it like a mission with daily SOPs, family briefings, and a support network on call. The work is tactical, the payoff is human: fewer emotional flashbacks, less 4F scrambling, and more nights where everyone actually sleeps.

Vignette: A Survivor Teaches Boundaries

When a household has reclaimed a measure of safety, the next mission is clear: teach other people how to deal with the veteran or survivor so the home stays secure. Think of this as training friendly forces to respect the rules of engagement for your nervous system. That's where teaching boundaries through lived example comes in.

Inner Safety Signals: Your body talks first. A tight throat, a hollow stomach, or a sudden fog of panic are not personality flaws — they're alarm buoys from the amygdala and brainstem saying, "This feels unsafe." The amygdala is a small almondshaped cluster of nuclei deep within the temporal lobe that evaluates threat and triggers rapid emotional responses. The brainstem, the oldest part of the brain, controls essential functions such as heart rate and breathing and coordinates the rapid protective reactions of the body. These signals often precede conscious thought and are the same circuitry behind emotional flashbacks—intense, vivid reexperiencing of a past trauma that can be triggered by a sudden noise, scent, or sensation—and the classic 4F reactions: fight, flight, freeze, or fawn. Learning to read those cues is like learning to read wind and terrain before moving across a field—it's survival information.

Communicating Boundaries: Be clear, concise, and steady. Use "I" statements that name the sensation and the request: "I get overwhelmed when people enter without notice. Please call first." Say it like an order you expect to be followed; enforce it the same way you would enforce an SOP. Consistency trains the social environment faster than any single speech.

Adapting Pace to the Nervous System: Progress is not a sprint; it's a series of small, graded exposures. Set micro-goals—two-minute social calls, then ten; a visit that lasts an hour, then longer. Measure by how your baseline arousal changes, not by how fast someone else thinks you should move.

Balancing Vulnerability and Firmness: You can show the map without giving up the fort. Sharing a memory or a trigger is vulnerability; refusing a certain type of exposure is firmness. Both build trust if offered on your terms.

Vulnerability without boundaries risks re-traumatizing; boundaries without vulnerability leave others unsure how to help.

Practical Scripts (tactical rehearsals)

- Unannounced visits: "I appreciate you checking in. I need a heads-up before visits—could you call first?"
- Pressure to disclose: "I'm not ready to talk about that. I'll tell you when I can."
- Offers of 'help' that feel intrusive: "Thanks. I'll take you up on that when I'm ready."

Modeling Safe Engagement: Actions teach louder than speeches. If the veteran enforces a simple rule—no surprise drop-ins—and treats others politely but firmly when the rule is tested, children and partners learn the pattern: limits equal safety. That lowers household hypervigilance and reduces Complex secondary PTSD for family members who otherwise pick up constant alert signals.

A final field note: treat boundary work like marksmanship. Practice, call your shots, adjust your stance, and celebrate the clean hits. Over time, a household that models clear, compassionate boundaries becomes a training ground for calm—one where both veterans and families get to breathe, repair, and rebuild.

Vignette: The Moment of Healing and Afterglow

After months of practicing boundaries and running after-action checks on your own nervous system, something odd happens: the alarms stop blaring long enough for you to hear silence. For a lot of vets this is the unexpected turning point — not fireworks, not a Hollywood montage — more like an afterglow that sneaks up at 0300 and stays. Heart rate that used to spike at the sound of a truck idling begins to settle. The body, which had been on permanent red alert, slowly reorients, like a damaged convoy finally finding a clear road.

Trauma can lock the amygdala – the brain's rapid threatdetector – into a perpetual "threat detect" mode, while the hippocampus, which timestamps and contextualizes memories, and the prefrontal cortex (PFC), the executive center that regulates attention, emotion, and decisionmaking, are pushed to the sidelines. The result is emotional flashbacks—intrusive, vividly replayed memories that drop you into a remembered fight without the presentday context. The body's default motor options in these moments are the 4F responses: fight, flight, freeze, and fawn. Healing begins when those systems start communicating again: the PFC nudges the amygdala, the hippocampus says, "That was then, this is now," and the body stops acting like it's under immediate fire. That reengagement of the brain's circuitry produces a "reboot of self." Pieces of identity that felt shattered—husband, squad leader, dad, friend—start reconnecting like pins on a map. Small freedoms become meaningful intel: stepping outside without scanning every shadow, savoring a morning coffee, laughing in a room full of people without guilt. These are not trivial; they're signs that the nervous system is learning new rules, and the brain's restored dialogue between amygdala, hippocampus, and PFC underlies the personal transformation.

These brief outward changes—reconnection of roles, relaxed vigilance, and the return of simple pleasures—mirror the restored dialogue between the amygdala, hippocampus, and prefrontal cortex that had been silenced by trauma.

Practical tactics for when the afterglow is faint or fades back in:

- Use quick regulation drills: box breathing, slow exhale drills, or a 5-4-3-2-1 sensory check to steady the system. Treat them like pre-mission checks.

- Practice graded exposure: brief, controlled re-entry into feared situations, paired with a practiced grounding sequence.

- Prebrief family and close teammates: agree on safe words, time-limited check-ins, and when to back off. That teaches others how to be a support element instead of additional threats.

Secondary CPTSD in families shows up as partner hypervigilance, overprotectiveness, or emotional withdrawal. Complex PostTraumatic Stress Disorder (CPTSD) is an extension of PTSD that includes disturbances in affect regulation, negative selfconcept, and interpersonal relationships; in a family setting, these symptoms manifest in a partner or child who constantly scans for danger, shields loved ones excessively, or pulls away emotionally. Countermeasures are education, clear boundaries, and shared small wins—family therapy, missionstyle habit building, and rituals that signal safety. Healing isn't a single medal ceremony. It's a string of small operational successes that, collected over time, rebuild a life soldiers and their families can trust again.

Therapy Options Overview

The persistent echo of complex trauma shapes not only our past but our present, often manifesting as an inner world prone to emotional flashbacks and wired for the survival responses of fight, flight, freeze, or fawn. For those carrying these imprints, whether from early life adversity or intensified by adult experiences like military service, the path to healing is not a single road but a network of carefully chosen routes. We find such routes in a range of therapeutic modalities designed to address the deep patterns of complex PTSD. These include structured approaches such as Eye Movement Desensitization and Reprocessing (EMDR), which works to reprocess distressing memories, alongside the body-centered practices of somatic therapies that regulate the nervous system and build internal safety. We also consider cognitive behavioral therapy (CBT) and dialectical behavior therapy (DBT), adapted to manage hyperarousal, avoidance, and relational disruption. Acceptance and commitment therapy (ACT) offers ways to engage with distress and guide actions by values, while narrative therapy helps rewrite life stories to reclaim agency. Additionally, we consider the supportive role of medications and the power of group and family contexts in creating safe spaces for healing. This collective of evidence-based methods, when applied with careful consideration for safety, stabilization, and individualized pacing, empowers individuals to gradually reclaim control over their internal world, moving from a reactive stance to one of intentional healing. We begin by examining EMDR, a method designed to gently reprocess those memories that hold us captive.

EMDR and Reprocessing

We were three mornings into a group session when one of the young veterans went quiet, eyes darting like a man listening for artillery in a quiet street. Ten seconds later he was sobbing, not about a firefight but about being six and locked in a bedroom while a parent raged. The room went still. That is the thing about complex trauma: combat can pull the trigger on childhood wounds, and childhood wounds can make combat feel worse. If you've felt that slipperiness — being in two timeframes at once — you're not alone.

EMDR: The basics

Imagine being able to rewire your brain's response to those memories, to hit a sort of internal "refresh" on the terror and shame that keep pulling you back. Eye Movement Desensitization and Reprocessing (EMDR) is a structured, evidencebased method that does just that for many people with complex PTSD (CPTSD). It isn't a magic patch or instant fix; it's a methodical approach that trains the brain to process stuck memories differently, reducing the emotional charge and returning control.

A phased approach to healing

EMDR runs on phases, and thinking of it like learning to swim helps: you don't jump into the deep end before you can float. Phase one builds stabilization — safety, grounding, and coping skills so you can handle waves without panicking. Phase two is preparation: picking target memories, mapping emotions, and introducing bilateral stimulation (BLS). Phase three is reprocessing: using BLS to engage both hemispheres and let the memory reorganize into something less threatening.

The three core steps look like this:

- Stabilization — get safe and steady.
- Preparation — pick targets and practice BLS.
- Reprocessing — apply BLS to reduce distress and integrate the memory.

How bilateral stimulation works

Bilateral stimulation — eye movements, alternating taps, or tones — is the engine of EMDR. It activates both hemispheres, allowing the brain to integrate fragmented traumatic memories that are locked in reactive circuits. Picture a memory stuck in a boobytrapped bunker: BLS opens the gate so the brain can walk through, neutralize hazards, and seal the bunker with new management. For details on the underlying neurobiology, see Neurobiology of Trauma: Brain and Body.

Childhood patterns, emotional flashbacks, and the 4Fs

See Emotional Flashbacks: Names and Recognitions for a definition of emotional flashbacks. EMDR adapted for children and combattraumatized veterans addresses these patterns and safety needs during processing. For children, it may involve playbased or artassisted EMDR to make bilateral stimulation engaging and less intimidating; for veterans, it often relies on strong grounding anchors and carefully paced eye movements to prevent overwhelm. By integrating these techniques, EMDR can help recalibrate the 4F circuitry and reduce emotional flashbacks, supporting recovery from CPTSD.

On session safety and handling flashbacks

See Emotional Flashbacks: Names and Recognitions for a definition of emotional flashbacks. EMDR practitioners monitor arousal, pace interventions, and employ safety protocols such as clear stop signals, scheduled breaks, onthespot grounding tools, and postsession support. For soldiers in therapy, practical moves include arranging a trusted buddy to checkin after sessions, establishing a "call me" plan with family, and rehearsing a safeplace visualization before leaving a clinic.

Evidence and outcomes for veterans and families

The 4F response—fight, flight, freeze, fawn—describes the instinctive reactions to threat that are central to trauma and CPTSD. EMDR has produced meaningful symptom reduction across CPTSD groups, including veterans, and is adapted to different populations: with children, practitioners employ playbased or artassisted techniques that use ageappropriate, symbolic activities to access and process distressing material safely; with veterans, clinicians emphasize grounding anchors, pacing, and practical stabilization to manage activation and maintain engagement. Families are affected as well—spouses and children can develop complex secondary PTSD—so familyfocused education, clear boundaries, and shared coping plans help reduce that risk. See Emotional Flashbacks and 4F references.

Introducing the 4F response—Fight, Flight, Freeze, and Fawn—helps explain how trauma hijacks our bodies. EMDR is adapted to support children with playbased or artassisted techniques that let them process memories safely. For veterans, therapists use grounding anchors and paced sessions to maintain calm while addressing distressing experiences. These adaptations, along with the phased approach that prevents being swept under, are detailed in the Emotional Flashbacks guide and the 4F references.

Somatic Therapies: Experiencing the Body

Somatic Therapies: A Body-Centered Approach to Healing from Trauma

If EMDR is the map for where the minefields of memory are, somatic therapies are the defusing kit you carry in your hands. The 4F response—fight, flight, freeze, and fawn—[see The 4F Responses] describes the immediate physiological and psychological reactions to perceived threat that many trauma survivors have become accustomed to. For veterans with combatrelated PTSD, battle fatigue, or traumatic brain injury (TBI), and for people whose complex posttraumatic stress disorder (CPTSD) traces back to childhood, targeting the body makes sense. Trauma lives in muscles, breathing, posture, and the automatic reactions of the nervous system. Somatic work teaches the body to stop reacting as if under attack when the threat is long gone, thereby helping to reset the 4F response and reduce emotional flashbacks—intense, presentcentered reexperiencing of core emotions from early traumatic episodes.

The Power of Breath and Movement

When the 4F response kicks in, breathing becomes shallow and rapid, feeding panic. Use the following drills to counteract this physiological pattern and restore calm.

- Diaphragmatic sigh: Hands on belly, breathe in low to feel the abdomen expand, then let out a long audible sigh. Three full sighs resets vagal tone more reliably than brute willpower.

Add gentle movement—slow walking, yoga poses that open the chest, tai chi weight shifts—to re-teach the body safe ways to move and release trapped tension. For TBI survivors, modify range and pace; small, repeated motions beat aggressive stretches.

Boxbreathing (4444):

- Inhale for 4 seconds, hold for 4, exhale for 4, hold for 4. Repeat for five rounds. Use it as a premission calmdown or when a memory spikes.

- Diaphragmatic sigh: Inhale slowly through the nose for 4 seconds, then exhale slowly and fully through the mouth for 6–8 seconds, allowing the diaphragm to fall fully. Repeat 5–10 times to release tension and reset the autonomic nervous system.

Body-Based Safety: The Foundation of Trust

You can't process trauma if your body doesn't feel safe. Somatic therapists build "body-based safety" the same way an NCO builds trust: predictability, clear limits, and respect. Techniques include establishing a safe physical anchor (a chair with two feet on the floor and both hands visible), practiced grounding cues (a specific hand press on the thigh), and consent-based touch when appropriate. These are not soft skills—when a veteran's chest tightens and the throat closes, a practiced safety anchor is the difference between shutting down and staying present.

Interoceptive Training: Tuning into Internal Cues

Interoceptive training is a set of exercises that sharpen awareness of bodily sensations such as heartbeats, breathing patterns, and muscle tension. By learning to notice these internal cues, individuals can identify the early signs of the 4F response—fight, flight, freeze, or fawn—that often arise before a fullblown flashback. Emotional flashbacks are powerful, presentcentered reexperiencing of core emotions from early trauma; interoceptive training helps bring them into conscious awareness so they can be managed rather than overwhelmed. For those with traumatic brain injury (TBI) or complex posttraumatic stress disorder (CPTSD)—the latter being a disorder of emotional dysregulation, intrusive memories, and relational problems rooted in prolonged or repeated trauma—interoceptive work is particularly valuable because it grounds the nervous system and fosters a sense of bodily safety.

Interoceptive training alerts you to changes in your inner weather—heart rate, tightness, nausea, or that hardtoname dread under the ribs. Training this radar gives soldiers and families early warning, allowing them to interrupt reactions before they become fullblown flashbacks. Simple drills:

- Body scan (2–5 min): slowly shift attention from feet to head, naming sensations without judgment.

- Heartrate check: pulse for 15 seconds after a stressful thought to see how fast it jumps.

- Sensation labeling: Say aloud "warm," "tight," "shaky," which reduces limbic reactivity.

Simple interoceptive drills:

- Body scan (2–5 minutes): slow attention from feet to head, naming sensations without judgment.
- Heartrate check: take pulse for 15 seconds after a stressful thought to see how fast it jumps.
- Body scan (2–5 minutes): slowly shift attention from feet to head, naming sensations without judgment.

These steps build agency: when you sense the first stirrings of a 4F shift, you can apply breathing, posture, or a grounding cue instead of riding the wave.

Collaborative Somatic Therapies: The Power of Connection

Somatic work is rarely a solo op. A therapist trained in these methods acts like a seasoned squad leader—attuned to pacing, to consent, and to the client's readiness to move. For veterans with TBI or severe hyperarousal, the therapist adjusts intensity, uses shorter sets, and checks in frequently. Families dealing with Complex secondary PTSD can be included: partners learn to offer a calming cue, parents learn safe touch patterns for dysregulated children, and siblings learn how to avoid taking on caretaker roles that trigger fawning responses.

Tactical Tips for Daily Use (for soldiers and families)

- Pre-shift routine: three minutes of box breathing plus a posture check (shoulders back, feet grounded).
- On flashback trigger: 30second grounding—name 5 things you see, 4 you can touch, 3 you hear, 2 you smell, 1 you taste.

A flashback trigger is any stimulus—visual, auditory, tactile, olfactory, or even an internal thought—that awakens a vivid, presentcentered reexperience of trauma. When a trigger fires, the 4F response (fight, flight, freeze, fawn) can kick in automatically, and emotional flashbacks may surface, bringing intense, childlike feelings to the foreground. The grounding exercise listed above is a rapid, sensorybased tool that anchors you in the present moment, helping to interrupt the 4F cascade and reduce the intensity of emotional flashbacks.

Family protocol: one designated calming phrase and a physical cue (holding forearm) practiced in non-crisis times. This grounding exercise aligns with the 4F response framework (see The 4F Responses). For trigger definitions, see Emotional Flashbacks.

In the end, somatic therapies return the body to its rightful job: carrying the person forward, not running the war. For veterans and families dealing with CPTSD, this approach gives practical, immediate tools to reduce panic, improve regulation, and restore trust in the only machine you've got—your own body.

CBT and CPTSD Adaptations

CBT for CPTSD: A Field Manual for the Mind

If somatic work is the map for finding the body's safe ground, Cognitive Behavioral Therapy (CBT) adapted for Complex PTSD is the mission plan for the mind. Think of it as missionspecific training: you don't throw a rookie into the jungle and call it a win. CPTSD needs an approach adjusted for multiple injuries — childhood wounds mixed with combat scars — not the standardissue CBT brief.

Trauma-Specific Adaptations

See What CPTSD Really Means for a full definition. CBT adapted for CPTSD targets those entrenched beliefs and the patterns they produce. Clinicians pace cognitive work, pulling apart longrunning overgeneralizations and testing them with realworld experiments. For veterans, that might mean converting 'I can't trust anyone' into a hypothesis to test in lowrisk social tasks, then grading upward.

You do not start a clearing operation without securing the perimeter. In therapy, stabilization is that perimeter: sleep structure, predictable routines, crisis plans, and skills to lower hyperarousal. Therapists set clear, written safety plans and small-step goals so patients aren't flooded. For soldiers used to orders and schedules, a short daily checklist that includes sleep, movement, and a grounding practice can be as reassuring as a pre-mission brief.

Emotion Regulation Skills

CPTSD often produces emotional storms—a sudden surge of affect that feels like being back in a firefight. These storms arise when the nervous system jumps into a threat response, often engaging the 4F system (Freeze, Flight, Fight, Fawn). CBT brings practical tools: grounding anchors (54321 sensory checks), paced breathing, distraction techniques, and behavioral coping plans. Family members should learn these tools too; when a veteran uses a grounding cue, a spouse trained to mirror that cue can reduce escalation. Teachable, repeatable tactics win the day.

Cognitive Restructuring

CBT adaptations for CPTSD combine cognitive restructuring to tame emotional flashbacks (see Emotional Flashbacks: Names and Recognitions) with graded exposure that respects the 4F system (see The 4F Responses: Fight, Flight, Freeze, Fawn). A useful combat metaphor: replace an outdated SOP that gets you hurt with a revised one that keeps you alive. Exposure must be tailored to the specific 4F response that emerges during reencounter. A veteran who tends to fawn (overaccommodating to avoid conflict) needs gentle, short, controlled exposures with builtin regulatory breaks; someone who goes straight to fight requires a different pacing. The rule is gradual grading: short, controlled exposures; builtin regulatory breaks; labeling the 4F response when it shows up; and rehearsing a coping response immediately after. Think of it as rehearsing a clearing technique with rest stops, not a nonstop assault.

Exposure and Working with 4F Responses

Putting it into practice: tailor exposures and cognitive work to the person's dominant 4F pattern while keeping a predictable structure.

- Prepare with cognitive restructuring: before an exposure, spotlight the automatic thought tied to the target cue, evaluate evidence for and against it, and generate a calmer alternative to use during the exercise.
- Grade the exposure: break the target situation into small steps, keep each step short, and intersperse regulatory breaks (grounding, breathing, orientation).
- Label responses: when a 4F response appears, name it aloud or in session (e.g., "I notice a fawn response—I'm softening my boundaries to avoid conflict"), which reduces automaticity and opens space for choice.
- Rehearse coping immediately after: practice the chosen coping or alternative behavior right after the exposure so the prefrontal reframe is linked to the corrective experience.

Examples of tailoring:

- Fawn (over-accommodating to avoid conflict): start with brief role-plays and scripted boundary phrases, paired with cognitive work that challenges self-erasing thoughts; build length and unpredictability slowly.

- Fight: combine short approach exposures with grounding and behavioral limits on escalation; rehearse safe expression and post-exposure calming.

- Freeze: use very small activation tasks (micro-decisions, brief movements) that rebuild agency, paired with gentle cognitive challenges to catastrophic helplessness beliefs.

- Flight: structure proximity-based steps with safety signals and return-to-safety breaks, while testing beliefs about danger and escape.

Across all patterns, the aim is the same: strengthen the prefrontal ability to reappraise threatening cues and to replace outdated survival responses with flexible, safer alternatives through repeated, graded practice.

Interpersonal Considerations and Families

Interpersonal trauma shows up as trust fractures. Bring trusted allies into therapy when safe: a family member, a clinician who has earned credibility, or a peer who knows military culture. Establish written safety agreements for critical moments (stepping out, calling a support person) and clear boundaries. Families also suffer secondhand wounds — "Complex secondary PTSD" — so include them in psychoeducation, teach them grounding and distress-tolerance skills, and provide referral options for their own care.

Engaging Veterans: Speak Their Language

CBT works better when it speaks military. Frame therapy in terms of mission readiness, skills training, and courage under pressure. Honor service, validate problem-solving strengths, and present seeking help as a tactical decision that improves performance. That framing cuts shame and increases uptake.

Monitoring Progress

Track symptoms across domains: emotional regulation, hyperarousal, self-concept, and relationships. Use clinician-administered and self-report tools (for CPTSD, measures that capture multi-domain symptoms are most useful) and set functional benchmarks — nights slept, social outings, minutes of triggered but contained distress. Weekly logs and brief check-ins let the therapist adjust pacing and techniques before a setback becomes an ambush.

CBT for CPTSD is not a textbook script — it's a mission plan that adapts to the terrain, the unit, and the wounds. With ongoing assessment, clear safety protocols, and skills practiced both in clinic and at home, veterans and their families can reclaim a measure of calm and control without losing the hard-earned strengths that kept them alive.

DBT Therapies

If CBT is the map for finding safe ground after CPTSD, Dialectical Behavior Therapy (DBT) hands you the kit: compass, rope, and a set of practiced maneuvers to get through the bad weather. For combat veterans whose inner battlefield includes echoes of childhood harm, DBT can be a practical protocol — structured, skills-focused, and built to hold someone steady when emotions try to take them over.

What DBT is and why it fits CPTSD

DBT was developed by Marsha Linehan to help people manage intense emotions and selfdestructive patterns. For CPTSD — where trauma was repeated, longterm, or started in childhood — DBT adds acceptance and mindfulness to behavioral skills, which helps stop automatic reactions from running the show. Think of it as teaching the body and brain new rules of engagement when old alarms are still wired to go off.

Trauma-informed adaptations

When DBT is used with CPTSD, clinicians tweak the tempo and the guardrails:

- Tailored pacing: No forced confrontations. Progress is phased so exposure and processing don't crater stability.
- Containment: Tools to shut down runaway arousal in the moment — a portable kit for the autonomic nervous system.
- Trauma processing: Once a base of safety exists, targeted processing can reduce the charge of traumatic memories.

Stage-based structure

DBT for CPTSD usually follows staged work:

- Establish safety and stabilization — build routines, sleep strategies, and urgent coping plans.
- Trauma processing and integration — carefully guided work on painful memories while using skills to stay regulated.

- Consolidation and maintenance — practice plans for real-world stress and relapse prevention.

Core DBT skill blocks — tactical use

- Mindfulness: Simple drills (observe-breathe-describe) that interrupt automatic escalation.
- Emotion regulation: Labeling feelings, reducing reactivity, and planning for high-risk times.
- Distress tolerance: Short-term survival techniques — sensory anchors, paced breathing, and emergency scripts.
- Interpersonal effectiveness: Clear, scripted communication to reduce conflicts and rebuild trust with family and teammates.

Neurology in combat terms: emotional flashbacks and 4F responses

Emotional flashbacks are brief, vivid intrusions that feel like the traumatic event is happening again. They are triggered by sensory cues, stress, or physiological arousal and can last from seconds to minutes. The brain's limbic system—particularly the amygdala and hippocampus—reactivates the memory, while the prefrontal cortex, which normally modulates emotional responses, is often less engaged during a flashback.

The fourF responses—Fight, Flight, Freeze, and Fawn—are the brain's automatic survival strategies. Fight is the attempt to confront or eliminate a threat. Flight is the instinct to escape. Freeze is the momentary immobilization that can protect the individual by reducing detectability. Fawn, often called the "pleasing" response, involves appeasing the threat to reduce harm.

Traumatic brain injury (TBI) can amplify both flashbacks and 4F reactions. Damage to the frontal lobes impairs executive control, making it harder to regulate emotions. Subcortical injury can heighten hyperarousal, increasing the frequency and intensity of flashbacks, and can bias the individual toward reactive 4F strategies. Because TBI can blunt the usual cognitive checks, a person may cycle rapidly between flashback and 4F states.

These definitions provide the foundation for applying therapeutic techniques, monitoring symptoms, and designing interventions that target the neural circuitry underlying flashbacks and 4F reactions.

Emotional flashbacks are sudden neurobiological relapses in which the limbic system reactivates the autonomic pattern of a past threat, making the body feel as if the danger is present again. The 4F responses—fight, flight, freeze, fawn—are fast, prewired tactics the brain uses to survive. Traumatic brain injury can blunt the prefrontal cortex's capacity to inhibit these automatic reactions and slow the processing of new information.

Neurology in combat terms: emotional flashbacks and 4F responses

DBT's response to these challenges

Dialectical Behaviour Therapy trains slower, deliberate responses so the body's nervous system is given time to integrate new, regulated patterns before it seizes control. In people with traumatic brain injury, the stepwise pacing and repetition of DBT are especially valuable: they compensate for reduced processing speed and impaired inhibition, allowing the individual to rehearse each response at a pace that matches the brain's slower recovery window.

Targets and measurable outcomes

This section defines specific treatment targets and measurable outcomes for DBT interventions related to emotional flashbacks and 4F responses. Duplicate content has been removed and clarified so this block remains distinct. Examples of targets include reducing the frequency and intensity of emotional flashbacks, decreasing the number of 4F reactive episodes, improving distress tolerance and emotion regulation, and increasing adaptive coping and interpersonal functioning. Measurable outcomes include validated symptom scales, behavioral diaries or counts, clinician-rated functioning assessments, and individualized goal-based progress metrics collected at baseline and at regular intervals.

Dialectical Behavior Therapy (DBT) is a structured, evidencebased treatment that targets the neurobiological and behavioral patterns underlying posttraumatic symptoms. Its core skill modules—mindfulness, distress tolerance, emotion regulation, and interpersonal effectiveness—help patients lower the frequency and intensity of emotional flashbacks and reduce the grip of the fourF responses, while breaking the cycle of avoidance.

Emotional flashbacks are brief, vivid reexperiences of trauma that feel as though the event is happening again. They arise when the amygdala reactivates a stored memory while prefrontal control is diminished. FourF responses (Fight, Flight, Freeze, Fawn) are the brain's automatic survival strategies that can dominate when a flashback is triggered. A person with traumatic brain injury (TBI) may find these reactions more automatic because frontallobe damage impairs executive regulation.

DBT addresses hyperarousal (sleep disturbances, startle, generalized anxiety) by teaching grounding techniques and breathing exercises that recalibrate the autonomic nervous system. It also targets interpersonal disruption—conflicts with family or partners—by strengthening communication skills and fostering empathy.

Progress is tracked with symptom checklists that note the number and severity of flashbacks, the frequency of 4F episodes, and the quality of sleep. Functional goals include achieving at least four consecutive weeks of stable sleep, reducing domestic conflicts, and decreasing panic episodes in public settings.

Formats and family involvement

DBT works in groups (peer learning, squad cohesion) and individual sessions (personal pacing, trauma focus). For families, skills training and clear safety plans help address Complex secondary PTSD. Practical steps for families: learn grounding cues to offer, set short protective time-outs, use scripted check-ins, and join a skills group together when possible.

A final field note: DBT is disciplined practice. Like firearms training, it takes repetition in safe settings before the drills reliably work under fire. For many veterans and their families, that practice is what turns reactive survival into deliberate living.

ACT Therapies

ACT Therapies for CPTSD: A Practical Field Manual

Think of Acceptance and Commitment Therapy (ACT) as a compact field kit for the mind — light, robust, and built for use in hostile territory. For veterans and people carrying childhood wounds, ACT gives tools to move through traumatic material without getting pinned down by it.

Core Components and How They Work in Combat Terms

- Acceptance: Stop trying to knife away the pain. Acceptance is the basic radio check: acknowledge the signal (thoughts, images, sensations) without dropping your position. Neuro-wise, this reduces the avoidance loop that strengthens traumatic networks.

Refer to the definition in "Emotional Flashbacks: Names and Recognitions" for details on emotional flashbacks. For information on the 4F responses, see "The 4F Responses: Fight, Flight, Freeze, Fawn". The TBI definition can be found in "Traumatic Brain Injury". For Complex Secondary PTSD, see the section titled "Complex Secondary PTSD".

- ACT components: Mindfulness is a short, sharp patrol in the present that trains the brain to notice when an emotional flashback is starting — that sudden, vivid reexperiencing that feels like you're back in the fight — and hold position instead of firing on instinct. Cognitive defusion adds small drills to unhook from traumabased thoughts such as "I am ruined" or "I'm unsafe." Techniques include labeling thoughts ("there's a thought that…") and using silly voices to shrink them, creating distance from the trauma narrative and reducing the power of emotional flashbacks.

- Self-as-context: This is the commander's perspective. It helps you see thoughts and feelings as passing orders, not the entirety of who you are. That separation weakens fusion with traumabased identity.

- Values: Your mission statement. Values are not goals; they're the reasons you get out of bed. Naming them provides direction when the 4F system (fight, flight, freeze, fawn) hijacks your actions.

- Values: Your mission statement. Values are not goals; they're the reasons you get out of bed. Naming them provides direction when the 4F system (fight, flight, freeze, fawn) hijacks your actions.
- Committed action: The day-to-day patrols toward values. Small, consistent moves build momentum and resilience.

Putting ACT into Practice — A Veteran Example

Imagine a veteran who freezes during loud trucks. The protocol:

- Prepare with cognitive restructuring.
- Grade the exposure.
- Label the 4F response.
- Rehearse coping immediately after.
- Values check: "What matters—family safety, integrity, being present?" Pick one.
- Committed action: Take a 5-minute walk with a family member, even if it feels small. Repeat.

Tactical Drills for Soldiers and Families

- Morning two-minute values brief: each person names one value and one tiny action for the day.
- Stop-breathe-count: when a trigger hits, stop movement, breathe four counts, name sensation.
- Thought-labeling: practice at mess hall — call out thoughts in neutral terms.
- Safety and boundary plan: families map triggers, assign roles (who calls a calming code word, who steps in to help ground).

Complex Secondary PTSD in Families

Partners and children can develop secondary PTSD that mirrors the veteran's 4F patterns—fight, flight, freeze, fawn—when trauma bleeds into close units. Psychoeducation helps family members recognize emotional flashbacks and defensive behaviors so they don't take them personally. Practical interventions include shared values and tiny joint committed actions—a fiveminute ritual after dinner, a family grounding cue—to repair trust and build predictable safety. Families should also map triggers and assign roles in a safety plan: who calls a calming code word, who steps in to help ground.

Final Note: Start Small, Keep It Real

ACT isn't some ballroom sprint. It's trench work: short, regular drills that shift how the brain responds to threat. For soldiers and their units, the payoff is tactical — better functioning under stress, clearer choices, and fewer nights stuck reliving the firefight or childhood room you couldn't get out of.

Narrative Therapy and Meaning Making

If ACT gets you moving again, narrative therapy helps you take back the story you tell about why you move the way you do. Think of it as stripping the enemy's propaganda out of your personal debrief and reissuing your status report: who you are, what happened, and what you decide to do next.

Reclaiming the Narrative

Trauma writes itself into memory like a bad field report that keeps getting reprinted. Narrative therapy hands you the red pen. The basic move is simple but powerful: separate the traumatic event from the person who survived it. The event becomes an outside actor — something that happened to you, not a sentence that defines you. For someone who carried combat shame for years, this re-authoring can shift the weight off the chestplate. For childhood CPTSD, it allows the adult you to tell a different version of the same past, one that includes survival, resourcefulness, and the skills you used to get through.

Reframing Trauma Stories

Reframing means retelling with an emphasis on agency. A grunt who pinned a buddy under fire can tell a story that acknowledges error or loss without making those moments the headline of their identity. Practically: write the original account line by line, then rewrite each line from the perspective of an observer who knows the whole operation — including stressors, orders, and limits. This reduces shame and self-blame by restoring context.

Externalizing the Trauma

Give the trauma a name like an enemy unit: The Flashback Platoon, The Guilt Patrol. That sounds cheeky, but naming works. It creates distance. You can talk about The Flashback as something you counteract with tools, rather than something that lives in your bloodstream. Families benefit when they learn the language: "He's not being mean — The Freeze is acting up." This reduces personalization and opens room for practical responses.

Constructing a Coherent Life Narrative

The 4F responses—fight, flight, freeze, and fawn—are the body's automatic, nonconscious reactions to perceived threat. Fight means confronting or attacking the danger; flight means removing oneself from it; freeze is a temporary paralysis that protects by staying still; fawn is an overcompliance that seeks to please in order to reduce threat. Understanding these four states gives a framework for recognizing and managing them.

A coherent narrative stitches the traumatic patch into a larger uniform. Start a timeline exercise: list significant events, the 4F responses present at each, and the strengths you used or developed. Add a "what I learned" column. That turns a brutal episode into a chapter where competence, survival strategies, or later caregiving appear on record. Over time that timeline reads less like a single catastrophe and more like a mission log with objectives, setbacks, and accomplishments.

Therapist as Co-Commander

In narrative work the therapist functions as collaborator, not commander. They help question automatic stories, listen for themes of shame, and offer alternative descriptions that highlight resilience. For combat veterans, a therapist who understands tactics and military culture can translate clinical language into field terms that hold meaning.

Integrating 4F States into Narratives

The 4F responses—fight, flight, freeze, and fawn—are the body's instinctive reactions to threat. Fight involves confrontation, flight is withdrawal, freeze is a temporary paralysis, and fawn is excessive compliance aimed at appeasing the threat. Mapping these states helps clarify why they surface and how to counter them.

Don't skip the body. Map where fight, flight, freeze, and fawn show up: heart, chest, throat, or the urge to apologize. When these states are mapped into the story, they stop being mysterious sabotage and become predictable reactions with countermeasures. A practical drill: when a memory surfaces, note which 4F state is triggered, describe it in a sentence, and name one concrete action (breath count, step outside, call a support person) to interrupt the pattern.

Tactical Exercises for Soldiers and Families

- Two-line externalization: write "The problem is…" and "I am…" then swap and reframe.

The 4F responses—fight, flight, freeze, and fawn—are the body's instinctive reactions to threat. Fight means confronting or attacking the danger; flight means removing oneself from it; freeze is a temporary paralysis that protects by staying still; fawn is an overcompliance that seeks to please in order to reduce threat.

- Family briefing: teach relatives to say, "That's The Freeze — give space and say X," so responses are scripted and less personal.

- Timeline plus strengths: one page, dated entries, and one coping skill listed per entry.

Narrative therapy won't erase what happened, but it hands you a different radio channel. With practice, the volume of shame drops and the command to act from values and skill comes back on the air.

Medication and Adjuncts: When They Help

Stories and meaning are central to recovery, but sometimes the nervous system keeps shouting over the conversation. When hypervigilance, insomnia, or intrusive images are so loud that therapy can't get traction, medications and targeted adjuncts become the squad medic: stabilizing, reducing acute symptoms, and giving the person enough room to engage in the hard work of trauma-focused therapy.

Medications as tactical support

Antidepressants blunt physiological alarms and reduce baseline anxiety, dampening the body's fightorflight response and keeping the soldier's stress levels within operational limits. Complementary sleep adjuncts—such as prazosin—target the nighttime surge of trauma memories, cutting down nightmares and restoring uninterrupted sleep.

Nighttime reexperiencing, often marked by emotional flashbacks, can disrupt sleep and daily life. The four basic defensive responses (4F) are instinctive reactions to perceived threat; spikes during the night can trigger vivid nightmares and physiological arousal. Targeted sleep adjuncts such as prazosin cut down on nightmares and improve sleep continuity, while antidepressants blunt physiological alarms and reduce baseline anxiety, further easing daytime functioning. Together these prescriptions restore uninterrupted sleep, lower emotional flashbacks, clarify thinking, and expand the calm 4F response range during the day.

Nonpharmacological supports that matter

Medication works best when paired with nonpharmacologic supports. These are the fieldcraft of recovery:

- Consistent sleep routine and light control before bed (reduce screen glare; dim lights).
- Breathing drills and simple grounding methods interrupt the rapid bursts of instinctive responses—fight, flight, freeze, and fawn—that arise when the body perceives threat. By slowing the breath and

anchoring the mind in the present, these techniques help calm the nervous system and reduce the intensity of each 4F response.

- Regular physical conditioning and paced movement to burn off excess arousal and stabilize mood.

- Mindfulness and short behavioral exposures guided by a therapist to retrain the nervous system.

Practical orders for soldiers and their families

Coordinate care: keep the psychiatrist, therapist, and primary care provider talking to each other. If there's a TBI, include neurology or a specialty clinic. TBI changes medication tolerance and risk profiles.

- Track and report: maintain a brief symptom and side-effect log for the first 8–12 weeks. Bring it to appointments; it beats vague reports like "I'm worse" or "it's fine."

- Avoid abrupt changes: stopping some meds abruptly can trigger rebound anxiety or other hazards. Any taper should be supervised.

- Family plan: relatives and partners can develop "red flag" lists and coping scripts — concrete phrases to use when a surge hits (e.g., "You're safe here; breathe with me for five breaths"). Family members may develop complex secondary PTSD; their own supports and where needed clinical care are legitimate parts of the treatment plan.

Special considerations — TBI and interactions

Traumatic brain injury (TBI) affects not only cognition and behavior but also how patients respond to medications, communication, and social interactions. When working with or caring for someone with TBI, consider the following practical points:

- Communication and cognition: Expect variability in attention, processing speed, memory, and language. Use simple, direct language, allow extra time for responses, repeat key information, and check understanding by asking the person to summarize rather than simply nodding.

- Emotional and behavioral changes: Irritability, impulsivity, emotional lability, apathy, and personality change are common. Respond with calm, clear boundaries; avoid confrontational language; validate feelings while redirecting unsafe or inappropriate behavior.

- Sensory and fatigue issues: Sensory sensitivities and easily triggered fatigue can affect social interactions. Shorten sessions or visits, minimize sensory overload (noise, bright lights), and schedule more demanding tasks during peak alertness.
- Safety and decision-making capacity: TBI can impair judgement. Assess capacity for informed consent for treatments or social decisions; involve family or legal proxies when appropriate and document assessments.
- Medication interactions and medical considerations: TBI patients often take multiple medications (anticonvulsants, psychotropics, analgesics). Monitor for increased sensitivity, altered metabolism, and drug–drug interactions. Be alert for seizure risk and consult neurology or pharmacy for complex regimens.
- Social supports and caregiver involvement: Engage caregivers and support networks early. Provide clear written instructions and realistic expectations for recovery. Educate about common post-TBI changes to reduce misinterpretation of behaviors.
- Rehabilitation and interdisciplinary care: Coordinate with rehabilitation, neuropsychology, psychiatry, and social work. Tailor interaction strategies to the individual's cognitive profile and progress.

Document functional strengths and limitations, adapt communication and interventions accordingly, and reevaluate frequently as recovery and needs evolve.

Group and Family-Based Approaches

Group and FamilyBased Approaches Overview

The 4F responses—fight, flight, freeze, fawn—are automatic brain reactions that help a person survive threat, but in trauma they can become maladaptive. If meds are the issuespotting spotter and therapy the weapons system, group and family approaches are the support crew that keeps the mission running. For veterans and survivors of childhood trauma, being around people who "get it" cuts through isolation the way a platoon cuts through bad terrain. These settings directly address the 4F stress responses—fight, flight, freeze, fawn—by providing predictable social feedback that calms the alarm circuits in the brain.

Peer Support: The Squad You Didn't Know You Needed

The amygdala is the brain's alarm system, while the frontal cortex is the higherlevel regulator that can step back from fear. For a precise definition of emotional flashbacks, see Emotional flashbacks: Names and Recognitions. Peer groups act like a battle buddy: someone who shows up, validates the symptoms you feel, and models how to act when the body is on high alert. Hearing another veteran describe the same shame or avoidance lowers the internal threat signal, quieting the amygdala so the frontal cortex can actually think for a minute instead of screaming primitive commands. To get the most benefit, look for groups with clear leadership, confidentiality rules, and a mix of skills training and open processing.

Groups can be shortterm skills squads or longer processing teams. Skills groups teach grounding, paced breathing, and simple exposure techniques to reduce emotional flashbacks—those sudden relivings triggered by sensory cues when the brain treats the present like the past. Processing groups give space to unpack the trauma narrative safely. Veteran formats often emphasize camaraderie and practical problemsolving (how to sleep on a civilian schedule, how to handle loud crowds). Childhood trauma groups emphasize attachment repair and emotion regulation. Good groups mix both: practice in session, homework between sessions, and periodic leader checkins.

If you're a leader, set expectations the first night—checkins, time limits for sharing, and a flag for when someone needs a break. Whether you're a member or a leader, the goal is to normalize symptoms, reduce threat, and provide a structured, supportive environment where skills and processing can coexist.

Group Modalities: Skills, Processing, and Formats

Groups can be organized to meet specific needs: short-term skills squads focus on teaching and rehearsing concrete tools (grounding exercises, paced breathing, graded exposure) so members can reduce distress in the moment; longer processing groups provide structured, safe time to work through trauma narratives and the emotions around them. Formats vary by population and goals—veteran groups often center on mutual support and practical adjustments to civilian life, while groups for childhood trauma prioritize rebuilding secure attachment and teaching emotion regulation. The most effective groups intentionally blend approaches: session-based skills practice, opportunities to process experiences, homework to generalize gains, clear confidentiality and leadership, and routine checkins to monitor safety. Choose or design a group based on who it serves and what change is needed, and ensure leaders set and reinforce boundaries and supports from the first meeting.

Groups can be organized to meet specific needs: shortterm skills squads focus on teaching and rehearsing concrete tools (grounding exercises, paced breathing, graded exposure) so members can reduce distress in the moment; longer processing groups provide structured, safe time to work through trauma narratives and the emotions around them. Formats vary by population and goals—veteran groups often center on mutual support and practical adjustments to civilian life, while groups for childhood trauma prioritize rebuilding secure attachment and teaching emotion regulation. The most effective groups intentionally blend approaches: sessionbased skills practice, opportunities to process experiences, homework to generalize gains, clear confidentiality and leadership, and routine checkins to monitor safety. Choose or design a group based on who it serves and what change is needed, and ensure leaders set and reinforce boundaries and supports from the first meeting.

Camaraderie and Safety: Building a Band of Trust

Safety is tactical: predictable routines, clearly stated limits, and a culture that discourages shaming. Camaraderie grows when members share practical coping tips and tolerate awkward moments without judgment. For combat-exposed troops, informal rituals — a moment of silence, a nickname system, or a short debrief after intense memories — can anchor trust. Leaders should coach members in slowing down during flashbacks and giving simple, concrete support rather than platitudes.

Family-Based Approaches: Training the Home Front

Family involvement turns the home into a consistent support environment. Structured family therapy teaches household cues that reduce 4F triggers: agreed phrases for time-outs, nightly check-ins, and predictable responses to panic episodes. Create household scripts for common triggers (what to say when a loud noise occurs, who takes over childcare during a flashback). That consistency helps retrain the brain's threat map so the home becomes less reactive.

Ethical Considerations: Boundaries, Consent, and Roles

Family and group work needs strict rules. Obtain informed consent that spells out confidentiality limits, reporting duties, and expected behaviors. Define roles — facilitator, member, family supporter — so no one is left guessing who handles safety issues. If disclosures imply imminent harm, have a prearranged safety plan. For clinicians and unit leaders, maintain boundaries: support and presence, yes; therapy without training, no. Finally, watch for signs of Complex secondary PTSD in partners and children and provide referrals when the support net is stretched thin.

Put bluntly: no one should fight alone. With the right squad and a clearly agreed plan, social support becomes a weapon against trauma's worst reflexes.

Choosing a Therapist: Practical Considerations

Setting the Stage for Healing: a Field Briefing for Therapy

If therapy were a mission, the pre-deployment brief would cover objectives, tactics, and exit criteria. For CPTSD care that brief happens in the first few sessions. Clear goals, realistic timelines, and a safety plan are the kinds of intel that keep operations from going sideways — and they matter whether the trauma started in childhood or on the line of duty.

The Three Ps: Purpose, Process, Potential

Purpose: What's the client's immediate mission? Is it to stop nighttime panic, reduce emotional flashbacks during family dinners, regain trust with a partner, or improve concentration after a TBI? Be specific. "Feel less on edge" is a start; "sleep through the night two nights a week without waking in a sweat" is an objective you can measure.

Traumatic brain injury (TBI) refers to brain damage caused by an external force, which can alter cognition, emotion, and physiological regulation.

- Process: What tactics will be used? The therapist should describe modalities, session structure, homework, and how progress gets tracked. Will you run skills training like DBT or a stabilization block before trauma processing with EMDR or trauma-focused CBT? Who will handle medical coordination for TBI symptoms?
- Potential: Lay out foreseeable obstacles and strengths. Triggers tied to childhood abuse can mimic combat triggers; both can create a limbic system that jumps first and asks questions later. A clear map of likely roadblocks — flashbacks, avoidance, sleep disruption — plus personal resources (family support, unit camaraderie, physical fitness) helps set realistic expectations.

Realistic Recovery Timelines

Healing from CPTSD is not a sprint. Expect irregular advances and setbacks. Therapy often begins with stabilization — arming the nervous system with regulation skills — then moves to processing and integration. Research supports combined approaches: EMDR for target trauma processing, DBT for emotion and interpersonal skills, trauma-focused CBT for cognitive restructuring, and stabilizing practices to maintain safety. Celebrate small wins: reduced frequency of freeze responses, better sleep, or fewer episodes of emotionally shutting down at home are all mission-critical progress markers.

Picking the Right Therapist: Vetting Questions

Treat finding a therapist like choosing a team leader. Ask directly:

- What is your experience with CPTSD, childhood trauma, combat-related PTSD, and TBI?
- What specific training or certifications do you have (EMDR, DBT, trauma-focused CBT)?
- How do you coordinate with medical providers, the VA, or family therapists?
- Can you provide references or supervision details and how you stay current with trauma care?

Safety Protocols: Managing Emotional Flashbacks and 4F Responses

The 4F response model (Freeze, Fight, Flight, Fawn) outlines the four instinctive reactions the body may exhibit when threatened. Emotional flashbacks are intense, involuntary reexperiences of past trauma that can trigger this cascade. Understanding these mechanisms helps therapists and clients design grounding and safety strategies.

Emotional flashbacks feel like a sudden limbic takeover: amygdala activation, hippocampal context loss, and a prefrontal cortex that's offline. Emotional flashbacks are brief, intense reexperiences of trauma that arise when the limbic system—especially the amygdala—reactivates a memory trace without the contextual guidance of the hippocampus, while the prefrontal cortex, responsible for executive

control, is often disengaged. That's why grounding and safety plans are tactical essentials.

The 4F response model—Freeze, Fight, Flight, Fawn—describes the body's instinctive reactions to threat, often activated during flashbacks. Practical grounding tools to practice include the 5-4-3-2-1 sensory check (name five things you see, four you can touch...), paced breathing (box or 4-6-4 counts), progressive muscle tension-release, and a "safe-place script" to read aloud. Build a written safety plan that includes crisis contacts (local ER, VA Crisis Line, an assigned support person), steps for deescalation, and instructions about firearm access or weapon storage during highrisk periods. Cocreate boundaries for sessions — pacing, touch, and topics that need a slower approach — and sign off on them together.

Access, Insurance, and Reliable Referral Paths

Consistent care wins battles. Ask your provider about coverage specifics: what services are allowed, session caps, prior authorization needs, and out-of-network reimbursement. If cost is a barrier, ask about sliding-scale slots, community mental health clinics, or veteran services through the VA or nonprofits. A good therapist will give reliable referrals — other trauma specialists, TBI clinics, family therapists — and coordinate those hand-offs, so no one on the team is left guessing.

For families carrying "Complex secondary PTSD," use the same operational clarity: set goals for family therapy, establish communication scripts, and keep safety protocols visible at home. When the lines of communication are clear and the safety plan is posted where everyone can see it, everyone has a better shot at steady recovery.

No medals are handed out for signing up for therapy, but showing up and putting a plan in place feels a lot like mission accomplished.

Integrating Therapies into a Personal Plan

Personalized Approach and Foundational Steps

CPTSD is defined as Complex PostTraumatic Stress Disorder, a condition arising from repeated or prolonged trauma, often starting in childhood, that produces chronic emotional, behavioral, and physiological dysregulation. Think of early work with CPTSD like checking weapons and securing a perimeter before pushing forward. For people whose roots go back to childhood trauma, that means prioritizing safety, stabilization, and building trust before any deep memory work. Those first moves reduce the body's automatic 4F activation—fight, flight, freeze, and fawn—and quiet emotional flashbacks so the rest of the plan isn't done under full enemy fire.

What the brain is doing: a brief field report. Trauma primes the amygdala and weakens prefrontal control. Emotional flashbacks are wholebody activations where the nervous system acts as if the threat is present. The goal is to lower the 4F response with concrete first steps:

- Grounding: focus on 5 things you can see, 4 you can touch, 3 you can hear, 2 you can smell, 1 you can taste.
- Controlled breathing: 468 pattern – inhale 4, hold 6, exhale 8.
- Body scan: notice tension, release gently.
- Safeplace visualization: imagine a place where you feel calm and protected.
- Reengage the prefrontal: ask yourself simple questions (e.g., "What am I doing now?") to bring attention to the present.

Concrete first steps

- Secure the environment: Create a predictable, low-stimulus space at home and in therapy. Control light, noise, and timing so surprises don't spike arousal. Simple: set phone to Do Not Disturb for sessions and establish signal phrases for pausing a conversation.

- Build rapport gradually: Trust isn't declared like a ceasefire. It's earned through consistency, clear boundaries, and small, reliable actions—showing up on time, explaining what will happen, asking permission to proceed.

- Neuroeducation: Teach the person what their body is doing. Brief, normalizing explanations reduce shame and cut the illusion that they're "losing it." Use diagrams or short metaphors (e.g., "your alarm is stuck on high alert") so families also get the picture.

Practical tools to lower 4F and handle flashbacks

- Orienting and grounding: look around and name 5 things you see, 4 you can touch, 3 you hear, 2 you smell, 1 you taste. This sensory check-in brings current, nonthreatening input to the cortex and reduces amygdala activation.

- Slow, extended exhale breathing: inhale gently, then exhale longer (for example 4–6 seconds). A longer exhale stimulates the parasympathetic system and helps downshift arousal.

- Name what's happening: say aloud (or to yourself) "This is a flashback" or "I feel terrified right now." Labeling activates prefrontal networks and creates distance from automatic reactions.

- Anchor with safe sensation: hold a textured object, splash cold water on your wrists, or press your feet into the floor. Clear, grounding sensations tell the nervous system you are in the present.

- Gentle movement: small, controlled movements (rocking, marching in place, shaking out hands) can discharge trapped energy without escalating fight/flight.

- Soothing touch and posture: place a hand on your chest or hug your arms; adopt an open, supported posture. These signals can reduce alarm and help the brain assess safety.

- Simple orientation phrases: remind yourself of facts—your name, the date, where you are—until the cortex regains control.

- Set a tiny intention: choose one small, doable step (sit down, call a friend, drink water). Concrete action helps reintroduce choice and agency.

- Reduce stimulation and seek support: if possible, move to a quieter environment and tell a trusted person you need help or space.
- Aftercare: once calmer, allow gentle processing—journal a line or two, notice body sensations, and plan a grounding routine for next time.

These tools work together with the field report above: they provide present-moment, sensory information and simple cognitive labels that quiet the amygdala and invite the prefrontal cortex back online so you can think and choose rather than only react.

- Grounding: five-sense checks (name three things you see, two things you touch), cold-water splash, or a textured object carried in a pocket. These anchor the present.
- Breath control: box breathing or paced exhalations calm the vagus nerve. Practice for one minute until it becomes automatic under stress.
- Micro-movement: slow, controlled physical actions—shoulder rolls, feet presses—help discharge freeze and reduce tension without needing to relive memories.
- Safety scripts: short, rehearsed lines to use during flashbacks—"This is a flashback; I'm safe now; I will use my breathing"—can halt escalation.

Integrating therapies: what to bring to the field

- Skills-based therapies (CBT and DBT): teach thought checks, emotion regulation, distress tolerance, and interpersonal skills. These are the drill manual—useful, repeatable, measurable.
- Somatic approaches: body-based work releases stored tension. Techniques like progressive muscle relaxation, somatic tracking, or trauma-release exercises help the nervous system complete interrupted defensive responses.
- Experiential practices: mindfulness, yoga adapted for trauma, and creative expression (writing, drawing, music) give nonverbal ways to process feelings. Think of this as cross-training for emotional

regulation.

Pacing, duration, and coordinated care

Respect the soldier's tempo. Sessions may need to be shorter, more frequent, or start with stabilization-only blocks before trauma processing. Set micro-goals: 15–20 minute skill sessions, then build to standard lengths. Watch energy reserves: one intense memory processing session can require several recovery days.

Coordinate across providers like a small-unit operation. Share safety plans, use consistent language about triggers and coping tools, and schedule regular brief check-ins so everyone—therapist, primary care, family—has the same operating picture. Include families in briefings to reduce Complex secondary PTSD: teach them what helps, what to avoid, and simple support scripts ("I'm here; tell me one thing that helps you right now").

Veteran-friendly tempo

Veterans often prefer directness, clear structure, and respect for pacing that acknowledges military training and combat exposure. Use combat metaphors sparingly and honestly, avoid minimizing childhood trauma, and emphasize collaboration. Trust builds when clinicians show competence, predictability, and a willingness to sit with discomfort without rushing the work.

Small wins count. Log them. Debrief regularly. Treat stabilization as mission-critical intel—the better you secure that base, the farther you can go without getting ambushed by old alarms.

Choosing a Path: How to Decide

With an understanding of the therapeutic pathways available for complex trauma, attention turns from what methods exist to how one best prepares to engage with them. Effective healing is not a spontaneous act but a considered undertaking, akin to preparing for a critical mission. This requires a thorough personal assessment: a clear understanding of current safety and daily stability, a mapping of triggers and emotional flashbacks, and an honest evaluation of whether a chosen approach truly suits the unique challenges of complex PTSD.

This readiness extends to setting clear, meaningful goals that respect personal values and individual needs, alongside selecting clinicians whose experience matches the intricacies of complex trauma, including 4F responses and veteran-specific considerations. Practical planning becomes central, addressing access barriers, insurance concerns, and ensuring supports are in place. As the work progresses, careful tracking of non-linear change and sound contingency planning are essential to maintain safety and momentum. This preparation establishes the foundation, ensuring that when therapy begins, it does so with maximum support and minimal risk.

Assess Readiness and Fit

Reassess Readiness and Fit Honestly and Safely

Treat this like a pre-deployment brief: mission readiness matters. Before committing to trauma-focused work, run an honest check on whether the person is prepared to handle the heat. That means assessing current safety, daily stability, awareness of triggers, and whether the selected treatment actually fits the complexity of childhood-plus-combat trauma.

Prioritizing Safety by Stabilizing Daily Functioning

Think of stabilization as hardening the perimeter before an incursion. If sleep is a mess, appetite is gone, substance use is high, or housing is uncertain, trauma processing can worsen symptoms. Practical steps to shore up daily functioning:

- Sleep: establish a set wind-down routine, limit stimulants after midday, use nightmare-management tools (imagery rehearsal, scheduled awakenings) before starting trauma processing.
- Nutrition and movement: small, consistent meals and brief daily activity can reduce baseline arousal.
- Substance plan: if alcohol or drugs are coping tools, get a supported reduction plan in place with medical oversight.
- Safety plan: crisis contacts, a quiet place to go, and a list of grounding tools ready for when 4F activation spikes.

Veterans: address benefits, housing, and VA or community supports early. A buddy or family member who understands safety steps can be mission-critical.

Assessing Awareness of Emotional Flashbacks and Triggers

You can't fight an enemy you don't see coming. Emotional flashbacks are internal transports that feel like a sudden return to the original trauma and are triggered by cues such as smells, tones of voice, orders, crowded rooms, or anniversary dates. Keep a trigger log to note earlywarning signs so you can spot when a flashback is about to begin. (The practical tools that follow are intended to be incorporated into the practical healing plan.)

Quick field tools (integrate into the practical healing plan):

- Build a trigger log: note what happened, what sensations came up, and the intensity (0–10). Patterns emerge fast.
- Learn early-warning signs: jaw tension, stomach tightening, narrowed vision, old survival behaviors (freeze, appease).
- Practice grounding runs: 54321 sensory checks, breathing box, naming three facts in the room. Rehearse these when calm so they'll work when under fire. Use them immediately after noting an earlywarning sign on your trigger log. Include these practices in your practical healing plan and rehearse them regularly so they work under stress.

Checking Fit for CPTSD-Focused Therapies

Not every therapist or modality is the right tool for this target. Complex PTSD needs clinicians who understand layered trauma: childhood attachment ruptures plus combat exposure and sometimes TBI. Ask straight questions about experience with CPTSD, use rates of stabilizing interventions before exposure work, and whether they coordinate care with medical teams.

Therapies to consider: trauma-focused CBT models and EMDR have utility with CPTSD when delivered with pacing and stabilization. Also look for clinicians who use phased care—stabilization, processing, reintegration—not a rapid-fire push into trauma memory work. Veteran-friendly providers will pay attention to service culture and TBI issues.

Set Mission-Focused Goals That Match Values and Needs

Goals keep the operation on track. Make them concrete: specific, measurable, realistic, relevant, and timeframed. Example: "Reduce nightmare nights from five per week to two within eight weeks using imagery rehearsal and sleep hygiene." Track progress weekly and adjust tactics if the plan stalls.

Include family: Complex secondary PTSD shows up in spouses and kids. Set household goals—clear roles, safe words for high-arousal moments, and time-limited family skills sessions—to support recovery on all fronts.

Reassessing readiness and fit is ongoing—run regular after-action reviews with your clinician, caregiver, or unit. When the baseline is secure, triggers are understood, and the therapy fits the mission, the work can move forward with far less risk of coming apart under pressure.

Clarify Goals and Boundaries

Laying the groundwork for healing looks a lot like writing an OPORD for your head: purpose, tasks, limitations, and the timeline. Before you sprint into trauma work, draft clear objectives, spell out safety constraints, and state how much time you can commit — both in weekly sessions and in the homework that follows. That's not soft; it's tactical preparation.

Identifying goals and desired outcomes

Start with a plain-language mission statement: what will be different when therapy is doing its job? Do you want fewer panic episodes, better sleep, fewer nightmares, fewer fights at home, or the confidence to sit through a crowded room without shutting down? Keep it concrete. Bring a short list to your first session and be ready to prioritize it with your clinician.

Establishing safety limits and time commitments

Set your red lines early. Tell your therapist what you're not ready to discuss, how long a session can go before you need a check-in, and whether you want a grounding exercise at the end. Decide an initial time commitment — for example, eight weekly sessions with a review, — and a communication plan for crises. If it sounds militaristic, good: clear rules prevent friendly fire.

Prioritizing symptoms and contexts

Rank symptoms by how much they interfere with daily function: sleep loss, aggression, emotional numbing, flashbacks, substance use, relationship strain. Map those symptoms to contexts — home, work, public spaces, anniversaries. Target the highest-impact items first; treating a single, high-disruption symptom can create space for deeper work later.

Anticipating triggers and 4F reactions

Know your 4F responses — fight, flight, freeze, fawn — and label the situations that provoke each. For each response, build a short coping plan:

- Fight: breathing drills, delayed-response scripts, safe physical outlets.

- Flight: anchor rituals that keep you present, pre-planned exits that don't escalate shame.
- Freeze: micro-movements, sensory cues (cool water, textured object) to re-engage the body.
- Fawn: boundary scripts and role-play to practice saying no.

Treat these plans like battle drills: practice them in low-threat settings until they become automatic.

Setting boundaries and agreeing on pace

Agree on session frequency and acceptable homework load. Put limits on how much trauma detail is tackled in one sitting — for instance, one memory per session unless both parties consent to push. Use a "stop code" or hand signal when in-person work feels too intense. Pace is not a weakness; it's a method to prevent re-traumatization.

Matching goals with trauma-informed options

Match your prioritized goals to therapies that fit CPTSD and combat-related symptoms: CBT and trauma-focused CBT for restructuring thoughts and behavior; EMDR for reprocessing salient memories; adjunctive approaches (medication management, skills groups) when needed. Veterans with childhood-origin CPTSD may need longer stabilization phases before exposure work.

Collaboration, coordination, and consent

Build a small team: psychologist, psychiatrist, social worker, and trusted family or support-group members. Clarify who gets what information and how consent is renewed — written agreements help. Decide who handles medication changes, crisis contacts, and family sessions. Keep disclosure tight: name specific records to share and set regular reviews to renew or withdraw consent.

This is not onesizefitsall. It's mission planning with backup plans, safety checks, and clear objectives so you and your loved ones can tackle the problem with fewer surprises and less collateral damage.

Practical Steps to Start

With the groundwork in place, it's time to sketch a personal trauma-informed plan — a field manual for your recovery that fits your service record, childhood history, and household. Treat it like a pre-deployment checklist: clear objectives, safety protocols, trusted team, small drills, and an after-action review schedule.

Start with Safety and Expectations

First order: safety. Write down non-negotiables — people you won't debrief with, days you need off phone/email, limits on session types or exposure work. Pair those with realistic expectations: which symptoms you want reduced (sleep, startle, anger), and what "progress" looks like week-to-week. Call out physical needs too — sleep, meds, exercise — because the brain does better when basic systems are stable.

Trusted Supports and Clear Boundaries

List three trusted supports by name and role: clinician, battle buddy, family member. Next to each, note what you'll share with them (logs, crisis signals) and what you won't. Teach that person a one-line script for crises — e.g., "You're safe. I'm staying with you until you can steady." This gives families a short, usable role without overloading them. Families should also get a short primer on complex secondary PTSD: how mirror symptoms (hypervigilance, withdrawal, guilt) can show up, and why boundaries protect both sides.

Begin with Small, Regular Grounding Drills

Set up a daily 3–5 minute "grounding drill" as part of morning PT or coffee. Examples:

- 5-4-3-2-1 senses scan (name five things you can see, four you can touch, etc.)
- Box breathing: 4 in, 4 hold, 4 out, 4 hold
- Two-minute progressive muscle relax (clench, release)

Track which drills cut your arousal in real time. If a drill works in the barracks or living room, it will work on the street.

Document Triggers and Early Warning Signs

Create a one-page triggers log with columns: trigger, physical signs (tight chest, gut cold), emotional label, SUDS score (0–10), immediate coping step. Update it daily for two weeks to map patterns. This is reconnaissance: you're mapping the enemy before you draw up a plan.

A Bit on What's Happening in the Head

When an emotional flashback strikes, the amygdala and brainstem fire an alarm, interpreting the situation as an immediate threat. The hippocampus, which normally stores memories, is thrown into chaos, and past feelings surge into the present as if danger is here. This triggers the 4F package—fight, flight, freeze, fawn—before the prefrontal cortex can step in to label the scene as a memory. Grounding techniques give the cortex time to reframe the threat.

Tailoring Therapy and Tracking Progress

Treat therapy like field testing. Give any new approach a defined trial (6–8 sessions), then assess measurable markers: nights slept, flashback frequency, relationship conflict incidents. Use simple metrics a clinician can chart. If progress stalls, swap or add interventions; combine symptom-focused tools (sleep, agitation) with therapies addressing long-term patterns rooted in childhood and combat overlap.

A Short After-Action Checklist for Families

- Learn one calm, validating phrase. Use it.
- Keep a household safety plan visible.
- Rotate check-ins so no one becomes the lone responder.
- Seek family-focused therapy if the family shows strain.

Make the plan visible, review it weekly, and update it like an ops order. Small, steady actions win fights; the same applies here.

Questions for Prospective Therapists

When you're ready to bring a therapist into your personal plan, treat the intake like a mission brief. Think of these conversations as reconnaissance: you're sizing up whether this clinician understands the particular mix of childhood trauma and combat stress that creates complex PTSD in many veterans. Below are practical categories and specific questions to put on the table, with explanations so you know what a solid answer sounds like.

Experience with CPTSD and complex trauma

- Questions to ask:
- What experience do you have working with CPTSD and complex trauma?
- How do you recognize emotional flashbacks and 4F stress responses in clients?
- Can you share an example of how you've helped a client manage an emotional flashback or a 4F reaction?

Why this matters: Emotional flashbacks are limbicsystem hijacks, not simple memory recall. The amygdala and midbrain launch intense, presentfelt emotions that lack a clear narrative, and the hippocampus cannot organize them. A therapist who names this process and applies grounding, titration, and windowoftolerance work understands the neurology behind the symptoms and can differentiate true dissociation or fawning from noncompliance.

Approach to safety, containment, and trust

- Questions to ask:
- What steps do you take to establish safety and containment in sessions?
- How do you build trust with clients who've been burned by authority or peers?

Tell me about a time you adapted your approach for a veteran with complex needs and comorbid conditions.

What you want to hear: Concrete tools—session structure, crisis plan, predictable check-ins, clear consent around trauma processing—plus examples of pacing adjustments. Trust builds faster when therapy feels like a predictable formation drill rather than improvisational theater.

Validation of triggers and grounding techniques

- Questions to ask:
- How do you validate clients' triggers and experiences?
- What grounding techniques do you teach and when do you use them?
- Walk me through a real case where grounding reduced overwhelm.

Practical tip: Ask the therapist to demonstrate a two-minute grounding exercise during the first call (breath counting, sensory list, or orientation to the room). If they can coach you calmly through it, they're likely to be useful in the heat of an emotional flashback.

Evidence-based modalities and cultural fit

- Questions to ask:
- Which evidence-based methods do you use for CPTSD (CBT variants, trauma-focused CBT, EMDR, somatic approaches, DBT)?
- How do you adapt treatments to fit a veteran's culture and life experience?
- How do you coordinate care when medications or TBI are in play?

A good clinician combines therapies and explains why one method is chosen over another. They should relate techniques to combat realities—sleep disruption, hypervigilance, TBI-related concentration issues—and adjust protocols accordingly.

Collaboration and veteran sensitivity

- Questions to ask:
- How do you work with other providers (primary care, VA, neuropsychologists)?
- What experience do you have with veteran and family care, and how do you stay current on trauma research?
- Family-focused question:
- How do you support spouses and loved ones who may be showing complex secondary PTSD?

Look for willingness to coordinate care, include family education sessions, and provide concrete tools for partners who often carry secondary trauma. A therapist who refuses to connect with medical teams or ignores family dynamics is a risk to your stability.

Final tactical moves: treat the first few sessions as a probationary period. Keep a checklist of answers and trust the ones that include clear examples, concrete tools, and a stated plan for safety. If the fit isn't there, it's okay to switch—this piece of your plan deserves the same standards you used in the field.

Cultural Safety and Trauma-Informed Care

Cultural Safety: The Foundation of Trauma-Informed Care

If you've ever stepped into an intake room and felt like the person across from you had read one manual and was trying to fit you into a different war story, you know how fast a session can go south. Think of cultural safety as basic mission planning: if the intel is wrong, the whole op is compromised. For veterans with CPTSD — especially those whose roots include childhood wounds — being met with cultural awareness can mean the difference between opening up and shutting down into a hardened shell.

CPTSD is defined as Complex PostTraumatic Stress Disorder, a condition arising from repeated or prolonged trauma, often starting in childhood, that produces chronic emotional, behavioral, and physiological dysregulation.

Why it matters

When a therapist overlooks a client's cultural background, the resulting emotional flashback can trigger a 4F response—fight, flight, freeze, or fawn—just as described earlier. The present conversation then feels like an old threat, retraumatizing the client. Recognizing this danger, clients and families can prepare practical defenses: list likely identitybased triggers, agree on a pause signal, and map grounding moves (54321, tactile objects, breathing cadence). These tools let the nervous system relearn safety and prevent rupture.

Practical steps for crews (clients and families)

- Ask the clinician how they learn about different backgrounds and traditions. If their answer is "I treat everyone the same," that's a red flag. You don't want a one-size-fits-all SOP in a theater full of unique terrain.

In the practical toolkit for managing triggers, one useful approach is to build a trigger plan that identifies likely triggers tied to identity or beliefs. The plan includes a preagreed pause signal and grounding moves such as 54321, a tactile object, or a breathing cadence. Practicing the pause signal at home allows family members to call a timeout before an argument escalates into a rupture.

- Build a trigger plan: list likely triggers tied to identity or beliefs, set a preagreed pause signal in session, and map grounding moves (54321, tactile object, breathing cadence). Practice the pause signal at home so family members can call a timeout before an argument becomes a rupture.
- Use the pause signal immediately when the therapist's comment feels culturally insensitive—this stops the 4F cascade before it turns into a flashback.
- After the pause, revisit the grounding moves together to reestablish safety, reinforcing the client's sense of control and reducing the chance of retraumatization.

Therapists can weave culturally sensitive rituals—such as prayer, music, food, or a veteran's specific salute—into the broader practical techniques to enhance repair work, helping clients feel seen and deepening the therapeutic bond. At the same time, centering client control means prioritizing the client's agency throughout the intervention: letting the client set the pace, choose the techniques that resonate most, and decide when to pause or shift focus. This clientcentered stance supports the practical techniques outlined above and reinforces empowerment.

- Include rituals or traditions when helpful: prayer, music, food, or a veteran's specific salute may be part of repair work. Therapists who can incorporate these without awkwardness are doing the hard work right.

For trauma survivors, control was stolen. Return it by offering real choices: type of therapy, pacing of exposure work, who attends sessions, and whether spiritual or family practices are included. Control reduces the brain's need to go straight to 4F responses. Families should be offered education meetings that explain how secondary trauma shows up and what safe support looks like without taking over the survivor's autonomy.

Validation as tactical medicine

Validation is a frontline procedure: acknowledge the meaning of a client's experience, name the pain, and mark it true. It's not agreement — it's recognition. Saying, "That would terrify me too," or "I hear that you felt powerless then and now" calms the limbic system faster than any explanation.

Staff training and ongoing practice

Therapists and clinic staff must commit to regular training in cultural humility and bias awareness. That means supervision with community experts, review of missteps, and regular feedback from veterans and families. Clinics should adopt after-action reviews when a session harms rather than helps — analyze what happened, who was impacted, and how to change practice.

Keeping it alive

Cultural safety is not a tick-box. It needs constant upkeep: self-checks for bias, consultation when unsure, and asking clients for input on what made them feel safe. For veterans and their families, demand that level of care. Treat it like your buddy's life depended on it — sometimes it does.

Access, Insurance, and Barriers

Access and cultural safety matter, but none of that helps if you can't get an appointment. For veterans and survivors of childhood trauma, the fight to receive CPTSD care often looks like a logistics operation with paperwork instead of rucksacks. Here are clear, field-ready tactics to close that gap.

Understanding insurance and treatment options

Insurance policies differ on what therapies are covered. Some plans pay for trauma-focused CBT or EMDR; others list only general therapy. Before you book:

- Call your insurer with the diagnosis code handy (your provider can help). Ask which CPTSD-relevant modalities are covered, what prior authorization requires, and what your copay and deductible will be.
- If the insurer balks at covering a CPTSD-specific approach, request a written denial and the appeal process. A concise clinical letter from your therapist that explains why a particular modality is medically necessary can change outcomes.

For veterans: the VA offers many services but has eligibility rules and wait windows. Use the VA patient advocate office if you hit roadblocks; they can fast-track intake in some cases.

Practical barriers and tactical fixes

Emotional flashbacks and the 4F stress responses (fight, flight, freeze, fawn) can turn everyday tasks—phone calls, filling forms, waiting rooms—into overwhelming battles. To overcome these practical barriers, consider:

- Telehealth whenever possible. If an inperson visit is needed, ask about transportation vouchers, community rides, or flexible locations.
- Flexible scheduling: request evening or weekend slots, or book a brief intake to ease anxiety. Many clinics offer secure text or email booking so you can avoid panictriggering calls.
- Childcare: ask if sessions can be held while children are nearby

or if the clinic offers resources. Alternatively, arrange a temporary babysitting swap with family members.

Finding CPTSD-specialized providers

CPTSD needs clinicians who understand both childhood trauma and combat exposure. Tactics:

- Get referrals from primary care, fellow vets, or military family groups.
- Verify training: look for providers trained in EMDR, trauma-focused CBT, sensorimotor therapy, or attachment-based work.
- Use veteran and PTSD directories; filter by trauma specialties and telehealth availability.

VA versus private options — trade-offs

VA care often costs less but may have longer waits and eligibility checkpoints. Private plans usually give more provider choice and faster scheduling but can mean higher out-of-pocket costs. If both are available, consider hybrid care: short-term private sessions while waiting for long-term VA placement, then transfer records and treatment plans.

Cutting stigma and shortening waits

Normalizing help-seeking within units and families reduces shame. Encourage leaders and spouses to model therapy use. If wait times are long, apply these measures: ask for a short-term triage session, contact multiple clinics simultaneously, and use peer-support groups to hold the line until formal care begins.

Supporting families (complex secondary PTSD)

Families commonly carry stress from a veteran's CPTSD. Family members should seek their own support, learn about emotional flashbacks and 4F responses, set clear boundaries, and join family therapy or support groups. Treat family care as a tactical element of the overall treatment plan.

When the system feels like an obstacle course, use the tools above like a field manual: prepare, call with a plan, bring an advocate, and don't accept "no" without an appeal. Getting into care is the first mission—once you're in, the therapy can do the next part.

Measuring Progress and Adjusting

Measuring progress with CPTSD is less like checking off a to-do list and more like reading after-action reports from a chaotic patrol: some days the unit comes back intact, other days you're counting equipment and morale. The unpredictability stems from brain changes caused by repeated trauma. Repeated threats sensitize the amygdala—the brain's alarm bell—fragment hippocampal memory so events feel stuck or out of order, and weaken prefrontal control, making it harder to calm the alarm. These shifts create emotional flashbacks and the 4F reactions—fight, flight, freeze, and fawn—as defined earlier. Tracking these reactions with a simple 2–3 minute entry—frequency, intensity (1–10), duration, context—provides data that links the neural changes to measurable progress.

Trauma-informed pacing accepts that the brain repairs itself slowly. Think of recovery like a field medic rebuilding a platoon: you patch, you stabilize, you rehabilitate. Rushing exposures or skills without stabilization risks setbacks. A trauma-informed plan prioritizes safety markers first: sleep baseline, reliable support, and a short list of coping practices that actually work for the individual under stress.

Practical tracking that respects that pacing is multi-domain. Use a simple daily card or app that logs four fields:

- Symptoms: count nightmares, anxiety spikes, and emotional flashbacks.
- Functioning: note whether basic tasks happened — food, hygiene, work.
- Relationships: rate social contact quality and any conflicts.
- Coping skills: which tools were used and how effective they were.

Make entries brief — a 2–3 minute check is enough. For emotional flashbacks and 4F events, use the same mini-format every time: frequency (how many today), intensity (1–10 scale), duration (minutes), and context (who/what triggered it). Because these metrics mirror the brain's shifting states caused by trauma, they give therapists and families real, actionable data, not just feelings.

Set goals that are flexible and person-centered. Anchor them to safety and war-tested values: keep the team safe, maintain the household, preserve honor. Examples: short-term — attend a small gathering and leave after 45 minutes if overwhelmed; long-term — build a daily 20-minute self-care routine three times a week. Adjust targets when sleep dips or TBI-related cognitive fog appears; if memory or concentration is an issue after a blast, simplify tracking (use voice notes, check-boxes, or a color-coded magnet on the fridge).

Families should track too. Complex secondary PTSD shows up as hypervigilance, guilt, or emotional shutdown in partners and kids. A family log can mirror the veteran's: note tense interactions, nights of poor sleep, and when supportive strategies helped. Teach household members the 4F language so responses are less personal and more tactical: "I see a freeze; I'll give two minutes, then offer a grounding cue."

Finally, celebrate small wins like a sergeant praising a recruit — a 10-minute walk, one night of better sleep, or a successful phone call. Those micro-victories rebuild trust in the self. Keep reporting, keep adjusting the plan, and keep the tempo slow enough for the brain to heal but steady enough for life to continue.

What if It Feels Risky: Contingency Plans

Contingency Planning for Risky Therapy Decisions — Mission Brief

Treat risky therapy moves like a recon mission: you plan the objective, map the exit routes, and have a medevac on standby. Contingency planning is the battlefield check that keeps you from getting pinned down by a surge of emotional flashbacks or a full freezeflightfightfawn reaction. Below are field-ready sections you can use to build a practical safety plan with your clinician and family.

Assessing Personal Risk Tolerance and Safety — Know Your Red Lines

Start with a frank prebrief about what you can handle. Ask yourself which topics make my chest clamp, cause my vision to narrow, and make my hands shake. Which ones send me into fawn or freeze? Write these triggers down and share them with your therapist. That creates a clear operational boundary — your emotional safety net. For vets with childhood CPTSD overlapping combat trauma, some triggers will be old-guard (abandonment, shame) and some will be combatspecific (loud bangs, command voices). Both matter.

Identifying Thresholds for Stopping or Pausing Therapy — Stop Orders

Set concrete stop orders before the session. Example triggers for a pause: • If emotional flashbacks spike in intensity above an 8 out of 10.

- If emotional flashbacks spike in intensity above an 8 out of 10.
- If you experience more than three major dissociative episodes in a day.
- If suicidal thoughts appear or worsen.

Agreeing on these thresholds ahead of time removes guesswork in the moment and gives your therapist permission to slow the pace or shift tactics.

Planning Crisis Support and Emergency Rules — Who's on the Wire

Draft an emergency SOP with contacts and clear roles:

- Primary contact (name, phone): immediate checkin.
- Secondary contact: arrives if primary unavailable.
- Clinician emergency protocol: who to call and when.
- Local crisis numbers and nearest ER with TBIaware staff.

Draft an emergency SOP (Standard Operating Procedure) with contacts and clear roles.

- Primary contact (name, phone): immediate check-in.
- Secondary contact: arrives if primary unavailable.
- Clinician emergency protocol: who to call and when.
- Local crisis numbers and nearest ER with TBI-aware staff.

Train your family or battle buddy on signs that mean "this is beyond our capabilities" and rehearse the steps once a month so the response is automatic.

Establishing In-Session Grounding and Breathing Techniques — Immediate Stabilization

Keep a short toolbox for the chairside:

- breath drill: inhale four seconds, hold four seconds, exhale six seconds, repeat three times.
- Grounding script: list five things you can see, four you can touch, three you can hear, two you can smell, one you can taste.
- Physical anchor: feet flat, palms pressed, name your current location and time aloud.

These are tactical moves to slow arousal and stop a runaway freezeflightfightfawn cascade.

Choosing Modalities with Gradual Exposure and Pacing — Phased Ops

Pick therapies that allow phased exposure. Start with containment and coping drills, then progress to memory work in small, controlled increments. Good clinicians will use micro-exposures, short sessions, and frequent check-ins so you never feel forced into a breach.

Collaborating with Trauma-Informed Clinicians and Peers — Build the Team

Work with clinicians who understand both combat-related and childhood CPTSD, and plug into peer groups where families and peers learn signs of complex secondary PTSD. Share the contingency plan with your therapist and a trusted peer so support is not a single point of failure. When everyone knows the SOP, the chances of an uncontrolled event drop sharply.

Final thought: contingency planning isn't a lack of courage — it's tactical discipline. You wouldn't clear a building without a plan; treat your therapy the same way.

12-Month Healing Plan: Months 1–8

The world can feel like a perpetual battleground when past alarms override present calm. This section details a structured way to rebuild security, inside and out. It begins by fortifying your personal space with immediate safety measures and clear boundaries, giving your nervous system a chance to stand down from its constant watch.

We then move to strengthening the vital link between mind and body, using controlled breathing and body awareness to disarm emotional flashbacks. Next, we address how to define your needs and communicate them clearly within your most important connections, practicing the language of safety in all interactions. Consistent, restorative sleep becomes a central anchor for the nervous system's repair. As your inner world stabilizes, we turn to the important work of redefining identity, discovering guiding principles that stand firm against the echoes of trauma. Creative expression provides a way for processing difficult memories safely, while a structured method for building trust in others allows for secure, reliable bonds. Throughout these steps, nurturing kindness toward yourself becomes a steadying practice, countering the critical voices of trauma with soothing, personal rituals.

Month 1: Grounding and Safety Fundamentals

Month 1: Grounding and Safety Foundations for CPTSD

If you've ever jumped at a car backfire and found yourself standing by the kitchen doorway, you know how old alarms can sound like new threats. That split-second hijack—heart pounding, muscles ready, mind replaying threats—is the kind of thing we'll put a stop to in Month 1. This phase is about building a cozy fortress around your day-to-day life: predictable, defensible, and comfortable enough that your nervous system can stop running point every hour.

Establishing a Safety-Conscious Practice

Think of a calm room in your head: low light, predictable rhythm, no surprise triggers. For combat veterans and people with childhood-based CPTSD, stability is not luxury—it's a medical intervention. Start by setting a daily routine that the body can count on: wake time, meals, movement, and a pre-bed ritual. Learn your personal safety signals—the small physical or emotional cues that mean your system is moving toward overload. Maybe your jaw tightens, your breathing shallows, or an old shame pops up out of nowhere. When those signals appear, intervene before the smoke clears into panic.

Creating a Personal Grounding Toolkit

A toolbox on the nightstand beats empty hands when the alarm goes off. Try a handful of reliable tools and keep the ones that work:

- Deep breathing exercises (box breathing, slow diaphragmatic breaths)
- Progressive muscle relaxation (scanandrelease like unwiring tense muscles)
- Mindfulness meditation (short, anchored practices; three minutes works)
- Physical activity (a brisk walk, shadow-boxing, tactical PT)

- Creative work (scribbling a line, sketching an angry stick figure, hammering a nail)

Treat these like drills: run them daily so they're second nature during a trigger.

Establishing a Daily Safety Plan and Boundaries

A daily safety plan protects your recovery zone. List people, places, and actions that drain you; appoint specific windows for social contact; schedule downtime. Boundaries are not selfish; they provide perimeter security. Tell your unit (or family) the new operating orders: "No calls after 9 p.m. unless code red." Say no to invites you can't handle. If TBI or battle fatigue complicates concentration, keep plans shorter and simpler.

Sleep Hygiene and Routine

Sleep is where regulation repairs itself. Set a consistent sleep schedule. Create a wind-down routine—reading, slow breathing, low light. Avoid screens before bed. Cool, dark, quiet works better than overheating your brain with late-night briefings.

Nutrition and Physical Self-Care

Food and movement change how your body responds to stress. Aim for whole foods, steady hydration, and regular, modest exercise—walking, yoga, or PT drills adapted to tolerance. Use relaxation techniques before and after physical work to prevent pushing into hyperarousal.

Families and Secondary CPTSD

Partners and children pick up the signals and can develop complex secondary stress. Train families in safety signals, include them in a household toolkit, and set mutual boundaries. Simple actions—shared bedtime routines, agreed no-tech hours, and designated calm spaces—reduce spillover.

Practical reading that links combat fatigue and CPTSD includes Battle Fatigue: Understanding PTSD and Finding a Cure by Paul D. Walker (2014) and Arsenal of Hope: Tactics for Taking on PTSD, Together by Jen Satterly (2018). These works connect field experience with practical tactics you can adapt during Month 1.

Month 1 is about stopping the bleed: stabilizing your nervous system, setting reliable routines, and arming yourself and your family with simple, repeatable skills. Drill the basics until they become reflex.

Month 2: Breathwork and Body Awareness

Month 2: Breathwork and Body Awareness for Healing

If Month 1 was about building a defensive perimeter—lights on, rations stacked, clear watch shifts—Month 2 hands you a basic weapon most people forget they already have: your breath. For combat troops this is familiar: steady breathing before a long patrol. For many veterans with CPTSD, childhood trauma added more booby traps to the body, so the nervous system trips alarms at small things. The fix isn't mythical; it's physiological and trainable.

How trauma alters the system

Trauma primes the autonomic nervous system (ANS) to prefer high alert. That shows up as the 4Fs: fight, flight, freeze, and fawn. Emotional flashbacks aren't mental hallucinations so much as a limbic hijack—the amygdala screams, the prefrontal cortex takes a knee, and the body replays survival stuff from the past. Breathwork sends a direct signal to the parasympathetic system (hello, vagus nerve), dialing down hyperarousal and giving the frontal brain a chance to reenter command.

Practical breath tools: box breathing and the longer exhale

- Box breathing (field-friendly): Inhale 4 counts — hold 4 — exhale 4 — hold 4. Think of it as clearing comms: steady, predictable, repeatable. Start with one or two rounds and build to five.
- Longer exhale: Breathe in for 4, breathe out for 6–8. The longer exhale nudges parasympathetic tone and slows that fight-or-flight engine.

Pair breathwork with a body scan

Combine breathing with a short body scan to find where trauma stores tension. Lie or sit. With each inhalation, bring attention to a body region; exhale and soften. Move head → neck → shoulders → chest → belly → hips → legs → feet. Pause where you feel tight; two breaths into that spot, then move on. Keep it gentle; the goal is noticing, not forcing release.

Gentle grounding cues

Grounding keeps you in the present so the body scan doesn't flip into overwhelm. Use simple anchors:

- Feet on the floor: press and sense weight.
- 5-second sensory check: name aloud one thing you feel, see, hear, smell, taste.
- Cold cue: hold a can of chilled water or splash cool water on your face.

Controlled exposure and self-compassion

Start small when re-contacting body sensations. Use a 0–10 rating for discomfort and keep the work under six. Increase intensity by tiny increments across days. Pair exposure with self-compassion cues such as: "This is hard. I'm safe right now," or "I'm doing exactly what I can." Say them out loud if it helps—spoken words anchor the cortex.

Tracking and after-action reports

Carry a pocket notebook. For each micro-session jot: date/time, technique used, body areas noticed, SUDS rating, triggers nearby, and how long you practiced. Small logs reveal patterns and help you report to a therapist or family member with specifics.

Micro-practice protocols (5–10 minutes)

- Pre-shift: 5 minutes box breathing and shoulder scan before a stressful meeting or appointment.
- Midday reset: 8-minute longer-exhale session with feet-on-floor grounding.
- Bedtime wind-down: 5-minute body scan lying down, paired with slow exhalations.

Family tactics: Complex secondary PTSD and team training

Partners and family can learn the drills. Run short shared practices: twominute breath checks, oneperson guided practice. Family members should avoid pushing exposure—keep them in support/observer roles and teach phrases that comfort without minimizing.

Family Tactics: Addressing Complex Secondary PTSD

- Practice one micro-session daily.
- Keep a notebook for quick logs.
- Use grounding anchors before and after scans.
- Bring a family member into one guided practice.

These are field-tested, low-tech tactics you can carry in pocket or pack. Like any drill, consistency builds tolerance; repeated small exposures with calm breathing teach the nervous system there's another option besides constant alert.

Month 3: Boundaries and Relationship Scripts

CPTSD is defined as Complex PostTraumatic Stress Disorder, a condition arising from repeated or prolonged trauma, often starting in childhood, that produces chronic emotional, behavioral, and physiological dysregulation. Transitioning from breath and body awareness, the next front in combatting hidden scars is establishing clear boundaries — think of them as your rules of engagement for personal space and emotional safety. For soldiers with PTSD and CPTSD rooted in childhood trauma, boundaries are not an optional courtesy; they are a survival protocol that reduces ambiguity when emotional flashbacks or 4F responses flare.

Establishing Personal Boundary Needs and Non-Negotiables

Start like a recon mission. Ask yourself:

- What restores me emotionally and physically?
- Which behaviors put me on alert or shutdown?
- What is non-negotiable for me in close bonds?

Write those answers down. You might discover you need an hour of solitude after intense social contact, or that certain jokes trigger panic. These are not weaknesses; they are intelligence. When childhood complex trauma and combat trauma overlap, the brain often misreads social cues—clear personal limits cut down misfires.

Clarifying What You Will and Won't Tolerate

Turn your limits into plain-language orders. Short, firm statements reduce grey zones that provoke resentments or sudden shutdown:

- "I won't stay in yelling arguments. I'll step outside for 20 minutes."
- "I need a heads-up before visitors; surprise crowds trigger me."

These are practical directives for others. They reduce the likelihood of activating a freeze, flee, fight, or fawn reaction during a conflict.

Tactical Strategies for Emotional Flashbacks and 4F Responses in Relationships

When an emotional flashback hits, act like a pressurecooker in reverse with these fieldready tactics:

- Ground yourself: name 3 sounds, 2 textures under your hands, 1 nearby smell.
- Speak with "I" language: "I'm in a flashback. I need to pause this talk." This cuts automatic reactivity.
- Preagree on shortterm selfcare: walk outside, play a playlist, do a breathing drill, and schedule a checkin afterward.

These techniques help both the veteran and loved ones avoid getting pulled into an escalating pattern that produces complex secondary PTSD.

Crafting Scripts and Using Templates

Scripts reduce ad-lib reactions. Use a simple template:

- Clear need: "I need…"
- Example of the trigger: "When X happens…"
- Proposed solution: "Can we do Y instead?"

Example script: "I need space when I start to dissociate. When voices rise, I'll step into the yard for 15 minutes. I'll come back and we'll finish this calmly." Keep scripts short, factual, and repeatable.

Practice and Role-Play in Safe Settings

Treat practice like a drill. Role-play with a trusted friend, partner, or therapist. Start with low-stress scenarios and increase intensity gradually. Rehearse the script until it sounds like an SOP and not a reactive plea. Add small humor to ease tension—military crews use banter to steady nerves; you can too.

Implementing Safety Cues

Agree on a discreet signal for pause: a hand gesture, a two-word phrase, or a timeout card. The signal grants immediate permission to stop, breathe, and use grounding tools. Make the protocol non-judgmental: no forced explanations required in the moment.

Tracking Progress and Refining Scripts

Conduct an AAR (after-action review) once a week. Log incidents, which scripts worked, what triggered a 4F event, and one tweak for next time. Over time, this pattern recognition reduces surprises and strengthens trust within families affected by complex secondary PTSD.

Boundaries are not punishment; they're tactical moves that protect readiness, relationships, and healing. Set them, rehearse them, track them—and treat refinement like mission planning: practical, repetitive, and purpose-driven.

Month 4: Sleep Hygiene and Restoration

Sleep will never be as sexy as a weapons systems brief, but for veterans and their families it's the single most reliable tool in the kit for calming a worn-out nervous system. Think of sleep as the field maintenance your brain gets every night: oiling circuits, filing away what needs to be kept, and scrapping what's dangerous to keep around. For those living with CPTSD — whether the trauma came from a childhood household or a patrol zone — sleep helps the brain separate the raw emotion from the facts of an experience. When that process runs better, hypervigilance and frequent awakenings relax their grip.

A quick word on brains with battle scars: TBI and ongoing hyperarousal change sleep architecture. Nightmares, fragmented sleep, loud-noise sensitivity, and trouble falling or staying asleep are common. Emotional flashbacks and 4F responses fire up the same systems that sabotage sleep. Fixing sleep won't erase trauma, but it gives those systems breathing room to recover and to learn safety signals again.

Tactical sleep plan

- Set a tight sleep window. Pick a bedtime, wake time, and keep them within a 30minute window every day, even on days off. Your circadian clock is a disciplinarian; it performs best with the same orders day after day.

- Shift slowly. If you need to move your schedule, adjust by 15 minutes per night so your body doesn't declare mutiny.

- Keep a log. For two weeks, jot bedtime, wake time, sleep quality, nightmares, coffee and nicotine timing, and any meds. Bring that to your clinician — it's hard data soldiers understand.

Bedtime ritual: make it a predictable sequence

Treat the ritual like a premission checklist. Repetition tells the body it's safe to downshift. Sample sequence:

- Doff "uniform": change into comfortable clothes.
- Warm wash or quick shower — water signals reset.
- Low light: dim lamps, reduce blue-spectrum sources.
- 10–20 minutes of unwinding: light reading, breathing work, or journaling one sentence about what's occupying your mind.
- Lights out at scheduled time.

Pre-sleep routines that work in the field

- Breathing drills: box breathing or paced diaphragmatic breathing, for five minutes, reduces sympathetic arousal. Veterans know this as the calm-before-engagement trick applied to sleep.
- Progressive muscle relaxation: tense-and-release from toes to jaw to drop tension that stubbornly clings after combat or childhood stress.
- Grounding items: a weighted blanket or a familiar garment can cue safety for some; white noise or earplugs help those with noise sensitivity.
- Aromatherapy: a few drops of lavender on a pillow or diffuser can be soothing for many.

Limit stimulants and screens

- Cut caffeine at least 6—8 hours before lights out. That watchcafé habit is understandable; move the last cup earlier when possible.

Avoid nicotine close to bedtime; it's a stimulant and disrupts sleep.

- Heavy meals two to three hours before bed can disrupt sleep architecture; plan lighter evening meals.
- Screens: aim for a screen-free wind-down hour. If that's impossible, use blue-light filters and prefer audiobooks or calming music over scrolling.

For families and partners

Coordination matters. Children and partners are affected when one household member is up and down at night. Shared bedtime rituals, dimming the house lights at a set hour, and keeping night-time check-ins brief can protect everyone's sleep. Complex secondary PTSD shows up in bedrooms as much as living rooms; a household plan reduces collateral damage.

If nightmares, severe insomnia, or TBI-related sleep problems persist, push the issue with your provider. There are targeted treatments and sleep-focused therapies worth deploying. Good sleep isn't optional for recovery — it's the base camp from which the rest of the work moves forward.

Month 5: Meaning-Making and Identity Exploration

Month Five: Meaning-Making and Identity — Setting the ZFrame

After stabilizing sleep and calming the nervous system, this month shifts focus to who you are when the alarm isn't set to fight-or-flight. Think of it as mission planning for the person you want to be: clear objectives, small maneuvers, and regular after-action checks. This is where meaning-making and identity work get tactical.

Guiding Principles: Your Operational Code

Pick four guiding principles, to act like rules of engagement when triggers hit and the 4F responses kick in. Keep them short, memorized, and tattooed in your brain like a mission brief.

- Self-compassion: speak to yourself with the same basic decency you'd give a wounded squadmate.
- Courage: move toward exposure in controlled, bite-size steps.
- Resilience: treat setbacks as intel — study, adjust, move on.
- Authenticity: refuse role-playing that costs you pieces of yourself.

Say these aloud during a low-stress period; use them as a short code when emotional flashbacks or a fawn response tries to override judgment.

How the Brain Screams—and How that Affects Identity

Quick field note on the hardware: emotional flashbacks are not memory playback; they're an amygdala-triggered hijack that dumps old feeling-states into current time, making a safe kitchen feel like a combat zone. The 4F suite — fight, flight, freeze, fawn — is wired to protect, but chronic activation can split identity into "trauma mode" and "day-to-day mode." The fix is not to erase either side but to integrate them so the frontal cortex can make decisions instead of the alarm circuits.

Reframing Identity: Strengths, Roles, and Bonds

Stop listing only wounds. Make three columns on a sheet of paper:

- Strengths: skills, grit, tactics you used to survive (problem-solving under pressure, loyalty, steady hands).
- Roles: current positions that matter (parent, partner, coach, mechanic, veteran).
- Meaningful relationships: people who offer support, challenge, or unconditional backup.

Use an AAR (after-action review) format: what went well, what went poorly, what to change next time. Run this review weekly for a month. The goal: replace a single trauma-driven script with a catalog of functioning parts you can call on.

Narrative Integration: Practical Steps

- Timeline exercise: write a short timeline with dates or phases. Add one-line notes about what those periods taught you.
- Pattern spotting: circle repeated themes (control, abandonment, hypervigilance) and note one new behavior you'd like instead.
- Rewriting the narrative: craft a brief paragraph that starts, "I am someone who…" and includes at least two strengths and one value. Keep it on your phone or pinned on the fridge.

These moves help stitch memories and values into a coherent story so the pieces stop arguing with each other.

Building Coherence and Self-Compassion

Make daily choices reflect core values: pick one small action each day that matches a value (call a friend, fix that dented fence, show up for a practice). Track it like a mission log. When the inner critic shows up, use a two-step rebuttal: name the thought, then offer a compassionate counterstatement (short, factual, and nonjudgmental).

Family Briefing: Addressing Complex Secondary PTSD

Families carry combat stress too. Hold a civilian-style briefing: explain triggers, describe likely reactions, set boundaries, and create shared calming rituals (a five-minute check-in, a nonnegotiable bedtime routine). Encourage family therapy or support groups; schedule these like appointments.

Closing Drill

This month is about building an identity that includes the veteran and the child, the survivor and the citizen. Run the exercises, debrief weekly, and treat setbacks as intel for the next operation. Small, consistent acts of self-compassion and meaning-making win more ground than grand declarations.

Month 6: Creativity and Expression Projects

Month Six: Creativity, Nonverbal Processing, and Sensory Stabilization

After the work on identity and values, the sixth month shifts into hands-on, nonverbal territory. Think less briefing slide, more field exercise for the nervous system. The goal here is simple: use creative, sensory tasks to access difficult memories without getting overrun by limbic surges or a full 4F mobilization.

Accessing Difficult Memories Safely

Nonverbal methods let the brain speak in images, rhythm, and touch when words get wired up. Use these tools with a safety plan: check your baseline (breathing, pulse, a 30-second grounding check), set a timer, and have a named stop-signal (a word or gesture you give yourself permission to use).

- Visual journaling: Fill a notebook with marks, color fields, torn paper, and captions. No editing. Use color to mark intensity (red = hot), shapes for patterns (circles = returning memories), and a single line to note when sensations spike. If language is needed, short labels work—this is processing, not a report.

- Stream-of-consciousness drawing: Ten to fifteen minutes, no goal except movement. Keep your wrist moving. This lowers the verbal cortex input and lets the right hemisphere map sensations.

- Poetry and spoken-word: Short lines, repeated refrains, or a one-minute monologue can hold the feeling in a container. Record it if you like; playback can provide distance and data.

Grounding and Safety through Sensory-Based Projects

Sensory activities regulate the body. They pull the brain into the present and reduce limbic hijack.

- Tactile tasks: knitting or crochet, clay modeling, or even planting a seed or potting a small plant. The steady, repetitive motion helps stabilize heart rate and vagal tone. If TBI affects fine motor control, choose larger, gross-motor versions (rolling clay, digging a patch of earth).

- Sensory exploration: walk barefoot on safe ground, listen to a playlist of nature sounds or steady rhythm tracks, and keep a small bottle of a scent you find calming for quick inhalation. These are tools to pull attention back into the body when an emotional flashback threatens.

Stabilizing 4F Responses and Flashbacks

Tactile and proprioceptive input interrupts fight, flight, freeze, and fawn spikes.

- Weighted blanket or compression wrap: deep pressure slows down arousal circuits.
- Tactile anchors: a pillow or comfort object to hold, a textured pocket stone to rub, or a rhythmic task (stringing beads, hammering pegs) to re-establish control.

Practical rules: if symptoms climb, stop creative processing and use a grounding protocol (5-4-3-2-1, paced breathing, or a short physical task) before returning.

Building Personal Narratives

Creative formats help reframe trauma with agency.

- Journaling prompts: write a short note to your younger self with three things you would tell them now; list where support sits on a given day.
- Creative writing and visual narratives: draft a short scene or a comic strip that places you as an active agent—no heroism required, just choice.
- Keep it private or share selectively. Families can co-create a visual map of stressors and coping tools—this is part of addressing complex secondary PTSD in partners and children.

Documenting Progress and Collaboration

Track work with a monthly portfolio of pages, recordings, and photos. Set a weekly 15-minute check-in to note changes in triggers, sleep, and reactivity. Share pieces with a trusted comrade, therapist, or family member—ask for feedback that is specific and kind. Peer creative groups for veterans can reduce isolation; family sessions can help secondary trauma surface in a contained way.

One last order: no one is grading your output. This phase is about sensory grounding and reclaiming control—one small, messy piece at a time.

Month 7: Trust-Building in Relationships

Month 7: Building Trust and Safety in Bonds

After a month of drawing, journaling, and tactile grounding, it's time to put some people in your corner. For combat vets and anyone with Complex PTSD rooted in childhood trauma, trust can feel like a scarce supply, something you guard like a weapons cache. Yet reliable human contact is one of the most effective tools for downshifting a rattled nervous system and cutting the frequency of emotional flashbacks and 4F surges (fight, flight, freeze, fawn).

How safe bonds actually calm you—chronic threat exposure wires the amygdala to overreact and the prefrontal cortex to recede. When someone proves predictable and nonthreatening, your body gets a steady stream of signals that it's safe: cortisol and adrenaline drop, breathing steadies, and the brain's top-down control can reengage. That biochemical change is what shrinks hypervigilance and makes emotional flashbacks less frequent and shorter.

The power of dependable allies

Picture a support person who knows your triggers and doesn't make a big deal when you go quiet. That person reduces the odds of a full-blown 4F episode. Building a reliable support network is missioncritical for PTSD management. Likewise, assembling a "team" of trusted people who can act like a predictable support element during highstress moments.

Clarifying boundaries and picking secure confidants

This is where tactics beat hope. Lay out your limits clearly: what you can handle, what sets you off, and what you need when arousal spikes. Pick confidants who show consistency—people who follow through, don't flinch at hard topics, and respect agreed limits.

Practical drill:

- Make a disclosure ladder: Level 1 (surface small talk), Level 2 (personal struggles), Level 3 (trauma specifics). Share only up the ladder as trust proves steady.

"I'm triggered. I need space, timeout, or checkin."

- Use "I" statements: "I feel unsafe when…" keeps you in the driver's seat and cuts off defensive reactions.

Practicing paced disclosure and social exposure

Start small. Share a tiny detail at first and measure the response. If the other person stays calm and consistent, move one rung up the ladder. Treat it like exposure drills in training: incremental, predictable, repeatable.

Nonverbal trust signals

Words matter, but nonverbal cues are field radios. Create and agree on signals that mean "safe," "pause," or "need help." Examples:

- A steady hand squeeze = "I'm grounded."
- A set check-in routine (text at 2100) = predictability.

Calm tone, steady eye contact, and small predictable rituals (making coffee together) that repeat reliably.

Including trauma-informed professionals

Bring in pros when needed to design boundaries and safety plans. Clinicians versed in CPTSD can map triggers, coach families, and create fallback plans if things escalated. For vets, a clinician who understands TBI and combat trauma is ideal. For families dealing with complex secondary PTSD, professionals can teach containment strategies, secondary exposure reduction, and paced communication practices.

Tactical checklist for the month

- Draft a one-page trust plan with your team.
- Practice the disclosure ladder once a week.

- Agree on two nonverbal signals and rehearse them.
- Schedule a family psychoeducation session with a trauma-informed clinician.

Keep it practical, keep it predictable, and treat trust-building like an operation: small, deliberate moves that stack into real safety.

Month 8: Self-Compassion and Rituals

Practical Self-Compassion: Talk to Yourself Like a Wingman

SelfCompassion and Grounding Rituals

If you expect a buddy to cover your six in a firefight, start covering your own emotional six. Compassionate selftalk is not fluff; it's an operational order you repeat until it becomes habit. Emotional flashbacks and 4F responses (fight, flight, freeze, fawn) are driven by the amygdala flipping the emergency switch while the prefrontal cortex is on cooldown. Saying calming, factual phrases rewires that response over time by nudging higher brain centers back online.

Morning QuickRead

Begin each day with a brief review of your core values or a short inspiring quote—just a few lines to set the mental framework.

Box Breathing

4444 rhythm: inhale for 4 counts, hold for 4, exhale for 4, hold for 4. Repeat for three cycles. This activates the vagus nerve and steadies the nervous system.

Sensory Anchor

Carry a small item—a dog tag, smooth stone, or lavender scent vial. When triggered, press it into your palm and focus on the texture or scent to bring attention back to the present.

Action Ritual

Spend five minutes on a repetitive, calming task: folding a blanket, slow pushups, knitting. The rhythm restores bodily equilibrium.

Safe Corner

Designate a quiet spot with a blanket and earplugs. When needed, take three deep exhalations and rest for five minutes to reset before reengaging.

Try this protocol:

- Morning quick-read: 60 seconds. Stand, inhale slowly, and deliver one line aloud: "I'm doing the best I can today." Repeat once.
- Midday check: 30 seconds. Quiet breath, two statements: one factual ("I ate; I slept") and one kind ("I deserve rest").
- Night debrief: 2 minutes. Note one thing that went well and say, "I handled that."

These scripts are simple, repeatable, and built for brown-bag mental maintenance.

Grounding and Safety Rituals: Fieldcraft for the Nervous System

If you expect a buddy to cover your six in a firefight, start covering your own emotional six. Compassionate self-talk is not fluff; it's an operational order you repeat until it becomes habit. Emotional flashbacks and 4F responses (fight, flight, freeze, fawn) are driven by the amygdala flipping the emergency switch while the prefrontal cortex is on cooldown. Saying calming, factual phrases rewires that response over time by nudging higher brain centers back online.

Make a short, repeatable routine that combines self-compassion with simple grounding protocols. Practice it daily (a morning quick-read) and use it in the moment when triggered. Examples and a compact protocol:

- Morning quick-read: one to three short compassionate lines you read aloud each morning to prime the nervous system (e.g., "I am safe right now. My breath grounds me. I can handle this.").
- Box breathing: 4-4-4-4 (inhale-hold-exhale-hold) for three cycles.
- Sensory anchor: carry a small item (dog tag, smooth stone, scent vial with lavender) and press it into your palm when you feel triggered.

- Action ritual: five minutes of a repetitive, calming task — folding a blanket, slow push-ups, knitting — something that returns rhythm to the body.
- Safe corner: a defined spot with a blanket and earplugs where a person takes three deep exhalations and rests for five minutes.

Use the morning quick-read to make compassionate phrases automatic; use the breathing, anchor, action task, or safe corner to redirect the body and bring attention back to the present when the amygdala has flipped the switch. Repetition turns these fieldcraft measures into reliable, on-demand tools for the nervous system.

These techniques reduce heart rate, interrupt panic loops, and help the brain shift from alarm mode back to baseline.

Honoring Different Trauma Histories

Military trauma and childhood-rooted CPTSD often produce the same alarms, but origins change the script. A combat vet might react to loud noises; a survivor of early neglect might react to perceived abandonment. Design rituals that respect that history: if scents trigger memory, pick neutral anchors; if touch is comforting, set clear consent rules with family. For families, this means creating rituals that everyone can opt into without pressure—like a five-minute check-in at dinner or an agreed hand signal when someone needs space.

Tactical Routines for Families and Secondary CPTSD

Complex secondary PTSD shows up in partners and kids like fatigue, hypervigilance, or taking blame. Make family rituals simple:

Journaling: Track the Small Wins

A battle log for the inner fight. Keep entries short: date, trigger, response, ritual used, outcome. Celebrate micro-wins (got through a grocery trip, three deep breaths stopped a panic) and note patterns. Over weeks you'll map triggers and see what reduces flashbacks and which rituals actually work. Bring these notes to clinicians to sharpen treatment plans.

No single ritual fits all. Treat these like SOPs: test, adjust, and report back to your team — family, trusted friends, and trauma-informed clinicians — until you find a set that keeps you steady on days that matter.

Daily Practices, Checklists, and Reflections

Understanding the constant watch your nervous system maintains is the first step toward reclaiming inner security. This section moves from awareness to action, laying out practical, daily strategies to stabilize your internal world. We will establish foundational morning and evening rituals to anchor your days, offering concrete ways to check in with your breath and body, effectively disarming emotional flashbacks and autonomic stress responses. From grounding through mindful sensory engagement and deliberate movement to setting clear boundaries and refining sleep patterns, each practice builds upon the last, providing a reliable framework for sustained calm. These repeatable actions not only counter hypervigilance but also help you track incremental progress, turning insight into enduring self-regulation.

Morning and Evening Grounding Checklists

Morning Grounding Foundations: Establishing Daily Stabilization Anchors

Morning can feel like a combat zone because the brain jumps into emergency mode: the amygdala fires, tagging memories as urgent, while the prefrontal cortex is still halfasleep and cannot calm the surge. In plain terms, the emotional parts of the brain flag memories as urgent, and the thinking parts lag behind. To anchor yourself, follow this breathbased wakeful check:

- While still in bed or at the bedside, inhale slowly through the nose for a steady count (e.g., 4). Exhale through the mouth for a slightly longer count (e.g., 6). Repeat three times.
- Scan your posture and body tension: are your shoulders hunched like you're bracing for mortar? Drop them by choice, feel your spine lengthen and your feet connect to the floor.
- Run a quick "activation list": heart racing, tight jaw, cold sweats, foggy thinking. If any are present, slow the breathing and bring attention to a sensory anchor—such as the feel of your breath, the weight of your feet on the floor, or the scent of your pillow.
- If activation is mild, assign a small, doable task for the first 15 minutes (fill a water bottle, step outside for 60 seconds, put on a favorite shirt). Lowcomplexity tasks help the prefrontal cortex boot up.

This is not therapy theater. It's a tactical pre-mission check to prevent an emotional flashback from taking command before you even stand up. Paul D. Walker's work on battle fatigue underscores how a predictable start-of-day routine reduces runaway activation — consider this your field manual for personal stability.

Grounding with Trusted Sensory Anchors: Pack Two or Three

Anchors are simple, repeatable sensory cues that pull the brain out of autopilot and into a regulated state. Pick 2–3 items or sensations you can use anywhere.

Examples soldiers use.

- Texture: a worn leather strap, a smooth river stone, the edge of a wooden rosary, or a dog tag you rub between fingers.
- Scent: a small vial of sandalwood, lavender, or your grandmother's cologne tucked in a pocket.
- Sound: a 15-second audio clip (ocean, boots-on-gravel, a short marching cadence) stored on your phone.

How to train them

- Pair the anchor with calm breathing three times daily for a week: inhale, exhale, engage the anchor, and say a grounding phrase (short and concrete).
- Use anchors proactively—not only in crisis; conditioning increases their reliability when the amygdala tries to pull you.

Families and caregivers: learn your veteran's anchors and use them intentionally during stressful moments. For complex secondary PTSD (caregivers who absorb stress), pick a family anchor the whole household can use for short resets.

Evening Reflection and Reset Checklist: Close Out Your Watch

The evening check is a tactical debrief. Keep it crisp and useful.

Suggested checklist

- Triggers encountered today (one-line each).
- Relief strategies tried and how effective they were (rate 1–5).
- Three intentions for tomorrow (one must be self-care).

- Prep actions: lay out clothes, set alarm with a 15-minute buffer, place anchors where you'll see them.

Prompts that matter

- What signaled I was escalating today?
- Which anchor brought me down and how fast?
- What small win did I get (made a call, showed up to a training, lasted through dinner).

For families: include a two-minute check-in where everyone names one stressor and one comfort. That builds a shared rhythm and helps spot secondary trauma signs early.

Run this protocol for two weeks and log the data. You don't need full recovery in a fortnight, but tracking patterns turns chaotic mornings and sleepless nights into predictable operations you can manage. Small, consistent actions beat heroic single efforts every time.

Journaling Prompts for Insight

Journaling for Insight: Uncovering Hidden Patterns and Finding Peace

CPTSD is defined as Complex PostTraumatic Stress Disorder, a condition arising from repeated or prolonged trauma, often starting in childhood, that produces chronic emotional, behavioral, and physiological dysregulation. Think of a journal as a quiet field notebook — an operations log for your nervous system. It's a private, simple, factual record where you note what happened inside you when no one else was watching. For service members, veterans, and people whose trauma began in childhood, journaling turns chaotic emotional flashbacks into recognizable signals: it exposes repeating triggers, catalogs bodily reactions, and connects thoughts, feelings, and sensations. That connection of mind and body calms a hypervigilant nervous system by engaging the thinking brain, making memories less mysterious and less dangerous.

To make the process practical, start each entry with a concise template that ties emotion to trigger, body, thought, urge, memory, grounding, and pattern. Use the following four short lines (or a single list if you prefer):

- Feeling: name the emotion (e.g., anger, shame, hollow) and rate intensity 1–10.
- Trigger: what happened just before this started? (event, person, memory cue)
- Body: where do you feel it? Describe quality (tight, hot, sinking, buzzing).
- Thought: the dominant thought or sentence running through your head.
- Urge/behavior: what do you want to do or avoid right now?
- Memory content: any images, sounds, or scenes that surfaced?
- Grounding/action: one small thing you can do now (breaths, walk, hold an object).
- Pattern note: has this happened before? When? (brief)

Keep entries honest and patternfocused—not blame—and keep them short when concentration is limited (TBI, exhaustion).

Connecting Emotions to Triggers and CPTSD Patterns – Revised

These prompts train the prefrontal cortex to re-engage with the amygdala's alarm system. Over time the list of "just-before" events reveals recurring patterns—verbal tone, crowded places, certain anniversaries—that read like enemy intel.

Identifying Emotional Flashbacks without Labeling

Language matters. Swap "I'm having a flashback" for "I'm receiving a signal" or "I'm escalating." That shift reduces shame and keeps you in problem-solving mode. A journal entry might read: "Signal at 0900—heart racing, hands cold. Thought: I'm unsafe. Action taken: 3-minute paced breathing." That's reconnaissance, not a verdict.

Recording Bodily Sensations Linked to Stress Responses

Be specific and concise when you record sensations:

- Location: point to where it is (chest, throat, stomach, arms).
- Intensity: rate 1–10.
- Quality: tight, hot, numb, tingling, heavy, fluttering, etc.
- Movement: is it spreading, rising, sinking, pulsating?
- Modifiers: what makes it better or worse (breath, posture, people, time)?
- Time course: when did it start and how long did it last?

Link each sensation to the feeling and the trigger. Over time you'll see patterns you can plan for — and quick grounding actions that reliably help (5 deep breaths, name 5 things, press feet into floor).

Record your 4F reactions in the field notebook:

- Fight: clenched jaw, flushed face, irritability.
- Flight: pacing, restlessness, need to leave rooms.

- Freeze: numb bladder, slow speech, shut-down.
- Fawn: over-apologizing, people-pleasing, loss of boundaries.

Write the physical details every time. The body is the first radio; the journal is the decoding manual.

Tracking Timing and Duration of Emotional States

Log start and stop times. "Anxiety 1015–1100" gives you data to predict peaks and plan countermeasures—when to schedule downtime, when to avoid social triggers. A tally over two weeks tells you whether mornings, mealtimes, or weekends are highrisk windows.

Noticing Cognitive Distortions as Transient Stories

Cognitive distortions are wartime propaganda your old brain broadcasts. In your journal, label them "stories" and interrogate them: evidence for, evidence against, alternative statement. Example:

- Story: "I'm a failure."
- Evidence for: missed deadline.
- Evidence against: past mission successes, support from team.
- Alternative: "I messed up one task; I have skills to fix it."

Setting Micro-Goals for Tomorrow's Self-Regulation

End each entry with one micro-goal—small, specific, and doable. Examples: five minutes of box breathing at 0700; phone call to one supportive person; 20-minute walk after lunch. For families and caregivers, micro-goals can be signals of support: "I'll check in at 1800" or "I'll bring a calming playlist." Small wins compound.

Practical tweaks for brain injury and fatigue: use bullets, keep entries under six lines, or record voice memos that you later transcribe. Keep the journal accessible—pocket-sized or on your phone—and treat it like essential kit. No one hands out medals for silent suffering; an honest log is a tactical tool that gives you the advantage back.

Breath and Body Scan Routines

Anchoring the Nervous System: Breath and Body Scans

Think of breath and body scans as two pieces of kit you can carry into any moment of chaos—no batteries required. Breathing slowly signals the vagus nerve to lower threat level, while body scans remind the nervous system that the environment is safe. For troops with childhoodorigin CPTSD, these practices act like a field radio calling in a ceasefire between the sympathetic charge and the parasympathetic brakes. They don't erase the threat history, but they buy you time and options when a stress response kicks up.

How breath actually calms the storm

When adrenaline and alarm systems light up, the brain reads the body as "on mission." Slowing the breath sends a clear signal through the vagus nerve: threat level lowered. Clinically, paced breathing increases heartrate variability and nudges the system away from fight/flight/freeze toward a state where reason and safety checks can run. In plain terms: breathing slower gives the executive brain a window to take over from the ancient wiring that wants instant action.

Paced-breathing drills (practical, no fluff)

Here are two field-tested patterns you can use when tension spikes or as pre-mission prep. Try both and see which feels less like punishment.

- Extended exhale (for acute spikes): Sit or stand with feet planted. Inhale through the nose to a count of 4. Exhale through the mouth to a count of 6. Repeat 6–10 cycles. The longer exhale helps engage the calming circuits.

- Box-light (quick baseline reset): Inhale for 4, hold 4 (softly), exhale 4, hold 4. Do 4 rounds. Use this when you need something short you can do standing in line or during a family argument.

Do not force breath into weird shapes. The goal is steady, not heroic. If holding breath or counts feels triggering, shorten counts to what your body can manage; small wins win campaigns.

Body scans: clearing the sector

A body scan is a systematic check of what the vehicle (your body) is doing. Move attention slowly from toes to head, or do a focused check on areas that hold tension — jaw, shoulders, belly. Note sensations without issuing orders: "tightness," "aching," "nothing." Breathe into the spot, soften if possible. For people who dissociate, anchor first: press feet into the floor, hold a cold mug, or say out loud three things you see in the room before scanning.

Nonjudgmental awareness — the rules of engagement

Treat sensations like intelligence reports, not enemy combatants. Don't label a tense chest as "weakness." Observe it, gather data, and adjust tactics. This reduces rumination and prevents escalation from thought to full-blown alarm.

Daily routines and tactical integration

Make the practice part of your pre-op and off-duty routine: two to five minutes of breathing on waking, a short body scan before sleep, and a one-minute breath check during breaks. Use triggers as reminders — a siren, a family argument, going to the VA — and run a quick drill instead of riding the wave.

Bringing family into the plan

Families are often the co-operators in this conflict zone. Offer brief guided sessions with consent: "Can I do a two-minute breathing drill with you?" If caregivers are showing signs of secondary stress, they need drills too; regulation spreads. Keep guidance simple, avoid pushing, and make it a shared task rather than a correction.

A final field note: progress is measured by increased choices, not by perfect stillness. The breath and the scan are tools you can take anywhere — barracks, kitchen, car — and use to reclaim a moment of safety when the past tries to take over the present.

Sleep Routine Templates

Establishing a Nightly Sleep Framework: Orders for Lights Out

If you were on a night patrol, you'd have a plan, a timeline, and contingency signals. Treat sleep the same way—this is mission planning for your nervous system. When the brain has been on high alert for years, it needs predictable cues to stand down. The following framework turns vague "try to relax" advice into a hard SOP you can use every night.

Set the Schedule: Fixed Lights-Out

Pick a fixed bedtime and stick with it like a duty roster. Go to bed and get up at the same times every day, weekend included. Consistency trains the body clock so falling asleep becomes less of a firefight and more of a routine handoff. If sleep is MIA, keep the rollout time consistent; short naps should be limited to avoid wrecking the schedule.

Wind-Down Ritual: Your Pre-Sleep Recon

Create a 30–60 minute wind-down ritual that signals "stand down" to your brain. Examples that have worked for veterans:

- Low-effort reading (no combat thrillers); dim light.
- Warm shower or bath to lower core temperature.
- Gentle stretching or a brief guided relaxation.
- Slow breathing for five minutes to lower 4F activation.

Pick two or three activities and do them in the same order each night. This repetition is the cue your brain learns to link to rest.

Build a Cadence to Reduce Nighttime Triggers

Emotional flashbacks and sudden arousal often flare up when the mind is unstructured. A steady pre-sleep cadence—same time, same activities—reduces the chances of those internal alarms firing. If flashbacks occur, pause the ritual and use a short grounding set: 5 slow breaths, feet on the floor, name three neutral objects in the room, then resume.

Make the Bedroom a Safe Forward Operating Base

Treat the bedroom like a secure billet. Practical measures:

- Keep familiar comforting items nearby (a worn blanket, a photo that soothes).
- Use dim, warm lighting in the hour before bed.
- Introduce calming scents such as lavender if that works for you.
- Ensure temperature and noise are controlled; earplugs or a white-noise device can help.

Limit Stimulants and Screen Time

Avoid screens for at least two hours before bed. The blue light and the brain's tendency to run missions on social media or news feeds are bad combinations. Avoid caffeine and nicotine within two hours of lights-out. If a stimulant is medically required, discuss timing with your provider.

Pre-Sleep Tools: Journaling and Slow Breathing

Carry out a brief check-in before bed. Spend five minutes writing a short list of what's on your mind—no editing, just transfer it to paper. Follow with two to five minutes of slow, paced breathing (inhale 4, exhale 6) to downshift the nervous system. These tools reduce rumination and lower 4F arousal.

Nightly Reflection: A Small After-Action Report

End the ritual with a concise reflection: one thing that went tolerable today, one task for tomorrow, or three small things you appreciate. Keep it brief; the point is to close the mental file.

Managing Nightmares: A Practical Rescript Plan

Nightmares can be rehearsed and altered. Use this three-step plan:

- During the day, write a short, new ending for the nightmare that removes danger or adds escape.

- Rehearse the new script as a mental exercise for 5–10 minutes, visualizing the safer outcome.
- Anchor the rehearsal with a calming action—slow breathing or progressive muscle relaxation—so your body learns the alternative response.

Family Brief: How Loved Ones Can Support the Operation

Complex secondary PTSD affects partners and kids too. Give family members a short brief: what helps (soft lighting, quiet), what to avoid (sudden loud awakenings), and a simple code word to use if urgent. Share the rescript plan so loved ones can assist without escalating the threat response.

This framework won't fix everything in one night, but applied consistently it lowers the nightly threat score, cuts down on surprise arousals, and gives you a repeatable method to bring the nervous system in from the cold. Keep it compact, keep it routine, and treat sleep like the critical mission it is.

Movement Micro-Habits for Calm

If the nightly framework is your base camp, movement micro-habits are the patrols you send out through the day — short, low-risk actions that keep the nervous system from slipping back into a high-alert posture. These are not full workouts or long therapy sessions. Think of them as booby-trap checks for your body: quick, routine, and often preventing a bigger problem later.

Grounding through feet on the floor

There's a reason infantry drills begin with the feet. Planting your feet and noticing pressure is a fast way to pull the brain out of an emotional flashback and into the present. Try this when you feel tension rising: inhale, feel the soles against the floor, distribute your weight evenly between heels and balls of the feet, then exhale. Hold that attention for one full breath. Do it while standing in line for chow, sitting in a meeting, or before you get out of the truck after a long route. It's simple, discrete, and effective for reducing 4F activation (fight, flight, freeze, fawn).

Diaphragmatic breathing: a tactical pause

Breathing sounds boring until you're mid-flashback and your chest is a drum. Diaphragmatic breathing is the control band on that drum. Here's a compact drill: inhale through the nose for a count of 4, fill the belly, then exhale through the mouth for a count of 6. Repeat this 4–6 breaths. A former Special Ops coach I worked with put it bluntly: "You can't always call a ceasefire with your engine, but you can pull its choke." Slowing the exhale nudges the vagus nerve and drops heart rate, which helps shut down a runaway threat response.

Proprioceptive cues: press, tap, squeeze

Touch and pressure tell the brain you're anchored in a body and not under immediate threat. Small, repeatable cues can interrupt panic circuits.

- Tap your feet on the floor for 10–20 seconds.

- Press your palms into your thighs and hold for a breath.
- Squeeze a stress ball or clench and release a fist.
- Use a discreet fidget toy during meetings or long waits.

These actions stimulate proprioceptors in muscles and joints, sending safety signals back to the brain and helping reduce freeze and flight impulses.

Gentle movement snacks: rhythm resets

Short bouts of movement throughout the day reset circulation, mood, and motor arousal. They work like quick maintenance checks.

- Stretch arms overhead for 15 seconds.
- Roll shoulders back twice and breathe.
- Walk a block at a purposeful pace.
- Do 10 small jumping jacks or march in place for 30 seconds.

Keep them brief and regular — the goal is to release tension, not to exhaust yourself.

Posture resets: scheduled body checks

Posture affects how the brain interprets the world. Set a hourly reminder on your phone or watch to take a posture reset: stand tall, drop your shoulders, align your head over your spine, breathe a slow cycle of 4 in/6 out, and re-ground through your feet. Over time this reduces freeze tendencies and improves bodily awareness.

Getting the unit involved: family and secondary CPTSD

Families pick up the vibration of a veteran's nervous system; this is where Complex secondary PTSD shows up. Teach partners and kids simple micro-habits — a shared cue like tapping feet, a household rule to take three diaphragmatic breaths when conflict heats up, or passing a squeeze ball during stressful conversations. These practices not only help the veteran but reduce reactive patterns across the family unit.

All of these are low-cost, low-risk drills you can run every day. The compound effect feels small at first, then suddenly you notice fewer full-blown activations and more moments you can manage without calling in heavy support. Keep them short, make them routine, and treat them like mission checks: no excuses, just habit.

Mindful Eating and Mood

If movement micro-habits are the quick drills that stop the body from snapping to alarm, mindful eating is the chow hall SOP that keeps the whole squad steady. For veterans carrying combat scars and childhood complex trauma, meals can either trigger a drop back into old threat patterns or become a reliable anchor. The aim is to turn eating into a repeatable tactic for calming the nervous system.

When the brain is keyed up into 4F mode—fight, flight, freeze, fawn—appetite and impulses follow orders. Emotional dysregulation shows up as chaotic eating, bingeing, or numb stuffing to escape feelings. Smells, textures, and routines can cue emotional flashbacks: one bite and you're back in a replay. Mindful eating trains you to detect those triggers fast and choose a different response.

Use sensory cues like a reconnaissance check. Before the first bite, scan the plate: color, aroma, texture, temperature. Bring the food close and inhale—what stands out? Chew slowly. Notice how flavors change between chews. That crunch of an apple, the warmth of broth on a cold day—those are anchoring signals to the brain that you're present, not under attack.

Plan meals like you pack a mission bag for neurobiological stability. Each plate should include:

- solid protein to steady blood sugar and mood,
- complex carbohydrates for sustained energy,
- omega-3 sources (fish, walnuts, flax) to support brain function,
- fiber-rich vegetables and whole grains for gut health.

These elements work together to reduce anxiety spikes and blunt the impulse to self-soothe with junk.

Limit processed rations and caffeine around mealtimes. Processed foods and stimulants can provoke anxiety and heighten hypervigilance. If you run on coffee, separate it from hunger-driven meals; when possible pick whole, nourishing options during eating windows.

Adjust portions when fatigue or pain sets in. Low energy or flare-ups call for smaller, more frequent portions to prevent overeating and energy crashes. Field rule: if your body reports low reserves, take half now and another small portion later. No heroics.

Breathe and ground while you eat. Take three slow diaphragmatic breaths before the first bite. Pause halfway through the meal to check your breath and hunger. A simple grounding cue—say "steady here" silently—can interrupt an automatic stress reaction and keep you present.

Rituals reduce hurry and hyper-alertness. Light a candle, sit at a dedicated spot, or use a specific plate. Shared meals with a trusted person cut isolation; families can use the same rituals to ease complex secondary PTSD at home.

Keep a short log—two lines will do: hunger rating (1–10), mood, any triggers noticed. Over weeks this becomes actionable intel: patterns emerge and you can respond with compassion instead of criticism. Ask yourself, "What would I tell my buddy?" and answer that kindly.

Mindful eating isn't perfection; it's a practical stance. Treat meals as mini-missions—brief, tactical, aimed at keeping your system steady so you can face the day with more control and fewer surprise flashbacks.

Boundaries and Communication Scripts

Boundaries are the quiet sentries on the perimeter of your mind. After we talked about using meals to ground, an overactive nervous system, the next practical move is putting up fences that stop other people's chaos from barging into your headspace. For combat veterans and those carrying childhood wounds, clear limits do more than keep you comfortable — they lower the alarms in your brain so the 4F responses don't hijack the day.

When a threat cue fires the amygdala, the sympathetic branch revs up for fight or flight, while the dorsal vagal pathway pulls the plug for freeze. Fawning is a social survival trick that appeases the threat, driven by an overworked social engagement system. Emotional flashbacks arise when affect circuitry lights up without an explicit memory, triggering the same raw terror or shame. Boundaries interrupt this loop by reducing unpredictability, and signaling to your nervous system that you're in control of what happens next, breaking the automatic 4F pattern.

Step 1: Identify triggers and list safe alternatives

Begin by mapping the specific cues that activate your FightFlightFreezeFawn responses. Once you know what sets your nervous system off, create a list of concrete, calming actions or boundaries you can deploy—such as a pause, a grounding phrase, or a physical distance—to regain control before the automatic reaction takes hold.

Step 1: Identify your triggers. Make a tidy trigger sheet. Start small: list the people, places, tones, smells, or tasks that spike you, and give each a 1–10 intensity rating. Next to each trigger, write one simple alternative action: step outside, use a preagreed code word with your buddy, count breaths, or call a specific family member who grounds you. For example: crowded PX (8) → excuse self, go to truck for 10 minutes. This is tactical planning, not weakness.

Step 2: Practice boundary scripts

Scripts are like SOPs for emotions. Keep them short, calm, and repeatable under stress. Examples that work in the field and at home:

- "I need a minute. I'll come back when I'm calmer."
- "I'm not ok to talk about this right now. Let's pause."
- "That tone makes it hard for me to listen. Can we try that again more quietly?"

Run these out loud until they sound natural. Record them on your phone; listen to them as you would—premission briefings.

Step 3: Role-play with your team or family

Role-play a few scenes with someone you trust — spouse, sibling, battle buddy. Put on a timer, swap roles, and practice delivering and receiving boundaries. Make it safe: allow breaks for the person practicing. Use humor to lower stakes — bad acting is expected; that's the point. These rehearsals build muscle memory so real encounters feel less like ambushes.

Step 4: Use neutral, nonblaming language.

Neutral language reduces escalation. Frame things as: "When X happens, I feel Y; can we try Z?" — short, specific, and about the present. Refrain from piling historical grievances onto the moment; that invites a 4F response from the other person.

Step 5: Respect reciprocal boundaries

Boundaries work when everyone signs on. Ask your family what they need and honor their scripts. Complex secondary PTSD can look like mirrored hypervigilance or overprotectiveness in partners and kids; setting mutual limits prevents that feedback loop. Agree on signals for time-outs, and place a visible "calm card" in the house or on a phone.

Putting it together: your three-minute tactical plan

- Pull out your trigger sheet. 2) Choose one high-impact script and practice it aloud five times. 3) Role-play it once with a household member. 4) Put a one-line boundary note in your wallet: your script plus your exit plan. Small steps build safety. You're training new neural pathways — like clearing a lane under fire so the rest of your life can move without constant alarm. And if you can keep a platoon in formation, you can keep your head in the game.

Milestones, Reflections, and Next Steps

Milestones Anchor Steady Progress in CPTSD Healing

Think of milestones like mission checkpoints. You don't get to Bravo by sprinting blind; you move from checkpoint to checkpoint, take stock, fix the gear, and push on. For soldiers and families dealing with CPTSD — whether the trauma started in childhood or on the battlefield — checkpoints give structure, reduce overwhelm, and keep motivation from tanking when a setback hits.

Recording Incremental Gains

Small wins count. Use simple, repeatable measures that a tired brain will actually use under stress:

Daily mood: a 1–10 scale on a sticky note or phone app. A five feels different when you compare it across weeks.

- Sleep log: jot hours slept and sleep quality. Tiny improvements add up and matter to brain repair.
- Flashback frequency/intensity: record dates, triggers, what happened afterward.

These data points create a living record. When progress is slow, the log provides proof you moved forward rather than gaslighting yourself into thinking you're stuck. Treat it like an after-action report (AAR): what worked, what didn't, what to try next.

Logging Triggers, Emotional Flashbacks, and 4F Responses

An emotional flashback is the nervous system slamming back into a past state—sudden panic, shame, or helplessness that feels like being pulled into an earlier era of life. It is triggered by sights, smells, phrases, or situations that flip a switch. When the switch flips, the body selects a survival program: fight, flight, freeze, or fawn. Understanding this cycle lets you log triggers, internal reactions (thoughts, body sensations), and the 4F response, so you can craft preplanned countermeasures and practice them until the response becomes less automatic.

Celebrating Resilience

Ritualize small celebrations. Medal ceremonies are optional, but acknowledging resilience builds a better self-image than constant self-criticism. Mark three straight nights of better sleep, call out a calm response to a trigger in the family AAR, or treat yourself to a comfort you actually enjoy. Families should also make space to recognize the unseen labor of supporting someone with CPTSD; that keeps care from turning into resentment.

Monthly Milestones

Set monthly objectives that are realistic and flexible. Think in terms of three priorities: safety (sleep, triggers), skills (grounding, boundary scripts), and connection (one positive social contact). Factor in seasonal stressors or known cycles from deployments or family events. Run a monthly AAR: what changed, what's next, and what needs immediate attention. Adjust goals rather than punish missed targets.

Reflections and Neurobiological Integration

Quiet reflection is not fluffy. Repeated reflection, journaling, safe recall with a therapist, and mindfulness-style practice help brains reprocess stuck states so circuits rewire. Call it neurobiological integration: safe, repeated practice helps the nervous system learn that reminders no longer mean total danger. Use brief, guided exercises — five minutes of paced breathing, a ten-minute grounding routine — and stack them into daily life.

Next Steps and Daily Practices

Convert insight into habit. Build routines that mix predictability with room for real-life mess:

- Morning-check-in: mood + one small coping plan for the day.
- Midday grounding: a twominute breathing or bodyscan exercise.
- Evening AAR: what went well, what to tweak.

Keep the plan simple and editable. When 4F reactions spike, fall back on the scripts and safety steps you practiced. Families should make an agreed "safety protocol" for high-stress moments so everyone knows their role. Over time, these small, tactical moves create steadier control and more days that feel livable rather than merely survivable.

Creative and Relational Healing

Healing from the deep imprints of trauma requires more than comprehension; it calls for methods to repattern the nervous system, cultivating new capacities for safety and connection. We turn now to those small, potent breakthrough moments in creative-relational healing, where a spark of imagination or a moment of authentic presence can interrupt old patterns of response. We will observe how simple acts of visual expression, the grounding power of rhythm and music, and the mindful application of breath and movement become anchors for regulation. These approaches help individuals shift from reactive states toward a present-moment sense of internal safety.

Supported by relational witnessing, these practices reduce hypervigilance and shame, quieting the body's defensive 4F responses and steadily building trust. We will discover how they aid memory integration without re-triggering, and how structured prompts, along with sharing in safe spaces, can support paced processing and the formation of new narratives. For those affected by childhood adversity or military stress, these methods establish neural regulation and reinforce coping mechanisms. The necessity of consent, clear communication through practical scripts, and a supportive, integrated care network will guide our understanding of pathways toward lasting well-being.

First-Person Vignettes: Breakthrough Moments

Drop the map and check your bearings: surviving combat and growing up under constant threat leave similar wiring in the brain. Combat stress, battle fatigue, TBI, and complex PTSD that traces back to childhood overlap in predictable ways — hypervigilance, shutdown, antsy anger, and emotional flashbacks that ambush you like an IED from the past. There are small, sharp moments that break those patterns. I call them breakthrough moments in creative-relational healing: brief instances where connection, presence, and a creative cue interrupt automatic defense and open a space for new responses.

Attunement: the quiet front line

Attunement means being present with another human in a way that says, "I see you. I'm with you." For soldiers raised in combat or childhood chaos, that presence registers as validation — a primitive signal the brain can use to lower the alarm. Validation and caregiver attunement help reduce the 4F responses: fight, flight, freeze, and fawn. Those responses are lifesavers in short bursts; repeated activation wires in hypervigilance, anxiety, and low mood. A steady attuned presence dampens arousal and expands trust over time.

Emotional flashbacks and neural mechanics

Emotional flashbacks are sudden floods of feeling—terror, shame, rage—with little or no conscious memory. Neurobiology explains how interoceptive signals—heart rate, gut tightness, muscle tone—trigger the limbic system and hijack the cortex. Training interoception through creative practice rewrites those circuits. Practical creative drills—such as guided body scans, rhythmic breathing paired with visual imagery, or expressive movement that focuses on bodily sensations—act as regulatory cues that interrupt the flood and help reengage the cortex, reducing the intensity of the emotional flashback.

Creativity as a regulatory cue — practical drills

Use these short, repeatable creative exercises to translate the understanding of emotional flashbacks into moment-to-moment regulation. Each drill focuses attention on bodily signals while engaging a simple creative channel, creating an alternative pathway that calms the limbic response.

- Two-minute grounding sketch: Set a timer for 2 minutes. Without lifting the pen, draw continuous contour lines of a nearby object while matching each stroke to your exhale. Purpose: bring attention to breath and muscle tone, anchoring interoception.
- Rhythm tapping (60 seconds): Tap a steady 4-beat rhythm with one hand while placing the other on your chest or belly to feel the pulse. Gradually slow the rhythm. Purpose: synchronize heart rate awareness with an external, controllable cue.
- Sensory labeling with color: Name aloud what you feel (e.g., "tightness," "heat") and assign a color, then shade a small square with that color for 90 seconds. Purpose: strengthen cortex-mediated naming and reduce limbic intensity.
- Micro-improvisation (30–60 seconds): Hum or play a short, improvised phrase on an instrument, focusing on how the air moves and where tension is held. Purpose: redirect affect through safe creative expression that engages interoception.
- Movement mapping (1–3 minutes): Move slowly and notice muscle tone; draw a quick body map marking areas of tightness, then deliberately soften those areas while drawing. Purpose: link proprioception to intentional regulation.

Practice these drills both as preventative daily routines and as quick interventions during a "sudden flood of feeling" to help retrain neural responses.

Renamed identifier: 1641a

Creativity is a calm flag for the nervous system. No arts degree required. Try three-minute marker drills: draw a single line while tracking your breath; notice tight spots in your body and name them out loud; families: mirror a one-sentence validation ("That looked like a hard day for you") and hold silence for two beats. These tactics teach neural regulation by linking sensory cues to safety.

Vignettes of transformation

A veteran paints a rooftop he can't forget; later he points to a color and says the name of an emotion he'd been carrying. In a group session, ex-squadmates work in silence, then laugh at a shared mess-up; that shared attention becomes trust. These small moments begin to rewire wounded systems, bridging military experience with CPTSD research and giving practical routes for soldiers and families to act.

Art Journaling and Visual Expression

Healing Through Journaling: Fieldnotes for the Inner Front

Think of an art journal like a pocket notebook issued in theater — only this one gets your feelings written, sketched, or glued, not coordinates. For soldiers and veterans dealing with combat trauma, CPTSD, or TBI, art journaling helps move attention out of numbing and replaying into a present felt sense: grounding, body awareness, and calmer arousal.

Emotional flashbacks are body-based replays: the nervous system can bypass higher-order checks and go straight to a 4F response — fight, flight, freeze, fawn. Art journaling works because repeated, low-threat pages become safety cues; simple, sensory-focused practices train the autonomic nervous system (ANS) to form new pathways that reduce hyperarousal and shorten the length of triggered states. By shifting attention to touch, color, and small tasks, you interrupt the automatic 4F loop and give your cortex time to re-engage.

Practical drills you can use today

- 5-minute drawing: set a timer for five minutes and make continuous marks (lines, shapes, scribbles). No meaning required—focus on movement and rhythm to calm the body.
- Sensory prompt checklist: on a journal page, list 5 things you see, 4 you hear, 3 you feel, 2 you smell, 1 you taste. Add a quick sketch or color wash for each item to anchor sensation in the body.
- Color-intensity boxes: draw 5 small squares, assign colors to intensity levels (1–10) and fill in how you feel now; revisit later to watch intensity drop.
- Breath-and-mark: take three slow, deep breaths, then make one intentional stroke or dot after each exhale. Repeat until breathing and marks synchronize.

Do these practices briefly and regularly. The goal is not art quality but repeated, safe sensory experience that retrains the ANS and provides a grounded alternative when the body defaults to a 4F response.

Emotional flashbacks are bodybased replays that trigger the 4F response—fight, flight, freeze, fawn—without the brain's higherorder checks. Regular art journaling trains the autonomic nervous system by providing lowthreat practice; each page becomes a safety cue that rewires pathways to reduce hyperarousal.

Practical drills you can use today

• 5minute drawing: sketch anything that comes to mind for five minutes; let the motion anchor the body.

• Sensory prompts: note five things you can see, four you can touch, three you can hear, two you can smell, one you can taste. The sensory details shift focus from the flashback to the present, calming the nervous system.

- Start small: five minutes of drawing a shape, shading a corner, or writing one sentence about a sensation (tight jaw, heavy chest). Think paced, incremental work that honors developmental needs — like staging exposures, not storming the hill.
- Sensory prompts: note sounds, textures, temperature. These anchor the present and interrupt flashbacks without re-exposing the brain to trauma details.
- Narrative prompts for veterans: "Where in your body is that memory?" "What was small and safe in that moment?" These encourage coherent meaning-making while avoiding retraumatization.

Sharing the page: relational work that counts

Showing a piece to a trusted clinician or peer reinforces safety signals. Relational sharing builds attunement and reduces isolation — and that helps families who get pulled into complex secondary PTSD. For spouses and kids, co-journaling sessions with clear boundaries (time-limited, non-probing) can provide mutual regulation without turning everyone into an on-call clinician.

Adapt visuals for different histories

Offer options: collage, photos, stick figures, textured items, or simple markers. Age and culture matter; let people choose the tool that gives them agency. For military readers, treat materials like gear: pick what works, keep it accessible, and rotate when it stops helping.

For further reading by those who want tactical manuals and lived experience, see Battle Fatigue: Understanding PTSD and Finding a Cure (Paul D. Walker, Ret. Col.) and Arsenal of Hope: Tactics for Taking on PTSD, Together (Jen Satterly). Both complement journaling approaches and give concrete strategies for unit- and family-level recovery.

In short: a worn notebook, a quiet five minutes, and a trusted listener can be as effective as a tactical plan for a mission: simple, repeatable, and life-saving.

Music, Rhythm, and Mood Regulation

The ear is as much a front line as the eye in recovery work. After pages of visual methods, let's turn to another tool that moves through the body: music and rhythm. For combat vets and families dealing with CPTSD—whether from childhood wounds or battlefield scars—rhythm can act like an ordered patrol through a chaotic nervous system.

A steady, regular beat calms the autonomic nervous system, shifting it from fight/flight/freeze/fawn toward safety. This reduces hypervigilance and dampens the intensity of emotional flashbacks. The technique—melodic grounding—takes advantage of this effect by humming a familiar tune, vocalizing a short phrase, or repeating a twonote pattern. Producing sound focuses attention on the present body and breath, further trimming sensory memories and acting as a quick, focused intervention against panic.

Melodic grounding: a field technique

When dissociation or an emotional flashback hits, rely on a simple melodic grounding technique: choose a recognizable tune or a twonote pattern, keep the tempo slow and even, and hum or speak it until you feel steadier. The steady beat signals safety to the nervous system, reduces hypervigilance, and brings attention back to the body and breath, weakening the hold of sensory memories.

Breath-guided rhythm: syncing systems

Combine humming with paced breathing to get better results. Breathe in for five counts, hum on the out-breath for five, repeat. This simple sync improves heart-rate variability and steadying signals between brainstem and cortex. Clinically, it's a low-risk intervention you can teach in session and use in the field.

Build a personal playlist that works

Create playlists for specific tasks: calming during sleep, grounding during flashbacks, or energizing for physical rehab. Match tempo to function (slower for down-regulation). For folks with TBI or sound sensitivity, keep volume low, avoid sudden changes, and choose instruments or recordings with clear, simple lines.

Rhythm as a relational tool

Group drumming, clapping patterns, or synchronized marching drills can re-establish trust and attachment—important for veterans and families experiencing complex secondary CPTSD. These activities send non-verbal cues of safety and predictability, useful in therapy groups or family sessions.

Tactical takeaway: experiment with short, repeatable sound-and-breath routines; build a few context-specific playlists; and when working with families, use simple rhythmic exercises to rebuild attunement. Music won't replace therapy or medical care, but used like a reliable piece of kit, it gives soldiers and loved ones another way to steady the body and re-engage with life.

Movement, Breath, and Somatic Practice

If rhythm steadied the room, the next step is to steady the vehicle: your own body. For veterans and families dealing with CPTSD—and for the soldier whose childhood armor never came off—the combination of movement, breath, and somatic work is a front-line tactic for re-establishing nervous system control and a sense of safety.

Interoception and the Felt Sense

Think of interoception as the instrument panel inside your chest and abdomen. When those gauges are readable, you catch a rising panic before it becomes a full 4F eruption. Training that sensorium—practicing feltsense awareness—builds emotional literacy: you name rising heat, tightness, or hollowness and choose a response instead of reacting on instinct. A quick drill: pause, place a hand on the belly, and silently report three sensations (temperature, pressure, movement). That small checkin teaches your system what to look for.

You can then anchor that awareness in a breathing protocol that calms the 4F response. Inhale for four counts, hold one, exhale for six, and repeat five times. For hyperarousal, focus on a slow, generous exhale until your shoulders drop. If you feel fainting or freezing, use short reset breaths—three quick inhales followed by a long exhale—to break stuck immobility. Diaphragmatic cues help: feel the breath push the lower ribs and belly out, not the chest up. By pairing feltsense awareness with these rhythmic breaths, you give your nervous system clear signals to shift from danger to calm.

Trauma-Informed Pacing and Gentle Movement

Start small. Trauma-informed pacing means consent, micro-doses, and time for recovery after each practice. A useful sequence: one minute of breath work, thirty seconds of standing hip rolls, then rest. No heroics. Slow, repetitive movements—neck circles, hip rocks, toe planting—prevent flooding and build tolerance.

Postures, Grounding, and Embodiment

Postures that anchor you: feet shoulder-width, knees soft, pelvis neutral, weight sinking into the heels. Clench-and-release the glutes for five seconds to feel the ground under you. For battle-fatigue or TBI survivors, these postures restore pelvic stability and a sense of containment when surroundings feel unsafe.

Relational Cues and Titrated Exposure

In groups or therapy, consented touch (a palm on the shoulder), steady voice cadence, and mirroring signal safety. When emotional flashbacks surface, the approach is titrated exposure: introduce small reminders in a controlled setting, pair them with grounding and breath, and only increase intensity when stability is intact.

Daily Home Practice for Soldiers and Families

Short, consistent beats win wars here: two minutes of belly breaths upon waking, three minutes of mindful walking with hands on chest mid-day, evening posture checks before bed. Families can practice together—brief drills that teach secondary CPTSD sufferers how to regulate alongside the veteran. Small, repeated practices create durable regulation under pressure.

Photography and Storytelling

Photography and Storytelling: Field Tools for Relational Healing

When I tell soldiers to bring a camera into therapy, some imagine a sniper scope. Relax: this is more like reconnaissance for the inner terrain. Photography and storytelling let people externalize what's stuck inside—turning hot, confusing sensations into objects that can be looked at, handled, and discussed without being swallowed by them.

Externalizing Internal States through Photography

Photography and storytelling are creative tools that help externalize internal states, slow flashbacks, and sequence memories in a manageable way. By turning feelings into concrete images or brief narratives, the brain can focus on a stable cue rather than an immediate emotional surge. Start with safe photographic subjects—shadows, boots, a faded baseball cap—take a photo, note any bodily sensations at the moment, then breathe and label the feeling. Treat each photo as a twominute recon: photo, breath check, label, store securely. Parallel to this, use short "story capsules": three sentences that name an event, describe one bodily sensation, and end with a safe outcome. Read one aloud a day, then expand slightly the next; pacing the exposure gives the nervous system time to tolerate detail without flipping into fight/flight/freeze/faint. Together, photography and storytelling create a structured, sensoryrich narrative that reduces overwhelm and supports trauma recovery.

The Role of Storytelling in Trauma Narratives

Stories help sequence memory; when paired with images they make an experience both concrete and tolerable. Use short, controlled story exercises—three-sentence capsules that name an event, one bodily sensation, and one safe outcome—and link each capsule to a photo you took as an external cue.

Suggested rhythm:

- Day 1: read the capsule aloud while looking at the photo.
- Day 2: add one line of detail or repeat it twice, keeping focus on breath and bodily sensation.
- Continue only as long as the intensity stays manageable.

This paced pairing of image and story reduces overwhelm by giving the nervous system time to tolerate increasing detail, turning automatic flash responses into moments you can observe, label, and contain.

Co-Creation and Relational Healing

Therapist and veteran cocreate artifacts—photo series, captions, shared timelines—working within clear boundaries and consent. Think of it as a joint op with strict rules of engagement: consent first, safe words, time limits, and agreed storage/privacy practices. Cocreation promotes grounding and redirects power into the veteran's hands.

Suggested rhythm:

- Begin with a short grounding exercise to orient the veteran.
- Explicitly outline roles, boundaries, and storage expectations.
- Conclude each session with a brief review of progress and next steps.

Therapist and veteran cocreate artifacts—photo series, captions, shared timelines—working within clear boundaries and consent. Think of it as a joint op with strict rules of engagement: consent first, safe words, time limits, and agreed storage/privacy practices. Cocreation promotes grounding and redirects power into the veteran's hands.

Suggested rhythm:

- Select the type of artifact (photo, caption, timeline) together.
- Use collaborative tools to edit and finalize content.
- Document and archive decisions to maintain privacy and consistency.

Building Trust and Vulnerability

Sharing images and drafts of stories is risky; do it slowly. Families can participate in small, supervised steps to avoid complex secondary PTSD—partners should be briefed on signs of vicarious distress and given their own support tasks. In therapy, mutual vulnerability breeds trust when the clinician respects limits and keeps the pace tolerable.

Suggested rhythm:

- Identify safe disclosure moments.
- Practice active listening and empathy.
- Monitor emotional cues and adjust pace accordingly.

Sharing images and drafts of stories is risky; do it slowly. Families can participate in small, supervised steps to avoid complex secondary PTSD—partners should be briefed on signs of vicarious distress and given their own support tasks. In therapy, mutual vulnerability breeds trust when the clinician respects limits and keeps the pace tolerable.

Suggested rhythm:

- Gradually introduce sharing sessions.
- Provide clear supervision and support structures for family members.
- Offer individual coping strategies for vicarious distress.

Practical Applications and Considerations

Suggested rhythm:

- Compile an implementation checklist tailored to each veteran.
- Ensure cultural sensitivity in all artifacts and interactions.
- Evaluate outcomes with both qualitative and quantitative measures.

Train clinicians in trauma-informed creative methods; for veterans with TBI, adapt tasks for attention and memory (fewer shots, larger printouts). Start with low-stakes assignments, use secure digital storage, and always include a grounding routine before and after sessions. In short: no recon without permission, no surprise debriefs, and keep the mission simple—externalize, label, share a little, rest.

Trust-Building, Boundaries, and Consent

Building a Safe Basecamp

Think of trust like a field-expedient shelter: if the poles wobble, the rain gets in. For service members coping with combat PTSD, battle fatigue, or TBI — and for those whose CPTSD roots go back to childhood — repair starts with predictable, nonjudgmental presence. That means showing up on time, keeping promises, and listening without trying to fix everything on the first pass. Small, steady reliability creates the conditions where the nervous system can stop being on constant alert.

Predictable Presence: Small Things, Big Trust

Predictable presence signals safety to a brain wired for threat. When a clinician texts a session reminder, a partner gently asks "how are you feeling?" without forcing answers, or a buddy sits quietly during a hard moment, these microanchors reduce surprise—the fuel for the 4F stress response: fight, flight, freeze, and fawn. By establishing such reliability, we create a foundation that empowers people to make consentfirst creative choices. In this safe, predictable environment, consentfirst creative tasks become opportunities to exercise agency, fostering empowerment and reducing the likelihood of emotional flashbacks that feel like reliving past threat.

Consent-first creative tasks are brief, structured activities offered only after explicit invitation and with predictable boundaries. Reliability — like clear instructions, scheduled check-ins, and an easy opt-out — signals safety; that predictability lowers surprise and reduces 4F responses, making it easier for someone to engage. Emphasize choice and power: describe the task, give alternatives (or a "pass" option), set a known time limit, and confirm consent before beginning. These practices respect boundary and agency while turning creative work into an empowering, low-risk way to connect, explore, or heal.

Creative activities work best when control stays with the veteran or family member. Make it consent-centered: offer options, ask for preferences, and accept a "not today" without pressure. Examples that have low threat but high payoff: taking photos of a route you walk, free-form drumming for two minutes, writing a one-paragraph letter you never send, or moving to a shared rhythm while seated. The point is agency — choosing the mission parameters and the pace.

Boundaries, Pacing, and the Brain

Boundaries protect the nervous system. Agree on session length, touch preferences, and safe words for increasing intensity. Use short exposures: two minutes of telling a memory, then five minutes of breathing and grounding. That pacing lets memory integration happen without triggering an emotional flashback loop.

Co-Regulation: Moving (and Breathing) Together

Co-regulation is simple and tactical: synchronize breath, rhythm, or movement. March in place together for a minute. Tap a steady four-beat on the table while the other person breathes with you. Shared creative tasks—collaborative sketching, paired drumming, or walking routes—help re-tune nervous systems. Families should know they can develop complex secondary PTSD; their own symptoms deserve validation and direct care. Practical rule: if someone is spiraling, pause creative work, use grounding (5 senses check), and re-set consent before continuing.

Short checklist to try tonight:

- Commit to one predictable action (text, arrival time).
- Offer two creative options; let them pick.
- Set a five-minute cap for hard material.
- Use a shared rhythm to come back to baseline.

No medals for sitting and breathing, but give it a try — it works.

Communicating Needs: Scripts and Scenarios

Foundational Scripts for Needs Communication: SOPs for Feelings

Think of these scripts as standard operating procedures for highemotion moments. When a brain flips into an emotional flashback—amygdala lighting up like a tripwire and prefrontal cortex temporarily out to lunch—the automatic 4F suite (fight, flight, freeze, fawn) takes over. A short, practiced Istatement can stop the escalation faster than yelling for help, acting as the onetwo punch that anchors the internal state and guides communication.

I-Statements and Needs Framing (Battle Drills)

Istatements are the onetwo punch that counters the 4F responses triggered by an emotional flashback. By stating what's happening inside you without accusing the other person, you interrupt fight, flight, freeze, or fawn and bring the situation back to a calm, premissionready state. Practice them like a premission checklist.

- "I feel scared when loud noises happen; I need a few minutes to breathe."
- "I'm overwhelmed right now; I need a break for ten minutes."

These lines name the internal state, then request an action. Simple. Clear. Hard to argue with.

Shifting Away from Blame

When triggered, blame is the enemy's propaganda — it multiplies defensiveness. Pause, breathe, and convert "You made me…" into "I feel…" If you catch yourself starting a sentence with "You always," swap it mid-sentence: "I'm getting tense. I need space."

Scripts for Common Needs Scenarios

Keep a handful of rehearsed phrases on the tip of your tongue or on a small card in your pocket.

- "I'm feeling overwhelmed; can we take a break and come back in 20 minutes?"
- "I need some physical space right now; can we sit apart for a bit?"
- "I'm scared — can you hold my hand or stay nearby until I calm down?"

Rehearsed Phrases for Emotional Flashbacks

Flashbacks short-circuit thinking. Short, direct requests work best.

- "I'm triggered. Can we slow down?"
- "I need you with me for a few minutes. Can you stay quiet and sit close?"

Pacing, Consent Signals, and Tactical Grounding

Use explicit pauses and check-ins as standard protocol: call out a pause, then actually take five. Establish simple consent signals with your partner — a raised hand, a word like "pause," or a thumbs-down meaning "stop." During high arousal, use grounding tools: name five things you see, breathe box counts (4–4–4), and repeat an I-statement.

Practicing in Relational Contexts (Drills with a Wingman)

Run role-plays with a trusted person or clinician. Run them like after-action drills: run the script, swap roles, give feedback. Families can learn "complex secondary PTSD" cues — how a parent's old CPTSD patterns echo in the home — and practice steady, slow responses that reduce escalation rather than intensifying it.

Final Tactical Tip: write your top three scripts on index cards. Memorize them like battle drills. When the brain floods, muscle memory of words can steady the system and create safer connections with the people who matter most.

Collaborators: Therapists, Advocates, and Allies

If the scripts and pacing drills are your field exercises, then integrated care is the operational unit that gets you home. Picture a small, steady squad: a therapist who acts as a relational guide, reading the map and offering the steady cadence of a walking checkpoint; an advocate who clears the route through red tape; and peers who carry your kit when your legs go rubber. This coordinated setup—therapist as guide and checkpoint, advocate as navigator, peers as support—reduces the risk of being overrun by emotional flashbacks or a 4F cascade—fight, flight, freeze, fawn—when the limbic system goes into autopilot.

Therapists as relational guides

A skilled clinician becomes a walking checkpoint: they contain the overload, match your pace, and introduce exposure in increments that your nervous system can tolerate. That containment is not soft talk; it's tactical. They calibrate breathing, use grounding drills, and offer paced recall so the limbic system learns that memory activation doesn't equal danger. This steady alliance helps prevent retriggering and permits real processing over time.

Advocates: the logistics specialists

Advocates move through bureaucracy so you don't have to. They can sort benefits, arrange housing, coordinate medical evaluations for TBI, and attend appointments as a second set of ears. Less stress on those fronts means more bandwidth for therapy. If paperwork makes you want to dig a foxhole, an advocate is the one who hands you a shovel and files the forms.

Peer support: buddy-system medicine

Fellow veterans and caregivers bring street-cred empathy. Hearing a peer say, "I had that reaction, too, and I'm still standing," cuts isolation fast. Peer groups also model coping tactics and offer practical tips—sleep routines after shift work, how to coach kids through an adult's emotional flashback—stuff clinicians may not live.

Trauma-informed collaboration: the rules of engagement

Effective care runs on consent, transparency, and agreed pacing. Hold a team brief: client goals, safety signals, exposure timeline, and contingency plans. Key principles to print and pin on the fridge:

- Safety: create physical and emotional space to debrief.
- Trust: consistent, predictable contact from providers and peers.
- Pacing: slow, measurable exposure steps tied to physiological markers.
- Collaboration: shared decision-making about what happens next.
- Trauma-informed care: minimize triggers and respect limits.

For families, watch for Complex secondary PTSD reactions—sleep loss, hypervigilance, or numbing—and get them included in briefs and basic training. Treat the household like a unit: simple signals, scheduled check-ins, and shared grounding practices beat chaos every time. Integrated care isn't glamorous, but it's the field-tested plan that helps you come back and stay back from the edge.

Relational Healing in Community

After the internal work of regulating the nervous system and finding anchors for personal safety, the vital next step grounds these gains within external relationships and the broader environment. Healing from the hidden scars of complex trauma asks for more than individual insight; it demands the steady construction of trust with others. This foundation isn't built on grand gestures but on consistent, deliberate actions that establish safety, ensure predictability, and mend ruptures with clear intent.

We will examine how reliable routines, transparent communication, and the protective architecture of clear boundaries counteract the destabilizing force of betrayal. This includes the power of shared rituals, the measured practice of vulnerability with consent, and the critical role of trauma-informed community supports. These practices offer a concrete path to manage emotional flashbacks and adapt to defensive 4F responses, creating environments where safety and trust can steadily take hold.

Rebuilding Trust after Betrayal

Rebuilding Trust: The Foundation of Healing from Hidden Scars

If integrated care is the platoon, then rebuilding trust is the supply line — without it, nothing moves. For veterans and those with childhood-onset CPTSD, betrayal shatters the basic expectation that others will act predictably. Repair isn't magic; it's heavy lifting: safety, consistency, and deliberate relational repair. Think of it like maintenance on a Humvee — dirty work, repetitive checks, and small parts matter.

Establishing Safety and Consistency

When betrayal fractures trust, the brain goes on high alert. Emotional flashbacks flick the threat switch: the amygdala screams, the hippocampus misfiles context, and the prefrontal cortex can't get the paperwork in order. That's when the 4F responses—fight, flight, freeze, fawn—show up like an old drill sergeant. The antidote is predictability: by restoring a sense of safety and consistency, we can rewire the nervous system and reduce the reflexive 4F reaction.

Practical drills to build that predictability

- Daily routine anchors – set three predictable moments each day (e.g., a morning coffee ritual, a midday walk, an evening winddown) to provide regular cues of safety.

- Safety rituals – create a short, calming ritual (a few deep breaths, a comforting phrase, a gentle stretch) to use whenever flashbacks flare.

- Grounding anchor – keep a tactile object (a smooth stone, a piece of fabric) that you can hold or touch to bring attention back to the present.

- Consistent communication – schedule regular checkins with a trusted partner or therapist, using the same format and tone each time to reinforce reliability.

By pairing the neurobiological understanding of betrayalinduced flashbacks with concrete, repeatable drills, the brain learns new, calmer responses, turning the old drill sergeant into a supportive coach.

Concrete drills:

- Daily check-in ritual (5 minutes at the same time): a brief, reliable connection that signals predictability and helps the hippocampus refile trust-related context.
- One-thing commitments: make a single, specific promise you can keep and follow through; repeated follow-through recalibrates expectations and rebuilds prefrontal-mediated trust.
- Conflict rules and pause words: agree on a clear timeout signal and a reconnection routine so emotional escalation is interrupted before the amygdala hijacks behavior.
- Transparent scheduling and notifications: share plans and changes in advance (or as soon as possible) to reduce uncertainty and prevent surprise-triggered flashbacks.
- Sensory anchors and routines: consistent bedtime, shared calendars, or small rituals (coffee together, a text at a set hour) create environmental predictability that soothes hypervigilance.
- Immediate repair sequence for slip-ups: acknowledge the harm, state what you will do differently, and follow through—this predictable repair pattern restores safety faster than explanations alone.

Transparency is field-expedient trust repair. Regular updates, clear explanations for changes, and honest admissions when mistakes happen reduce the hidden betrayals that trigger emotional flashbacks. When a partner explains the "why" of a decision, the hippocampus gets better cues and the present is less likely to collapse into the past.

Tactical transparency steps:

- Use short debriefs after tense interactions: what happened, what was intended, what will change. - Agree on "red flags" and tell each other when they pop up. - Keep information flow visible — shared calendars, briefed changes, written confirmations.

The Role of Community-Based Supports

Peers, mentors, and clinicians trained in CPTSD act like seasoned NCOs — they model steady behavior, validate experiences, and teach coping drills. For families, peer groups help normalize reactions and reduce complex secondary PTSD, where caregivers absorb the stress and start showing PTSDlike symptoms themselves.

Balancing Vulnerability and Safety

Vulnerability should be a measured exposure exercise, not a free-for-all. Create consent-based windows for disclosure: short, controlled shares with agreed boundaries. Use "safety words" or signals to pause the conversation. This protects against retraumatization while allowing repair.

The Power of Shared Rituals

Rituals are predictable safety exercises. Weekly meals, after-shift debriefs, or a Friday "gear check" for household plans create reliable experiences of care. Over time, these rituals rebuild trust by proving — again and again — that someone will show up.

Final field note: small, consistent actions beat big apologies every time. Trust rebuilds in inches: check in, be transparent, recruit community supports, protect vulnerability with consent, and set rituals that prove care on the regular. Your brain, and your unit at home, will thank you.

Interpersonal Boundaries and Safety Plans

If rebuilding trust was the field order, boundaries are the perimeter fences that keep the camp safe. To set up those fences, a soldier first identifies the unsafe elements in their environment and the trusted allies who can help reinforce the perimeter. With a CPTSD rooted in childhood and compounded by combat, clear interpersonal boundaries do more than keep people away—they create predictable conditions that reduce triggering interactions, keep emotional flashbacks in check, and make the watch feel safer.

Establishing Clear Interpersonal Boundaries

Begin by mapping unsafe elements and trusted support. List the interactions, places, or behaviors that leave you on high alert, then name the people or resources you can rely on to enforce limits or provide backup. Communicate limits clearly, enforce them consistently, and adjust the boundary plan as safety and relationships evolve—like repairing and reinforcing a perimeter fence to keep the camp secure.

Start by writing down what feels unsafe or draining. That's your recon: names, places, topics, and behaviors that trigger a spike in heart rate, breathing, or memory intrusions. Then list people and roles you can trust to respect those limits — a few reliable contacts are worth more than a hundred well-meaning strangers.

Defining Safe Limits and Finding Trusted Support

Safe limits might look like: no phone calls after 9 p.m., no surprise visits, or no conversations about certain events. Trusted support can be a combat buddy who understands military triggers, a therapist trained in CPTSD, a peer support group, or a family member who's practiced consent-based check-ins. The point is a small network you can reach during an emotional flashback so you aren't isolated.

Personal Safety Plan: Your SOP for Crises

Treat a safety plan like standard operating procedure. Keep a laminated copy and one in your phone.

- List of trusted contacts (names, numbers, preferred method: text/call)
- Step-by-step plan for an emotional flashback (leave the room, use a grounding script, call a contact)
- Coping tools and grounding techniques (short scripts you can say aloud)
- Safe places (physical locations where you feel secure)

Consent-Based Communication: Rules of Engagement

Communicate expectations up front. Ask for and give clear consent before plunging into heavy topics. Regular check-ins — a five-minute "status" at agreed times — reduce accidental breaches. Everyone should be able to say "no" or "not now" without penalty; teach family and peers to accept that reply at face value.

Limits on Disclosure

Control the pace of what you share. Use the "three-level" rule: mention a concern at Level 1 (surface), Level 2 (some detail), or Level 3 (full disclosure) and only move deeper when you feel safe. This prevents overwhelm and protects relationships from being overloaded.

Grounding Techniques: Regaining Present-Moment Safety

When the 4F responses (fight, flight, freeze, fawn) kick in, use quick, repeatable drills:

- Breathing: 4-4-8 or box breathing for two minutes
- Sensory focus: name five things you can see, four you can touch, three you can hear
- Gentle movement: slow marches in place, shoulder rolls, or a short walk

These tactics interrupt the old survival wiring and bring the nervous system back on post.

Adapting Boundaries to Different Contexts

Boundaries that work in a unit may need adjustment in civilian settings or with family. Veterans often re-learn social rules; that's fine. Adjust the specifics while keeping the core limits intact.

Families and Complex Secondary PTSD

Partners and kids can carry complex secondary PTSD. Families need their own boundaries and safety plans. Teach them the basics: what triggers you, how to do a consent check-in, and who to call. That practical training protects everyone.

Mission Maintenance: Regular Review

Set a cadence to review your plan — weekly at first, then monthly or after major events. Update contacts, tactics, and limits as relationships and needs change. Keeping the plan active is how a perimeter stays secure.

Support Systems: Family, Friends, and Peers

Support Systems Anchor Healing through Trusted Relationships

If combat taught us anything, it was that no one operates alone in the field. The same applies to the fight against trauma: recovery works best with a reliable team. For veterans carrying PTSD, battle fatigue, or TBI — and for adults whose CPTSD traces back to childhood — a small but steady network of trusted people provides stability, reality checks, and a place to land when the limbic system takes over.

Family and Friends: The Foundation

Family and close friends are the immediate perimeter. Simple acts — a partner sitting in the clinic waiting room, a sibling texting "check-in" after a trigger — break isolation and reduce the panic that follows an emotional flashback. Retired Colonel Paul D. Walker highlights this reality in Battle Fatigue: a supportive network often reduces symptom intensity and improves recovery outcomes for both PTSD and TBI. Practical order: pick two people who can show up reliably, brief them on warning signs, and agree on one simple response protocol.

Understanding Emotional Flashbacks (for the people on watch)

An emotional flashback isn't a cinematic replay; it's the brain switching to an earlier survival operating system. When the amygdala sounds the alarm, the prefrontal cortex loses grip, and the body shifts into a 4F pattern—fight, flight, freeze, or fawn. For someone whose trauma began in childhood, a smell or tone can trigger a state that mirrors a decadesold threat. Understanding this mechanism clarifies why the person may feel out of control, and it guides the way we communicate safely. Loved ones who recognize the pattern can help ground the person by calling out clear presenttime facts, offering a consensual safetouch cue, or leading a brief guidedbreathing exercise. These simple, intentional interactions establish a communication pattern that respects the survivor's neurological state and promotes healing.

Establishing Safe Communication Patterns

Knowing the brain has switched into an earlier survival operating system makes it easier to choose communication that helps rather than escalates. Practical patterns to establish in advance include:

- Agree on simple, specific grounding phrases or present-tense facts a partner can say (for example: "You are safe. We are at home. I'm here with you.").
- Prearrange clear, consented cues for consented touch or for "I'm here" nonverbal support (a hand squeeze, a particular word, or a tap).
- Use a calm, steady tone; avoid chastising, pressing for explanations, or asking "why" in the moment.
- Lead short, paced breathing or a guided grounding exercise rather than trying to reason with the person.
- Offer limited choices (stay here or go to a quiet room) instead of open-ended demands, and reduce sensory stimulation when possible.
- Check in afterward — when the person is calm and has given permission — to review what helped and adjust the plan.

These predictable, consent-based patterns convert the understanding of the flashback into concrete steps that restore safety and trust.

Communication that keeps the air clear looks like active listening, boundarychecks, and agreed safewords. Jen Satterly, in Arsenal of Hope, makes the case: safety in talk matters as much as what's said. Tactical tips: use short, nonjudgmental phrases during distress ("You're safe here," "Look at this clock with me"), keep a noquestion rule during flashbacks, and schedule regular checkins outside crisis times to discuss triggers and limits.

Collaborative Coping and Peer Support

Work together on coping routines that address nervous-system needs: coordinated movement (hikes, yoga-like stretches), co-regulation breathing drills, creative outlets, or shared tasks that restore agency. Peer groups — veteran-led or moderated — add a different kind of ammo: shared experience removes shame and provides hard-won tactics. Seek nonjudgmental groups at vet centers, community programs, or through trusted clinicians; these platforms reduce isolation and help both veterans and families feel understood.

Educating Caregivers and Guarding the Watch

Caregiving wears down even the toughest. Families should be taught the neurobiology of trauma, how to spot Complex secondary PTSD symptoms in themselves (sleep disruption, hypervigilance, rage), and how to rotate responsibilities. Set limits, keep a backup contact list, and build small rituals that restore normalcy. When families get support and training, everyone's operational readiness improves — including the person carrying the trauma.

Immediate mission items: name two trusted contacts, find one peer or family support group, and set one weekly shared activity to practice co-regulation. Small, steady actions create the perimeter that lets healing begin.

School and Workplace: Advocating for Needs

Advocate for Your Needs in Education and Work

If you made it through a combat zone, asking for adjustments at work or school shouldn't feel like walking into hostile territory — but for many with CPTSD, it does. Think of advocating as a mission briefing: define the objective, assemble the evidence, pick your team, and use clear signals when things get hot. A deadline, bright lights, or a critical supervisor can trigger a 4F response (fight, flight, freeze, fawn) or an emotional flashback that lands you back in a childhood or combat moment. That biological reality is why accommodations matter; they help create a safer environment by modifying those triggers.

Identifying Reasonable Accommodations

Start with a short intelgathering: list the tasks, settings, and stimuli that trigger symptoms. Then match practical fixes—reasonable accommodations such as extended deadlines, reduced lighting, or a supportive supervisor—to calm the 4F response and prevent flashbacks.

- Flexible hours or staggered deadlines for stress spikes.
- Reduced sensory inputs: quieter workspace, softer lighting, headphones.
- Break routines: scheduled pauses for grounding or therapy check-ins.
- Access to mental health support on-site or via telehealth.

These are not special favors; they're tools that keep you mission-capable.

Gathering Documentation

Paperwork wins battles you can't fight on instinct. Secure a diagnosis from a qualified clinician, recent treatment plans, and functional assessments that explain limits and workable adjustments. Keep copies in a folder (physical and encrypted digital). Update records after major changes so advocates — lawyers, disability offices, commanders, or school counselors — have current information.

Seeking Supportive Colleagues

Find at least two people at work or school who are discreet, empathetic, and willing to act as allies. They can buffer triggering situations, give you a heads-up before a meeting, or step in if a flashback happens. Approach them with short, plain language: what helps, what harms, and how they can assist without being a counselor.

Collaborative Planning with Trusted Allies

Build a simple plan with mentors, family, or your therapist: state objectives, list triggers, name accommodations, and assign roles. Families can experience Complex secondary PTSD; include them so they know how to help without becoming overwhelmed.

Using Clear, Trauma-Informed Communication

When you request adjustments, use predictable, calm language. Say what you need, why it helps, and propose specific solutions. Pause to allow processing time. Avoid long emotional monologues — stick to the facts and the requested fixes.

Setting Boundaries and Gradual Exposure

Set limits on workload, social obligations, and reactive tasks. Communicate those boundaries early and negotiate alternatives. For necessary stressors, build graded exposure: small steps, repeatable successes, and debriefs with a trusted ally or clinician.

Educating Peers and Supervisors about CPTSD

Offer brief, plain explanations of CPTSD and how emotional flashbacks or 4F reactions appear on the job. Give concrete examples of impact and practical fixes. Hand out a one-page summary and cite guidance like the EEOC's accommodations information so the request sits on policy, not opinion.

Advocacy is an operational task: plan it, document it, bring allies, and use clear signals under pressure. With a tactical approach, work and school can stop being threat zones and start acting like places you can function and grow.

Caregiving Roles and Boundaries

Boundaries: The Unsung Heroes of Caregiving Relationships

Think of boundaries as ROE for the home front — rules of engagement that stop small problems from turning into full-scale skirmishes. For veterans and family caregivers dealing with CPTSD rooted in childhood and compounded by combat exposure, boundaries protect mission readiness: the emotional stability of both parties.

When an emotional flashback triggers the amygdala, the hippocampus fails to contextualise the memory. The prefrontal cortex is sidelined, sending the body into one of the 4F modes: fight, flight, freeze, or fawn. The solution is to set clear, predictable boundaries that act as a deescalation protocol. By clarifying roles and responsibilities—essentially creating a mission brief for the home—you give the brain reliable cues. These boundaries limit surprise, supply trustworthy signals, and give the prefrontal cortex a fighting chance to assess present risk instead of replaying past assaults. In practice, that means mapping who handles medication, who monitors safety, and who offers emotional support so every caregiver knows their role and can act decisively when the 4F cascade begins.

Clarifying roles and responsibilities — a mission brief for home

Turn the neurobiological insight above into a simple operational plan. When an emotional flashback disables timestamping and executive control, predefining who does what reduces the need for splitsecond decisions and lowers reactivity. A compact mission brief might include:

- Designated responders: name one person to provide immediate grounding and one to monitor safety/logistics. Fewer decisionmakers reduce confusion.
- Concrete scripts: agree on short, calming phrases or signals (verbal or nonverbal) so responses are predictable and minimally stimulating.
- Boundaries and limits: set clear, consistent limits (what is and isn't acceptable during an episode) and a timelimited process for

addressing violations to protect everyone's safety.

- Predictable routines: predictable daily rhythms and response routines (where to go, what helps) supply reliable cues to the hippocampus and prefrontal cortex.
- Visible plan: post the plan or keep it in an easy place so any caregiver can follow it without improvising.
- Practice and debrief: rehearse the plan briefly and debrief after incidents to refine roles and restore trust.

By turning internal chaos into an external, simple protocol, caregiving teams give the brain the cues it needs to downregulate and return to presentfocused thinking.

- Draft a task list: morning meds, clinic rides, bill-paying, who calls the therapist. Make it specific.
- Decide who makes what calls when stress levels rise. Example script: "If I'm short of breath or dissociating, you handle the phone calls for that day."
- Set personal-space rules: knock, 10-minute cool-down after a trigger, or a designated quiet room.

Trauma-aware communication — short, predictable, and nonaggressive

Use neutral language and give warnings before sensitive topics. Try safety signals: a palm-up sign for "slow down," or a phrase like "Mission Check" before a debrief. Avoid vague requests; supplyable, time-bound statements work better ("I can sit through thirty minutes of this topic; then we pause.")

Safety planning and escalation

Write a simple plan: safe topics, agreed transportation for medical appointments, who to call if escalation occurs, and an explicit step for professional help. Keep emergency steps taped to the fridge. Treat the plan like a go-bag: accessible and rehearsed.

Caregiver self-care and preventing complex secondary CPTSD

Caregivers can develop battle fatigue of their own. Carve out regular R&R (no guilt), rotate duties with a backup, and get supervision or a peer group — think of it as after-action reporting. If family members show creeping hypervigilance, intrusive memories, or avoidance, get those symptoms assessed; early intervention prevents chronic problems.

Relational pacing — match speed to tolerance

Slow the tempo when the veteran signals distress; speed up when they're anchored. Small adjustments — a pause here, a 24-hour rule there — pay off in fewer flashbacks and more usable days.

Closing order: make boundaries written, practiced, and revisited. Treat them like mission plans — updated as conditions change, briefed before contact, and respected by all hands.

Community Healing Practices and Rituals

If relational pacing is the platoon's rule for moving through hostile territory, community healing is the base camp where the unit patches wounds, swaps stories, and plans the next sortie. For veterans with CPTSD — many of whom carry childhood trauma prints under their combat scars — getting back into a group that feels safe can cut the power of a trigger in half.

Community Healing Foundations for CPTSD Recovery

Shared rituals are lowtech, highimpact tools that act like standard operating procedures for lowering arousal. Lighting a candle, passing a bowl of soup, or sitting in a fiveminute circle where each person names one neutral fact about their day signal safety to the limbic system without forcing anyone to debrief. When a group breathes together, follows the same guided imagery, or maintains a steady cadence, the nervous systems coregulate. The simultaneous lowering of arousal creates a buffer that lets a person in high distress move from hypervigilance or numbness toward calm, reducing the intensity of emotional flashbacks and softening the 4F cascade—fight, flight, freeze, fawn. Think of a buddy tapping your helmet and saying, "Stand down." In practice, a short drill might be five counts in, seven counts out breathing, eyes softened, and a leader's voice set to "sergeant" rather than "therapist." Together, these rituals and synchronized attention form the foundation of community healing, grounding the limbic system and allowing collective resilience.

Relational Practices: Co-Regulation on the Line

Groups that practice synchronous attention — breathing together, following the same guided imagery, keeping a steady cadence — actually co-regulate. This shared rhythmic work is a core mechanic of community healing: when several people lower arousal together, it reduces the punch of emotional flashbacks and calms the 4F cascade: fight, flight, freeze, fawn. Make these practices routine, short, and predictable so they function as collective safety signals rather than forced processing. Short drill: five counts in, seven counts out breathing, eyes soft, leader voice set to "sergeant" not "therapist."

Slow Grounding, Breathing, and Sensory Anchors

Train these like basic combat skills. Slow grounding done together: name five things you can see, four you can touch, three you can hear, two you can smell, one you can taste — spoken slowly, deliberately. Sensory anchors are personal items — a smooth coin, a scent, a patch — used when dissociation or rage starts to climb. For TBI survivors, select anchors that avoid sensory overload; simple always wins.

Honoring Different Backgrounds and Spiritual Traditions

Rituals work when they honor personal histories. Invite participants to offer practices from their own backgrounds — a brief prayer, a song, a quiet gesture — but keep participation voluntary. That lowers the risk of retraumatizing someone and builds mutual trust across ranks and generations.

Sustainable Practice: Caregiver-to-Peer Mentorship

Make support stick by training caregivers and veteran peers as mentors. Mentorship teaches listening skills, how to spot signs of complex secondary PTSD in families, and safe escalation steps. Keep it practical: weekly buddy check-ins, a crisis roster, and oversight from a clinician or chaplain. When care moves from paid staff into peer networks, healing stays in the unit — like passing the radio after a long patrol.

Out in the field, healing works best when it's practiced, drilled, and kept simple. Groups that ritualize safety and train basic co-regulation can turn a chaotic nervous system into a team that knows how to stand down and look after one another.

Cultural Rituals in Relationships

Co-Creating Rituals with Family and Community: A Practical SOP

Think of ritualbuilding like mission planning for homefront ops: clear objectives, predictable timelines, and assigned roles. When a veteran's CPTSD overlaps with childhood trauma, the nervous system is always on high alert. Emotional flashbacks hijack a conversation like an IED stops a convoy—sudden, disorienting, and blocking progress. The antidote is a predictable ritual that signals safety to the brain and cuts the intensity of the 4F responses (fight, flight, freeze, fawn). Start by listing meaningful practices from the family's heritage and personal traditions—meals, songs, prayer, storytelling, or simple physical routines like a prebed hand squeeze. Invite elders and mentors to shape these practices; their presence models steady leadership and repairs relational patterns when old triggers arise. A nightly shared meal with a twominute headsup checkin is lowtech, highimpact: it teaches the brain that this time equals steadiness.

Establishing Shared Heritage Rituals

Start by listing meaningful practices from the family's heritage and personal traditions — meals, songs, prayer, storytelling, or simple physical routines like a pre-bed hand squeeze. Choose ones that are predictable and repeatable so they become reliable safety cues for a nervous system prone to emotional flashbacks. Invite elders and mentors to help shape these practices; their presence models steady leadership and provides relational repair when old patterns show up. A nightly shared meal with a two-minute heads-up check-in is low-tech, high-impact: brains learn that this time equals steadiness, conversations are less likely to be derailed by sudden emotional reactions, and relationships get regular opportunities to rebuild trust.

Predictable Rituals: Why Regularity Wins

Predictability lowers baseline arousal. Set the cadence — same time, same place, same trigger phrase — so nervous systems can trust the cue. For example: "Family check, two minutes." That phrase becomes a safety signal. When a trigger arrives, the ritual acts like a red plastic shield: it won't stop every flashback, but it reduces its force and buys time for regulated responses.

Honoring Ancestral Healing Practices and Integrating Traditions

Mix veteran practices (breath-and-ground drills, buddy checks) with ancestral routines (meditation, prayer, or traditional crafts). Combining traditions strengthens identity and reduces stigma for both the service member and family members facing complex secondary PTSD. Think of it as a hybrid patrol: some tools are old-school, some are modern, all are mission-relevant.

Tactical Steps: Involving Elders, Ritualizing Check-Ins, and Using Structured Pauses

- Convene a planning sit-down with trusted elders/mentors. Gather input; get buy-in.
- Draft a short emotional check-in script: name one feeling, one need, one small action. Time it (90 seconds each).
- Agree a pause protocol for conflicts: "Break/10" means ten minutes for a walk, breath set, or grounding anchor (touch an object, smell a scent). No debate during the break.
- Run the ritual on repeat until it becomes automatic.

Creating Community Rituals for Ongoing Safety

Set regular squad-style meetups: monthly support gatherings, neighborhood buddy checks, or hybrid groups that include therapists and elders. These rituals function as ongoing safety planning and expand the net of consistent care, reducing isolation for families carrying secondary trauma.

Small, steady practices are where recovery lives. Treat them like drills: keep them short, predictable, and backed by someone who can hold the line when the nervous system shorts out. A little routine goes a long way toward making home a secure base again.

Sustaining Growth Through Connection

Sustaining Growth through Connection

You didn't get to this point solo, and you don't recover solo. Recovery is like keeping a squad on patrol: you rely on teammates who call out danger, hand you bandages, and remind you of the rally point when your head fogs. That squad becomes the living map that interrupts emotional flashbacks and blunts 4F responses (fight, flight, freeze, fawn) when old threat patterns flare. Maintain this squad with regular, smallstep checkins—weekly therapist sessions, a daily fiveminute text, or a coffee with a trusted comrade—to keep the path clear.

Building Safe Communities Outside the Family

Combat vets and survivors of childhood trauma both benefit from places that run on predictable rhythms and shared language. Peer groups, veterans' circles, and trauma-aware community spaces offer that predictability. Picture a weekly circle where people start with a short ritual: name, one-sentence state report, two-minute grounding. That rhythm lowers surprise and creates a reality check against the mind's worst loops. Experiential learning—sharing, role-play, deliberate practice of calming drills—makes coping skills stick the way repetitive field training does.

Practicing Consistent, Small-Step Routines of Regular Contact

Regular contact is the squad's communication system; it reinforces the brain's "this is safe" wiring. Set a predictable cadence—weekly therapist sessions, daily checkin texts, or a threetimesaweek signal—to keep it simple. The goal is reliability, not perfection. These microroutines chip away at hypervigilance and slow down automatic 4F reactions.

Setting Boundaries that Support Mutual Care

Clear limits protect safety while allowing honest vulnerability. Teach a simple script to families: "When you raise your voice, I step away for 20 minutes. I'll come back and say, 'Ready to talk.'" Use code words for breaks and establish who handles what—emotional first responder vs. logistic support. Boundaries should be treated like SOPs: written, practiced, and reviewed.

Co-Regulation Strategies

Co-regulation is the buddy system for the nervous system. Two people doing rhythmic breathing, a slow walk, or paired exercises can downshift arousal faster than going it alone. Tactical drills: box breathing together for five cycles, hand on shoulder while counting seconds, or a ten-minute paced walk. For TBI and battle-fatigue cases, prefer low-impact, predictable activities and avoid overstimulating environments.

Honoring Veteran and Childhood Trauma Expertise

Accept that trauma shows up differently for military trauma, childhood abuse, or both. Communities and clinicians who specialize in veteran care and childhood trauma bring essential practical knowledge—PTSD tools that account for blast injury, TBI cognitive changes, or attachment wounds from early life. Seek out peer specialists, trauma-informed therapists, and groups that explicitly name those overlaps.

Tip checklist for squads at home:

- Set one predictable contact rhythm (daily text or weekly meet).
- Create a two-line break script for conflicts and practice it once a week.
- Pick two co-regulation drills to use when high arousal hits.
- Find at least one peer group or clinician who knows both combat and childhood trauma.

Small, steady connections are a form of tactical maintenance: they keep the system functioning and reduce the number of nighttime alarms that used to shove you into old survival patterns.

Meaning, Identity, and Legacy

The impact of trauma can break a life into many pieces, making a coherent story feel impossible. Yet, finding a way to understand and integrate these parts is central to healing. This section examines how we construct a unified self-story, one that connects past experiences to present identity and future purpose. It considers how to acknowledge trauma's lasting mark, yet move past its definition, building new meaning through genuine connections, a redefined sense of self, and service to others.

We will consider the important distinction between internal forgiveness and boundary-setting release, prioritizing safety for true recovery. The path also covers breaking intergenerational patterns through conscious awareness and clear communication within families. Finally, we examine how intentional practices, community ties, and a focus on lasting contributions build strength and hope for coming generations. This discussion offers direct ways to rebuild and reinforce a life, not just restoring it, but making it stronger than before.

Meaning-Making After Trauma

Meaning-Making: Reframing Trauma into a Coherent Self-Story

The first time I mistook a thunderclap for an enemy patrol, I laughed at myself in the dark and then couldn't tell if I was laughing or crying. That splitsecond mix of old wiring and new danger is the perfect hook for the work that follows: you are asked to take the fractured pieces of your life and weave them into a single, clear selfstory— one that shows how the past links to who you are now and what you do each day. CPTSD is defined as trauma that rewired early development, so defenses show up in adult life— in how you feel physically, how you handle stress, and how you connect with others. This definition will serve as the standard reference for all future mentions. An emotional flashback is not a visual replay; it's a sudden drop into the felt experience of earlier trauma—the ache, the shame, the terror— without full narrative context. When that happens, your body switches into a 4F mode and the present becomes old danger. Understanding that your nervous system is doing what it thinks kept you alive turns symptoms from personal failure into a malfunctioning circuit that can be rewired. By telling that single story, you give the nervous system a new map, helping to rewire those circuits.

Acknowledging Trauma's Impact

Step one is simple to say and hard to do: admit what happened and how it changed you. That means naming shifts in thinking, mood, and behavior without shame. In a squadroom or a therapist's office, the safest moves are honest ones. When veterans place their experiences into words in a non-judgmental setting, emotions get validated and the brain can start stitching fragmented memories together instead of shoving them into a locked drawer.

Good treatment. Grounding Therapy in Personal Experience and Present Functioning—sleep, work, and family roles.

Good treatment is not theoretical; it meets the person where they stand now. That means therapy that focuses on current functioning — sleep, work, family roles — and uses the veteran's own stories as material. Mindfulness-based practices help many with PTSD by calming hyperarousal and giving tools for when the brain flips into one of the 4F responses: fight, flight, freeze, or fawn. Traumatic brain injury adds another layer: memory gaps, slowed thinking, and irritability need practical drills and pacing, not platitudes.

Neurology in Plain Clothes: Emotional Flashbacks and the 4Fs

Building Meaning through Bonds and Belonging

Meaning grows through caregiving, trust, and steady ties. Unit cohesion and trusted family members provide the safety needed to rebuild identity. That's why treatment must include families: teaching them how to respond to flashbacks, set boundaries, and practice co-regulation.

Identity Shifts and Renegotiating Values

Trauma often forces a re-evaluation of values and roles. A soldier may no longer find meaning in the same missions; a parent might switch priorities. This is an opportunity to realign actions with what matters now. Practical steps: map pre- and post-trauma values, try new roles on a trial basis, and keep a log of small wins.

Legacy and Forward-Looking Purpose

Meaning-making can finish with service and reflection — mentoring other vets, volunteering, or building a family mission that includes resilience. Turning hard-earned survival into purpose creates a forward-looking life not defined by past wounds but informed by them.

Tactical actions to try today:

- Grounding: 5-4-3-2-1 sensory check when alarms ring.
- Breath work: 4second inhale, 6second exhale, three times before deciding.
- Trigger map: list places, smells, sounds that set off flashbacks and rank responses.
- Family brief: 10-minute daily check-in with one rule — no problem solving, only listening.

Those small, serviceable tools are how meaning gets built: one honest report, one regulated breath, one steady hand helping another across the line.

Forgiveness vs Release: What It Means

Forgiveness versus Release: what it means.

Think of forgiveness as internal maintenance and release as perimeter security. Both matter, but they operate on different layers of your nervous system and daily life. For combat veterans and survivors of childhood trauma, mixing these up can leave you either unsafe or carrying unnecessary emotional weight.

Forgiveness: the internal repair

Forgiveness happens inside your brain. It's a slow rewiring: the amygdala's alarm tone quiets while the prefrontal cortex relearns that the past threat isn't always present. This doesn't erase the event or excuse the perpetrator. Instead, it reduces the lingering charge—less adrenaline, fewer wakeful nights, fewer emotional flashbacks. To quiet the amygdala and rewire your brain, try:

- Name the emotion out loud: "I feel furious about X." Labeling recruits the cortex and reduces limbic intensity.
- Use brief cognitive reframes that are realistic, not Pollyanna: "They were wrong. I was harmed. I can refuse to carry that anger forever."
- Daily micro-practices: two minutes of paced breathing, then a sentence of self-compassion like a drill sergeant who's been taught kindness: "I did what I could with what I had."

Release: the tactical withdrawal

Tactical withdrawal is a safetyfocused strategy that limits exposure to triggers—such as smells, tones of voice, or postures—by setting clear boundaries, ceasing contact, and taking legal steps if needed. It gives you the room to stabilize while maintaining control. Field orders to implement it include:

- Use brief, unemotional scripted lines: "I'm not available for that conversation right now."

- Set physical and emotional perimeters.
- Remove or distance yourself from known triggers.
- Document any incidents and follow legal procedures if necessary.
- Scripted lines: "I'm not available for that conversation right now." Short, unemotional, repeatable.

You can forgive internally and still enforce a hard release externally. Forgiveness can reduce your internal suffering while release protects you from further harm and helps restore agency. For many with childhood-origin CPTSD, the brain's 4F responses — fight, flight, freeze, fawn — are over-primed by repeated early threats and later amplified by combat trauma. Release stops new threats; forgiveness lowers baseline arousal.

Family effects: complex secondary PTSD

Loved ones can get worn out by repeated sharing of trauma or by hypervigilant behaviors. Families need their own orders: set times for trauma talk, identify when to call a therapist, and use deescalation scripts. Caregivers should get training in boundaries and selfcare; Complex secondary PTSD is real and treatable with the same practical measures.

A final piece of fieldcraft: pair a physical anchor with mental practice. A two-count inhale/exhale plus a phrase — "I'm safe now" — gives the vagus nerve a cue to downshift. Tight boundaries plus steady inner work are the most reliable combo for regaining control and rebuilding identity after repeated wounds.

Redefining Identity Beyond Scars

Redefining Identity After Scars

If the last section was about letting go and protecting your perimeter, this one is about who you are when the dust settles. Combat, battle fatigue, TBI — and for many, childhood trauma — can become the headline of a person's life file. That headline can be changed, not erased. Think of it like a combat veteran who wakes up with a prosthetic and the same bad sense of humor: the wound is real, the scar is real, but it isn't the whole person.

The ongoing process of identity

Identity shifts slowly and in fits and starts. Neurobiology explains part of this: trauma strengthens fast, limbic-driven responses while weakening the prefrontal systems that hold long-term goals and values. Over time, with practice and exposure to new roles, those prefrontal circuits regain influence. Practically, that means identity can reorient — not instant, but possible. Small experiments count: one new project, one class, one mentorship role at a time.

Shifting focus from injury to an evolving self

This is tactical work. Start with a short inventory: skills, roles, relationships you value. Write them down. A former platoon medic still knows triage under fire; that skill maps to civilian emergency care. Leadership doesn't disappear because someone has a TBI; it just looks different — coaching, advocacy, training. Set micro-goals that put those competencies into real tasks: volunteer at the VA clinic, enroll in a certification, lead a peer-support group. These are low-risk drills that rewire identity.

Embracing valued roles

Adopt roles that carry meaning. Being a parent, partner, mentor, artist, or community leader provides multiple identity anchors so one survival story doesn't monopolize the whole file. Humor helps: one Marine I knew traded his war stories for woodworking tips and found people listened more to the furniture than the PTSD monologues. Families can help by highlighting strengths, not only symptoms.

Families and complex secondary PTSD

Emotional flashbacks are not memory playback; they're limbic hijacks — the amygdala lights up, the hippocampus misplaces context, and the prefrontal cortex is offline. The body goes into one of the 4Fs: fight, flight, freeze, or fawn. Tactical counters: quick grounding (5-4-3-2-1 senses), controlled breathing (box breaths for 60–90 seconds), orientation statements (I am safe, I am in my house, it is 2025), and a pre-packed safe plan (who to call, where to go). Repeated practice trains the prefrontal cortex to interrupt hijacks faster.

Partners and children can develop symptoms from living with a veteran's trauma activation—called complex secondary PTSD. Signs include hypervigilance at home, chronic guilt, emotional numbing, and peoplepleasing to avoid triggers. Tactical family moves: set clear boundaries, schedule checkins, provide psychoeducation on flashbacks and 4F reactions, and establish shared routines that restore predictability. Family therapy and peersupport groups help distribute the burden.

Trauma informs growth without defining the self

Trauma is part of the record, not the only file. Skills, relationships, and purpose persist — often ready to be redirected. As Jen Satterly notes about complex secondary PTSD, with the right support and strategies, healing and a renewed sense of purpose are possible. Practical focus, steady habits, and honest family communication create the conditions for an identity that carries scars but is stronger for what it learned.

Intergenerational Trauma: Breaking the Cycle

Conscious Awareness: The First Step to Breaking Intergenerational Trauma

When you finally notice the pattern — the anger that flares for no apparent reason, the habit of shutting down at family dinners, the kid who flinches when you raise your voice — that moment is like the first time you spot an IED marker from thirty meters out: slow your pace, call it in, change the route. That noticing is conscious awareness, and it's the operational order that starts breaking intergenerational trauma.

Understanding How Trauma Passes Through Families

Trauma passes through families via three intertwined routes: genes, the household environment, and learned behavior. Epigenetic changes can tweak stressresponse genes, so children inherit a system that's primed for alarm. When that genetic predisposition is coupled with a home that shuts down emotions or turns conflict into a daily briefing, the biology is reinforced into neural patterns—stronger synaptic pathways for anxiety and hypervigilance. Veterans who grew up with childhood CPTSD and later face combat trauma experience the same loop: the inherited stress circuitry, the learned coping strategies, and the chaotic environment of war all converge. This explains why combatrelated PTSD, battle fatigue, and childhood CPTSD often look similar: each can trigger emotional flashbacks—those sudden relivings of feeling rather than facts—and a 4F stress response (fight, flight, freeze, fawn) that hijacks reason.

If you're a veteran with childhood CPTSD overlapping combat trauma, emotional flashbacks can feel like being back on patrol without a map—you're reacting to a felt threat that isn't present. Naming the response—"This is an emotional flashback; I'm in 4F mode"—gives you a tactical advantage.

Breaking the Cycle Begins with Parent Self-Care and Self-Regulation

You can't be an effective squad leader at home if you're running on empty. Prioritize sleep, basic movement, and short, daily practices: box breathing for 60 seconds, three grounding senses (name 5 things you see, 4 you can touch, 3 you hear), and a five-minute check-in where you name one feeling out loud. Those simple actions are training drills in self-regulation.

Model accountability: apologize when you overreact, explain what triggered you, and show the repair. Kids learn emotion management by watching how adults handle stress — think of it as live-fire training for empathy.

Trauma-Informed Parenting, Routines, and Repairing Attachment

Trauma-informed parenting means doing more than not hitting the kid. It's anticipating triggers, offering choices, using calm language, and avoiding shaming. Establish routines that act like secure anchor points: consistent bedtime, shared meals, and a predictable weekly "sitrep" where everyone names highs and lows. Repairs to attachment are small and steady — show up, follow through, be predictable. That predictability rewires trust.

Age-Appropriate Conversations and Historical Context Without Blame

Tell the truth in a way your kid can handle. Explain that people respond differently to scary or hard things, and that some reactions come from family history, not their fault. When you discuss the past, focus on facts and understanding, not accusation. Naming patterns and context helps kids make choices instead of inheriting scripts.

Narratives, Community, and Translating Neuroscience into Practical Boundaries

Sharing stories — written, spoken, or through art — honors what happened while handing people tools to make different decisions. Veteran networks and community groups provide practical support and reduce isolation; hearing another veteran say, "I've been there" is like getting a supply drop. Learn basic neuroscience: stress rewires pathways, but neuroplasticity lets therapy and practice form new routes. Therapies such as cognitive approaches, EMDR, and somatic work can reshape stress responses over time.

Tactical Checklist (short)

- Notice the pattern; name the flashback or 4F state.
- Start small: 60-second breath, 3-grounding senses, nightly routine.
- Get help: therapy and peer groups from veteran networks.
- Model regulation: apologize, explain triggers, repair.
- Share age-appropriate history without blame; keep routines reliable.

Conscious awareness isn't sentimental. It's reconnaissance. Once you see the pattern, you can plan, train, and clear the path for the next generation to move forward.

Cultural and Spiritual Perspectives

Humility Toward Different Backgrounds: why it matters in trauma work

Think of a debrief where everyone at the table has different service records, hometowns, and faiths. Healing gets clumsy when we assume our way of understanding is the only valid one. Showing humility toward someone's background isn't soft. It's a tactical choice that lowers threat signals and opens a path to connection.

When Insensitivity Hurts

A quick way to shut down a fellow veteran (or a spouse, child, or buddy) is to swap their report for your own. "That happened to me" can feel like a grenade tossed into someone else's memory, redirecting attention and implying their experience is no longer unique. For people carrying trauma, that redirection often spikes shame and isolation, which feed the same arousal systems we're trying to calm. When childhood harm overlaps with combat stress, symptoms pile up and even small missteps in conversation can trigger an emotional flashback, where the mind replays old states of helplessness instead of the current facts. These negative impacts arise partly because such remarks ignore the veteran's meaning systems—faith, heritage, storytelling, rituals—that serve as anchors. Respecting and engaging those anchors can help break the cycle of shame and isolation.

Respecting Meaning Systems: faith, rituals, and storytelling

Beliefs and practices tied to heritage and faith frequently act as anchors, offering a sense of continuity and belonging. Ceremonies, shared meals, and storytelling can reframe painful episodes and help veterans reconcile actions taken under orders with who they want to be now. A simple squadlevel storytelling night—no judgment, only witness—can shift shame into a sense of joined survival. Rituals also help regulate arousal: slow breathing, repeated prayers, or grounding phrases send predictable signals to the nervous system, reducing 4F reactions (fight, flight, freeze, fawn). By actively honoring these cultural solutions, we counter the negative impact of insensitive remarks and create a supportive environment that nurtures healing and resilience.

Community Belonging as a Stabilizer

Support networks—church groups, unit reunions, veteran peer groups, neighborhood families—offer safety that lets people move past survival mode. When a person senses acceptance, neural circuits tied to threat quiet down and processing can begin. That's when therapy and practical skills make the biggest gains.

Practical Actions for Soldiers and Families

- Listen more than you speak. Let the other person lay out their full report before you offer an observation.
- Ask curious questions: "What helps you when that memory comes up?" not "Why are you like this?"
- Avoid assumptions about needs or beliefs; ask and check.
- Expose yourself to people from different backgrounds and traditions—attend a service, a dinner, a storytelling night—to widen the toolbox of coping practices.

Quick field check for emotional flashbacks

- Pause. Put one hand on your chest and one on your thigh—grounding.
- Name the state: "I'm noticing fight/flight/freeze/fawn."
- Breathe 4–4–6 (inhale 4, hold 4, exhale 6) while listing three things you can see in the room.
- Ask: "What would help me feel safe right now?" If you're the partner, offer options rather than fixes.

Complex secondary PTSD requires a holistic approach that addresses the whole person – mind, body, and spirit. Humility toward someone's background and beliefs isn't optional; it's a practical method to lower re-traumatization and build the trust that real healing needs.

Rituals and Traditions for Healing

Rituals: The Anchors of Safety and Meaning in Healing

Rituals act like lowthreat checklists for the nervous system. When sudden emotional flashbacks of shame, fear, or rage bypass the thinking brain, a predictable rhythm can calm the alarm circuits, feeding the brain a small, reliable sequence it can trust and reducing fightflightfreezefawn spikes so the frontal lobes can reengage. To create such a ritual, keep it simple: pick a clear cue (e.g., the kettle boils, the belt clips, the front door closes), perform a brief action (five deep breaths with a hand on the sternum, a twominute journal line, a tenminute steady walk), then give yourself a small reward (a sip of tea, a voicemail to a buddy, a pause to look out the window). For veterans with TBI, shorten actions and use tactile cues, timers, or largeprint checklists. The goal is reliability, not heroics.

Crafting Daily Rituals

Practical example: Morning "pre-brief" ritual

- Cue: alarm at same time
- Action: three diaphragmatic breaths, write one sentence about intention, stand and stretch
- Reward: one cup of coffee while listening to a favorite song

The Power of Memorial Traditions

Rituals do heavy lifting when it comes to processing loss and piecing together identity. Simple acts—lighting a candle, reading a name aloud, or keeping a box of letters—create a controlled space for grief and pride to be admitted. For families affected by secondary trauma, holding a short monthly story-sharing time lets the person with PTSD and their kin place events into a living narrative, not a chaotic loop of flashbacks. Keep memorials manageable: set a time limit, assign a moderator (could be a trusted friend or therapist), and allow people to pass when it's too much.

The Importance of Support

Rituals practiced alone can work, but shared rituals add safety. Choose companions who are vetted—therapist, support-group peer, or a trusted friend who understands triggers and boundaries. These allies can help regulate arousal in the moment (grounding cues, soft voice, guided breathing) and give accountability to keep the ritual consistent.

Adapting Rituals for Different Backgrounds

A healing ritual should fit personal history and beliefs. Swap elements so they match what feels meaningful: a walk for someone who mistrusts indoor silence, a brief prayer or a mindful breath for those with spiritual leanings, or a tactile object for someone with TBI. Universal patterns—predictable order, sensory cues, short duration—are what support the nervous system. That makes rituals flexible tools for veterans, their families, and anyone carrying complex trauma into adulthood.

Tactical takeaway: pick one micro-ritual, standardize the cue-action-reward, invite one vetted person to join once a week, and adjust for cognitive or physical limits. Small, consistent patterns win fights with the brain's alarm system more often than grand gestures.

Legacy Projects: Impact on Future Generations

Legacy Projects: Passing On Tools, Stories, and Calm

If rituals are the daily rations for the nervous system, legacy projects are the field manuals you hand down to the next squad — family, kids, mentors. These projects channel lived experience into practical skills, memory work, and safety cues that help break cycles of childhood trauma and service-related stress that feed Complex PTSD (CPTSD).

Sharing Adaptive Coping Strategies

A legacy project doesn't have to be glossy. A recorded fiveminute talk from a veteran explaining a breathing drill, a notebook of grounding techniques, or a simple card with "what to do when panic hits" can cut future suffering. By deliberately modeling mindfulness, paced breathing, or grounding steps and handing those tools to children, veterans create a purposeful transmission of resilience. They pass more than tips; they pass an actionable reflex for stress that beats rumination and emotional flashbacks — those sudden, overwhelming waves of feeling that hijack the present. In doing so, they embed wisdom that future generations can retrieve whenever the stress surge appears.

Modeling Resilience on Purpose

Modeling resilience on purpose means deliberately sharing coping tools and habits with younger generations, turning everyday interactions into lessons that future veterans will draw upon. When elders step forward, offering breathing drills or grounding strategies, they weave a living legacy that transcends time, ensuring that the wisdom of lived experience is not lost but becomes an actionable resource for the next generation.

Kids watch how adults handle pressure. If a parent describes how they used a mantra or a movement break after a bad memory, kids see resilience in action. Try a short family exercise: each member names one calming strategy and practices it together for a week. Expect grumbles — that's normal — but over time those rehearsals become go-to responses during 4F activation (fight, flight, freeze, fawn). Here the mentor role matters: steady, calm presence anchors the system.

Transmitting Values and Safety Cues

Legacy projects can encode safety cues — a phrase, a hand signal, a ritualized pause — that signal safety to a nervous system primed for danger. Record stories that highlight values like honesty, protection, and help-seeking. Attach a simple protocol to each story: when you feel X, do Y. These consistent templates guide behavior under stress and make emotional regulation less mysterious.

Cutting Future CPTSD Risk

When children receive clear templates for emotional regulation, labeling feelings, and requesting support, their brains build better stress responses. Teach emotion naming, a two-breath grounding, and a script for asking an adult for help. These small practices change neuronal wiring over time, lowering the odds that dysregulated stress will calcify into chronic CPTSD.

Honoring Lived Experience While Building Hope

Legacy projects let veterans honor difficult memories without getting stuck. Record interviews, scrapbooks, or short letters that acknowledge harm, state what was learned, and offer a plan for moving forward. That framing helps transform guilt and shame into a narrative of care and duty toward future generations.

Practical Steps for Getting Started

• Pick a medium (voice, video, notebook). • Identify one coping tactic to teach. • Create a safety cue and rehearse it. • Involve a trusted therapist or ally when stories touch deep triggers. • Practice with kids and mentors until it feels natural.

Complex secondary PTSD hits families when trauma spills over. Legacy projects act as a countermeasure: structured transmission of coping skills, steady mentoring during 4F spikes, and clear safety cues create intergenerational muscle memory for survival that does not cost emotional health.

Hope, Vision, and Future Orientation

If legacy projects set a marker on the map, hope is the compass that points you toward useful ground—something you can follow when symptoms fog up the GPS. Hope here is not a Hallmark poster; it's a practical, decisionmaking tool that helps you pick which battles to fight and which to stand down from. It is the future orientation that reshapes identity, guiding you to the places where you can build resilience and growth.

Future Orientation Reshapes Identity. When you use hope as a compass, you turn an abstract future orientation into a concrete identity change, choosing the battles that build the self you want to become.

When service members and caregivers focus on a tomorrow, the brain starts recruiting planning circuitry in the prefrontal cortex instead of defaulting to the amygdala's threat alarms. Retired Colonel Paul D. Walker put it plainly: "A clear sense of purpose and meaning can help individuals overcome even the most daunting challenges." In practical terms, set a mission: small, concrete, measurable objectives that point at who you want to be next month, next year. Treat these like patrol orders—short, repeatable, debriefable.

Tactics to Build a Future-Focused Self

- Choose one meaningful goal and break it into micro-steps. Want to run with your kid? Start with a 10-minute walk three times this week. Like clearing a jammed rifle, micro-actions clear psychological clutter.

- Use a written plan: timelines, contingencies, and simple metrics. Check it each morning as an operational brief.

- Assign accountability: a battle buddy, spouse, therapist, or mentor who receives progress updates and offers course corrections.

Identity Grows When the Past Is Integrated

Healing doesn't mean erasing the past. It means weaving it into a coherent narrative so it stops blowing up your present. Reframing is a combat technique—call it cognitive reconnaissance—where you identify what you learned, what you lost, and what you choose to carry forward.

How Narrative Coherence Lowers Flashback Frequency

A stable life story reduces surprise assaults from emotional flashbacks. When your brain recognizes a clear timeline (what happened, how you coped, what you plan to do), the 4F responses—fight, flight, freeze, fawn—lose their immediate trigger. Practically: rehearse your story out loud in safe settings; write short entries that connect past, present, future; and use "if-then" scripts for 4F activation (if my heart spikes, then 5 deep breaths and a 2-minute grounding drill).

Meaningful Goals for Families and Secondary CPTSD

Complex secondary PTSD—what family members pick up—can be tackled with shared objectives. Create family missions: a weekly dinner with no tactical talk, a joint legacy project, or mutual fitness goals. These provide structure amid 4F chaos and honor childhood resilience while building a tomorrow that holds everyone accountable and hopeful.

Seeing tomorrow reduces the grip of yesterday. For veterans, caregivers, and kids, practical hope puts work boots on optimism and turns vague wishing into operational change.

Synthesis and Personal Healing Charter

Moving beyond trauma's grip to truly construct a unified selfstory requires a direct approach. It means translating the science of recovery into your own experience, giving voice to emotional flashbacks, and mapping the 4F responses as they appear in your body. This segment provides the tactical framework to command your healing: from crafting a personal charter for daily self-work and establishing a rhythm of check-ins, to building strong support networks and preparing for crisis. Here, you will discover how to identify turning points, solidify a future identity rooted in values, and ensure your story becomes one of lasting purpose and resilience.

Integrating Learnings into a Personal Narrative

Framing Learning as a Personal Narrative

Think of your life story like an after-action report: you log what happened, what the gear did, and how you reacted. That report is yours to write. Turn clinical labels into sentences that make sense to you. Instead of letting textbook phrases float above you like a drone, drop them into your personal language so they sit where your memories live.

Naming Emotional Flashbacks

Start by mapping your triggers. Write down the sensory cue – sound, smell, place, or comment – that sparks a reaction, and list next to each cue the bodily signs you notice: heart racing, shallow breathing, cold hands, clenched stomach, tunnel vision. When you encounter that cue, pause and announce to yourself or a teammate: "This is an emotional flashback. I'm feeling anxious and small." The verbal label separates past from present, reclaims authority, and turns the secret into a visible, manageable signal. Practice the full sequence—cue → body signs → verbal label—so it becomes automatic under pressure, like a quick drill before a highstakes task.

Describing Triggers and Bodily Sensations

Connecting the 4F Responses to Body Memory

Your body keeps a file on how it used to survive. Fight, flight, freeze, and fawn—these are stored in muscle tension, breath pattern, and posture. A raised jaw and clenched fists suggest fight. A hollow chest and slowed voice suggest freeze. By naming these internal signals in everyday language ("I feel tight in my jaw, my breath is shallow, and my voice is slow"), you make the 4F responses visible to yourself and to others. Recognizing the signature gives you a counterorder: short tactical actions to interrupt the motor program. Try putting a hand on your sternum, taking a fourcount exhale, and pushing your feet into the ground. These physical interventions break the habitual response long enough to choose a different move, turning invisible body memory into a concrete, accessible tool.

Making CPTSD Concepts Accessible

Translating the 4F body language into everyday words helps people understand their own trauma responses. When you notice a clenched jaw, a hollow chest, or a slowed voice, describe it as "I'm feeling on edge" or "I'm holding my breath." This simple language bridges the gap between the internal physical reactions and an external, understandable narrative. By connecting body memory to clear, relatable terms, you empower both yourself and others to recognize, label, and respond to CPTSD symptoms in a more accessible way.

Describe CPTSD in straight terms: it's trauma that rewired early development so defenses show up in adult life—how you feel physically, how you handle stress, and how you connect with others. That phrase gives families language to talk about what's happening without medical jargon. Use plain metaphors: old alarms still ring in a new house. When families learn the alarm tones, they stop reacting like the house is burning and start using the panel to turn the siren off.

Identifying Turning Points

Mark moments when you did something different — small choices count: walking out of an argument instead of replaying it, asking for help, setting a boundary. Write these in your report as "turning points." They are proof you can break patterns. Circle them. Revisit them when the old programming gets loud.

Describing a Future Identity

Draft a one-paragraph mission statement for the person you want to be: values, daily habits, and how you show up with others. Make it specific and actionable: "I will pause for breath before replying; I will spend twenty minutes outside three times a week; I will check in with my partner after hard days." Treat that paragraph as a standing order and rehearse it, like practicing formation drills. That projection isn't fantasy — it's a plan of action to teach your body and those around you how to operate in this next chapter.

Crafting a Healing Charter or Pledge

Picture the ship again: rough seas, rain in your face, but you have a chart taped to the binnacle that lists not coordinates, but commitments. That chart is your Healing Charter — a compact, living order set you can read on the way to chow or when sirens of the past start wailing.

What a Healing Charter looks like

Healing Charter Framework

A Healing Charter is a onesentence mission that guides how you treat yourself when symptoms flare, followed by core values, daily practices, and clear boundaries.

Mission: I will choose safety and steady breathing before judgment.

Core values (≤5):

- Safety first
- Compassion for self
- Mindful presence
- Resilience without blame
- Connection to supportive allies

Daily practices:

- 10minute grounding exercise
- 20minute walk or movement
- One checkin with a trusted buddy

Boundaries: define donotcross lines for people, places, and tasks that trigger hyperactivation.

Use this framework to create your personal charter, adapting each component to fit your unique needs and goals.

Values that serve safety, not self-blame

Shift language in your charter from “I must fix this” to “I will keep myself safe.” That wording matters neurologically: when the brain hears threat, the 4F system (fight, flight, freeze, fawn) kicks the motor drives and chemistry into overdrive. If your values call for safety, your choices become tools to down-regulate that circuitry rather than punish it.

Boundaries as nervous-system armor

Treat boundaries like issued kit. Practical examples:

- Verbal boundary script: “I can do X, but not Y today.” Short, repeated, firm.
- Time boundary: block two daily windows for low-stimulus recovery.

Boundaries as nervous-system armor

Treat boundaries like issued kit. Practical examples:

- Verbal boundary script: “I can do X, but not Y today.” Short, repeated, firm.
- Time boundary: block two daily windows for low-stimulus recovery.
- Physical boundary: a seat or room designated for decompression.

Jen Satterly has emphasized boundary work in families with complex secondary PTSD; these are not selfish measures — they are physiological stabilizers.

Daily grounding and mindfulness drills (field-tested)

Make these non-negotiable drills:

Track progress tactically by recording the duration and intensity of each 54321 grounding session. Note any shifts in emotional state and adjust the number of rounds or senses used accordingly.

Use box breathing (4444 counts, three rounds) before decisionmaking. Log breathing depth, heart rate, and perceived safety, and use the data to finetune the count or add extra rounds for optimal calm.

- "Contact check": one text to a designated comrade saying, "I'm checked in," to break isolation.

Veteran's perspective: memory, purpose, and service continuity

For many who served, memory integration is tied to service identity. Use the charter to connect hard memories to ongoing purpose — small acts of service, mentoring younger vets, or compiling a memory book — so recollection has context and function rather than only pain.

Planning for repair-focused forgiveness

Forgiveness here is an operational plan, not a sentiment. Steps:

- Map the wound: name the trigger and the 4F reaction.
- Identify the unmet inner-child need (safety, comfort, hearing).
- Create a repair action (therapy session, apology letter, ritual).
- Repeat the action until the nervous system updates the memory's emotional charge.

A Healing Charter is practical, brief, and revisable. Treat it like any field SOP: test it, after-action it, and tweak until it keeps you steady when the weather turns foul.

Quarterly Check-Ins and Reassessment

Quarterly Healing Checkins: A CombatReady AAR for Your Recovery.

Treat a quarterly healing check-in like an After Action Review for your brain and body — except this time the mission is to keep you upright, asleep, and less likely to react like a startled private on night watch. Run these reviews every three months. They create a steady cadence that helps you pick up trends, celebrate hardwon gains, and retool tactics before stress spikes turn into a fullblown relapse.

Why regular reassessment matters

The brain's threat system doesn't file a oneoff report; it runs on patterns. Emotional flashbacks and 4F activations (fight, flight, freeze, fawn) show up in predictable ways when we track them, so regular reassessment is essential. A quarterly AfterAction Review (AAR) gives you the data to spot those patterns—when hyperarousal climbs, when sleep collapses, or which people or situations trigger a fawn response—so you can correct course with concrete steps rather than guesswork.

Quarterly checkin checklist:

- Collect data: sleep logs, number of emotional flashbacks, instances of 4F responses, medication adherence, therapy sessions attended, and physical training days.
- Score intensity: Use simple 0–10 scales for arousal and distress.
- Identify trends: Look for spikes in arousal, drops in sleep quality, or frequent fawn triggers.
- Develop corrective actions: Based on the trends, set specific, actionable steps (e.g., adjust sleep routine, modify therapy focus, or introduce new coping strategies).
- Document and review: Record your observations and plan next steps; repeat this cycle every quarter to maintain awareness and progress.

Checklist for a requarterly check-in

- Collect the data: sleep logs, number of emotional flashbacks, instances of 4F responses, meds adherence, therapy sessions attended, and physical training days. Use simple scales (0–10) for arousal and distress. For each record note frequency and context (who/what/where) and any coping used. At your quarterly review, chart these measures to spot patterns and convert them into 2–3 specific actions to implement and reassess at the next check-in.

- After Action Review: What went well? What didn't? What will we start, stop, and keep? Keep answers short and specific.

- Update the safety plan: revise boundaries, contacts for crisis, and grounding tools.

- Set measurable objectives for the next three months: nights of 7+ hours sleep, two grounding practices each week, one exposure task with therapist, three family debriefs.

Tracking progress the tactical way

Log triggers and successful responses. For each emotional flashback, note the stimulus, your 4F response, the grounding tool used, and how long it took to downshift. Over four quarters you'll see cycles — times of higher risk you can prepare for, and coping techniques that actually work.

Refining safety and grounding

Use the check-in to tweak sleep hygiene, exercise plans, and breathing drills. Try:

- Box breathing or tactical breathing: 4-4-4 cycles during early activation.

- A 5-4-3-2-1 sensory sweep when an emotional flashback hits.

- Consistent wake and sleep times with a wind-down ritual (no screens, low light).

If hyperarousal remains high, increase cardio or resistance training and consult your clinician about medication or sleep-focused therapy.

Revisiting identity, meaning, and legacy goals

Every quarter take ten minutes to check your sense of purpose. Ask: which roles matter most (veteran, parent, teammate)? What values guide decisions now? Use this time to tweak a personal mission statement and pick one project that honors service — mentoring a younger vet, volunteering, or a memory book. That project becomes a living way to integrate trauma memories into ongoing service.

Including families and addressing Complex secondary PTSD

Invite trusted family or partners to a scaled-down AAR. Let them report observations, list stress points, and propose support actions. Family members with secondary CPTSD benefit from their own quarterly check-ins; treat their needs with the same tactical planning.

Run these check-ins like you ran convoy briefings: concise, honest, and with clear objectives for the next leg. Small, regular adjustments win fights against chronic stress more reliably than huge, infrequent interventions.

Resilience Narratives: Sharing Your Story

The Power of Resilience Narratives: Healing Through Storytelling

Think of sharing your story like an AAR (after-action review). Done well, it sharpens unit cohesion and prevents repeat mistakes. Done poorly, it can spark old alarms and leave you exposed. For vets carrying childhood wounds layered under combat stress or TBI, telling stories can validate, reframe, and build connection — but only with the right precautions.

Establishing Safety Boundaries

Before you start speaking, establish a safe perimeter: pick a time, place, and listener that feel secure. Use a prearranged signal—a simple phrase or hand gesture—so you can pause or stop if internal reactions flare. Keep your initial disclosures short and structured: one anchor event, one feeling, one request (for empathy, feedback, or silence). Tell your listener what you need from them upfront. This commandandcontrol framework protects you from feeling overwhelmed and gives you a clear cue to notice the 4F reactions (fight, flight, freeze, fawn) that may surface during storytelling.

Understanding How 4F Reactions Show Up During Storytelling

During storytelling, the body can still react as if under fire—fight, flight, freeze, and fawn can surface midsentence—anger flares, you bolt, words lock up, or you downplay to keep the peace. These are automatic responses, not moral failures. The safety perimeter you set before you speak—choosing a secure time, place, and listener, and having a prearranged pause signal—acts as a first line of defense. Keep a grounding checklist nearby—breatheboxing, feet flat on the floor, a bottle of cold water—and use it the moment you sense an old pattern returning. That reduces the chance an emotional flashback hijacks the debrief.

Anchor Moments: Small Wins That Mark Progress

Anchor moments are the checkpoints you jot down after a telling: "Told my partner about the night in the FOB and didn't dissociate," or "Spoke for five minutes without the room going black." Record these. They are field evidence that your capacity to handle exposure is increasing. Share them with your therapist or story partner so the gains register outside your head.

Crafting a CPTSD-Informed Narrative

Keep authenticity, not drama, as your aim. Start with the facts that matter to you, avoid graphic replay unless you and your listener have agreed, and include what you learned or how you survived that way. Pace disclosures like a mission plan: recon first, limited contact, then deeper work when support is confirmed. Anchor moments are the checkpoints you jot down after a telling: 'Told my partner about the night in the FOB and didn't dissociate,' or 'Spoke for five minutes without the room going black.' Record these.

The Role of Story Partners and Choosing Listeners

Pick people who can hold fire — therapists, vetted battle buddies, or family members coached in listening skills. A good listener validates what happened without fixing it, asks clarifying questions, and follows your lead on next steps. Avoid audiences who push for quick solutions, lecture, or compare scars. For family members at risk of complex secondary PTSD, consider joint sessions where a clinician moderates and provides coping tools.

Practical Checklist Before You Tell

- Choose one objective for the session (validation, problem-solving, or emotional venting).
- Signal your stop-word and practice it once.
- Have a grounding technique ready and a follow-up plan (walk, call buddy, short therapy check-in).
- Note an anchor moment afterward and log it.

Storytelling is not therapy by itself, but when handled tactically it becomes a tool: it clarifies memory, reduces shame, and builds allies. Treat your narrative like mission-critical intel — share it with care, keep command of the room, and claim the moments that show you're getting stronger.

Resource Lists and Further Reading

If the previous chapters gave you permission to tell the story, consider this the supply drop: books, tools, apps, and community contacts that actually work when the alarm bells go off. Below is a compact, mission-oriented reference list — short on fluff, long on practical value — aimed at veterans, service families, and anyone dealing with CPTSD that links back to childhood roots as well as combat-related wounds.

Resource Kit: Foundational Texts

- The Body Keeps the Score (Bessel van der Kolk) — A field guide to how trauma sits in the nervous system and the body, with approaches that move beyond talk-only therapy.
- Attached (Amir Levine & Rachel Heller) — Useful for anyone who wants to understand adult attachment patterns that often trace back to childhood and show up in boots-on-the-ground relationships.
- Resilience (Eric Greitens) — Written by a former SEAL, short, direct, and full of practical mindset and habit tactics useful for reintegration and building steady routines.

Veteran-Focused Reads

- A military-perspective read — covers combat PTSD, battle fatigue, and TBI; straight talk that feels like advice from a senior NCO.
- A family-focused manual — targeted tactics for soldiers and families dealing with what is often called "complex secondary PTSD" — how trauma ricochets through units and households and what to do about it.

Practical Tools, Exercises, and Community Connections

- Mindfulness and meditation apps: Headspace, Calm, Insight Timer — short guided sessions (3–10 minutes) that can be run between tasks or before sleep. Think of them as a basic med kit for the brain.
- Grounding and breathing: Practice a 4-4-6 breathing or box breath

during an emotional flashback to quiet the fight/flight/freeze/fawn loop. Pair breathing with a sensory scan (name five things you can see, four you can touch, etc.).

- Journaling and expressive writing: Keep an "after-action" notebook for anchor moments — short entries noting what triggered you, what you did, and one small win. This creates an evidence log of progress.

- Support groups: Look for veteran peer groups, family-focused CPTSD groups, and TBI support networks. Peer-led meetings cut through clinical jargon and offer practical tips that actually fit military schedules.

Putting the Kit into Action — Tactical Tips for Soldiers and Families

- For emotional flashbacks: opt for shorter interventions, consistent routines, and apps with adjustable session lengths. Fatigue after cognitive work is normal, so plan restorative breaks.

- For households: run brief psychoeducation sessions at the kitchen table — explain 4F responses and share one coping tool per week so family members can support without taking it personally.

- For TBI: opt for shorter interventions, consistent routines, and apps with adjustable session lengths; fatigue after cognitive work is normal — plan restorative breaks.

A final note: treat these resources like mission tools. Pick a couple, practice them, and switch if they don't fit your tempo. The point is not to collect every book on the shelf but to build a kit that helps you and your people function better when the alarms sound.

Therapist, Peer, and Community Networks

Assembling the Platoon of Care

If you were back on base and the CO told you to put together a platoon, you'd pick people with different skills: shooters, comms, medics, and someone who can make coffee that isn't straight bilge. Think of healing from CPTSD the same way. No single person covers all the wounds—especially when trauma traces back to childhood and then a second dose of combat-carved stress shows up like an unwelcome drill sergeant. Build a multi-tier support team that covers clinical therapy, peer validation, and community resources, each with a clearly assigned role and a chain of communication.

Therapist–Peer–Community Coordination: the ops plan

Clinical care gives the map—diagnosis, neurologic framing of triggers, and evidencebased interventions. Peers give the terrain report—"This is how it feels when your chest tightens before a flashback." Community groups provide the logistics—places to meet, skills classes, and family supports. Those three elements work best when they coordinate. Practical moves you can use today:

- Standardize language. Teach family and peers to call what's happening an emotional flashback or a 4F shift (fight, flight, freeze, fawn). Consistent naming reduces confusion and decreases shame.

- Set a simple protocol for escalations: peer checkin → therapist message → crisis line/ER if safety risks escalates.

- Establish a single point of contact (a therapist, case manager, or peer leader) who keeps everyone informed with the veteran's consent. Think of that person as the unit's S-1 for mental health.

Understanding emotional flashbacks and the 4F shifts

An emotional flashback is a neurologic hijack of the limbic system, producing intense affect without the usual cortical narrative. The body reacts as if a threat were present, and the response falls into the four basic modes—fight, flight, freeze, and fawn. Early signs—clenched jaw, rapid breathing, withdrawal, sudden compliance—can be spotted by peers or family. When detected, short interventions can break the cycle: grounding cues ("name five things you can see"), paced breathing, or a preagreed safe phrase that signals "pause and breathe." Peerled groups can embed these techniques into tactical drills: practice grounding, rehearse safe phrases in roleplay, and validate each other's signals, turning knowledge of the 4F shifts into actionable, groupbased coping skills.

Peer-led groups: validation with tactical drills

Peer groups are where the "you're not crazy" memo happens. They normalize symptoms and provide real-world tips that therapists may not offer in session. Good peer leaders run meetings with rules: confidentiality, turn-taking, and a check-in/check-out to prevent flooding. Practical drills: role-play setting a boundary, practicing a 60-second grounding routine, or running a family briefing on what to do when an emotional flashback begins.

Community resources and the childhood/military overlap

Many vets carry childhood wounds that re-activate in high-stress environments. Community programs that recognize both sources of trauma—childhood CPTSD patterns and combat-related brain injury—can adapt services: longer-term group therapy, trauma-informed vocational training, and family workshops. Look for organizations that offer cross-trained staff (trauma therapists with military experience) or combined tracks for TBI and CPTSD.

Boundaries and safety planning: small items that save trust

Trust breaks when boundaries are vague. Create a short written safety plan: warning signs, calming steps, who to call, and locations that feel safe. Practice the plan once. Put boundary scripts on index cards for family: "I'm stepping back for 20 minutes. I'll come back when I'm calm." Designate an agreed safe room or a "signal" that means, "I need space." These details keep families from spinning into complex secondary trauma and give everyone a practical role in care.

Assembling this platoon takes time, paperwork, and patience—plus a few awkward family meetings. But with clear roles, consistent language about flashbacks and 4F responses, and a practiced safety plan, the team becomes something close to combat-ready for crises: coordinated, calm, and actually useful when the alarms go off.

Crisis Resources, Safety Planning

Crisis Safety Planning for CPTSD: Taking Control of Your Safety

If boundaries were your perimeter fence, a crisis safety plan is the standard operating procedure for when things go hot. This is practical work—lists, check-ins, rehearsals—so you and your support network know what to do when emotional flashbacks or a 4F spike hit.

Identifying Your Support Network

Make a concrete roster. Not "people who might help," but a prioritized list with names, phone numbers, best times to call, and the role each person fills: calm listener, driver, oncall caregiver, or professional contact who can provide clinical guidance. Have at least one contact who knows your safety plan and your limits. Brief them like you would a mission brief: what your triggers look like, how you signal for help, and any boundaries you need enforced. Families often carry complex secondary PTSD; assigning roles reduces ambiguity and prevents good intentions from turning into extra stress.

Creating a Personalized Crisis Response Plan

Write the plan down and post one copy where you'll find it. Include:

- Triggers and warning signs: specific situations, thoughts, bodily sensations, or behaviors that indicate a crisis is brewing. Use concrete cues—racing heart, dissociation, aggressive thoughts—so thresholds for action are clear.
- Step-by-step actions by severity: low-level grounding (5–4–3–2–1 sensory check), mid-level connection (call a contact, step outside to a prearranged safe spot), high-level escalation (contact crisis services or emergency care).
- Coping strategies that reliably work for you: short scripts to say out loud, calming routines, and physical activities that release tension.
- Resources and phone numbers: trusted contacts, your clinician, and

crisis lines.

Tie each step to a threshold. For example: "If I hit a 7/10 on my subjective distress scale or dissociate for more than five minutes, use steps B–D."

4F-Aware Coping Strategies

Know your default 4F response and prepare counters:

- Fight: Release tension with controlled physical training, shadowboxing, or a hard-handed task; then use brief cognitive checks to avoid verbal escalation.
- Flight: Preidentify safe exits and lowstimulus zones; carry a sensory kit so retreat feels deliberate, not shameful.
- Freeze: Use micromovements, slow diaphragmatic breaths, and verbal grounding phrases to reestablish body ownership.
- Fawn: Prepare short assertive lines and a selfcompassion practice to reduce automatic peoplepleasing.

Emotional flashbacks are not just memories; they're a brain-state where the amygdala and survival circuits treat present cues as threats. A safety plan translates that alarm into concrete actions that calm the system.

Planning for Safety in Triggering Environments

Before going into a known hot spot, run a quick recon: locate exits, identify a person to stay with, and set a signal for "time out." Build a calming routine to deploy immediately—noise-cancelling headphones, a familiar scent, a tactile object, or a five-minute breathing set. If you need to leave, have a prearranged route and a driver or rideshare option.

Crisis Resources and Accessibility

Keep crisis numbers handy and stored in your phone lock screen:

- National Suicide Prevention Lifeline (US): 1-800-273-TALK (8255)
- Crisis Text Line (US): text HOME to 741741

- Web chat services such as those from the National Alliance on Mental Illness (NAMI)

Practicing Drills and Regular Safety Plan Reviews

Treat the plan like routine kit maintenance. Schedule monthly check-ins with your network, run brief drills (call your support contact, walk through a calming routine), and update contacts or tactics as situations change. Rehearsal reduces panic and increases muscle memory—both literal and psychological.

If you want further field manuals on this topic, additional practical reads translate hard-earned experience into usable techniques for veterans and families.

Final Promises to Self and Next Steps

I Commit to Ongoing Healing with Compassionate Self-Ownership

Think of this as your operational order for longterm recovery: clear intent, realistic objectives, and rules of engagement that include kindness toward yourself. The amygdala rings a constant warning, the hippocampus blurs the timeline and context of memories, and the prefrontal cortex—the part that usually applies brakes—runs low on fuel. As a result, emotional flashbacks feel like being under fire again even when you're safe. Understanding this rewiring helps you own the process: you are not a victim of the brain, but the commander of the mission, capable of choosing gentleness and selfcompassion.

Accepting Imperfect Progress and Choosing Gentleness

Progress will have setbacks. That's standardissue, so treat this like sustained operations rather than a quick patrol. Set small, achievable objectives—fewer than you think you need—and give yourself credit for the ones you complete. When you stumble, practice the same calm briefing you'd want from a squad leader: factual, focused on next steps, not character assassination. Gentle selftalk works better than harsh selfdiscipline because chronic stress wires in guilt and shame, compassion helps rewire safety signals. Remember that the brain is rewired by CPTSD, but you own the process of recovery. By accepting imperfect progress and choosing gentleness, you create the safety cues your prefrontal cortex needs to retrain and reinforce selfownership.

Daily Grounding to Counter Emotional Flashbacks

Make grounding non-negotiable. Soldiers train drills until the reflex kicks in; replicate this process with anchors that pull you back to the present.

Five-step sensory scan: name five things you see, four you can touch, three you hear, two you smell, and one you taste. Run it like a quick patrol check.

Paced breathing: inhale for 4, hold for 2, exhale for 6. Repeat until you feel at rest.

- Body scan: sweep attention slowly from toes to crown, softening tension as you go.

These tactics calm the autonomic nervous system, helping the prefrontal cortex reconnect to control.

Identity Reformulation: Reclaiming Autonomy from Trauma

Trauma often steals decision-making and self-value. Reclaiming them is an active process. Start by separating what happened from who you are — list strengths and values that existed before and after trauma. Write a short personal statement (two or three lines) that you can read aloud each morning: it rewrites the script the brain keeps playing. For folks with TBI, keep statements concise and repeatable; repetition is the neurological equivalent of PT.

Setting Boundaries to Protect Recovery Space

Boundaries are defensive positions. Know your limits and communicate them with clear language and fallback plans. Practice short scripts: "I can't handle that topic right now" or "I need a break — I'll check in after 30 minutes." Use a buddy or family signal for extraction when environments become triggering. Protecting recovery may mean skipping an event or leaving early; that's tactical prudence, not weakness.

Creating a Personal Legacy

Turning hard experience into purpose heals at the cellular level. Options: mentor a younger vet, help run a family support group, or teach a life-skill class at a local center. Even small acts — telling your story at a squad reunion or writing a letter to your younger self — pull fractured identity back together and pass on lessons.

Engaging Professional Support and Establishing Routine Review

Lock in regular therapy sessions and peergroup meetings as part of your schedule, like PT or weapons maintenance. Track progress monthly: note wins, rework tactics that aren't helping, and adjust goals. Families should get education on complex secondary PTSD so they can set healthy boundaries and support effectively. When TBI is present, include cognitive rehabilitation and coordinate care across providers.

Commit to this with steady, pragmatic compassion. Take ownership of the work, but don't go it alone — your support network, clinicians, and peers are the squad that helps you hold ground and move forward.

Your Charter for Life

We began this book by examining the nature of hidden scars, those invisible wounds that shape our inner lives. We considered how these past experiences imprint themselves not just on our minds, but deeply within our nervous systems, affecting our daily experience and interactions. The understanding that the body itself holds these memories became a central thread, illustrating why a holistic approach to healing is not merely beneficial, but essential.

This book laid out a careful roadmap, not as a rigid instruction set, but as a guiding hand through the often-complex terrain of recovery. We looked at a variety of daily practices, simple yet powerful actions that, when consistently applied, can shift internal states and create space for repair. We heard directly from those who have walked similar paths, their voices offering validation and proof of resilience. We then considered the spectrum of therapeutic options available, offering insight into how each might serve a particular need, always emphasizing that the most effective path is one chosen with personal awareness and intent.

The structured plans, the checklists, and the reflective practices were presented as tools for self-discovery and consistent self-care. We saw how creative expression and the sustenance of genuine connection, both within personal circles and broader communities, contribute deeply to repair and growth. Moving past the immediate pain, we turned our attention to the deeper work of finding meaning, solidifying a new sense of identity, and considering the legacy one wishes to build from the crucible of past trials. The creation of your Personal Healing Charter, as detailed in the previous pages, reflects this commitment – a living document embodying your unique understanding and path forward.

The true impact of engaging with this material extends far beyond the mitigation of past suffering. It lies in the recognition of an inherent capacity for regeneration and strength within each person. The work described here is about reclamation – reclaiming agency, reclaiming peace, and reclaiming a future defined by intention rather than reaction. It is about understanding that healing is not a destination arrived at and then forgotten, but an active, ongoing process of self-attunement and compassion. By engaging with your inner experience, by listening to the subtle messages of your body, and by consciously choosing practices that serve your well-being, you cultivate a deeply rooted fortitude.

This ongoing attention to self, this patient tending of the inner garden, yields a quiet yet potent transformation. It shifts how you perceive the world and your place within it. It allows for the integration of past difficulties, not as burdens to be perpetually carried, but as parts of a larger, richer narrative that includes growth, wisdom, and compassion. The insights gained, the skills developed, and the self-awareness cultivated become resources you carry always, ready to meet life's unfolding circumstances with greater steadiness and grace.

As you step forward from these pages, carry with you the deep knowledge that your well-being is a worthy pursuit, deserving of your dedicated care. Continue to honor your own pace, to listen to your inner guidance, and to seek out connections that nourish your spirit. The work of healing is a lifelong commitment to oneself, a continuous unfolding of potential. May your days be marked by increasing moments of peace, genuine connection, and a steadfast belief in your enduring capacity for wholeness.